REIGN

Restoring Identity

40-Day Devotional

Restoring Identity

40-Day Devotional

KAT VAZQUEZ

Edited by: Jennifer Sawyer, Lindsay Hanson Cox
Cover art: Jordyn Myers, Yeni Torres

Reign: Restoring Identity made the choice to capitalize certain nouns and pronouns like Father, Son, Holy Spirit, Whose and He as a mark of honor to The Divinity. This adopted style may differ from those of other writers or book publishers. We have also decided not to capitalize the name satan. By this decision, we have chosen not give prominence or acknowledgment to the name or whatever it stands for. All artwork included inside REIGN's pages was purchased for the use of licensing rights.

Artist list: Eric Samuel Timm, Rebecca Friedlander, Antonio Pantoja, Jordyn Myers, Yeni Torres, Melissa Burch, Tessa Stiger.

Lightning Publishers
www.LightningPublishers.com

Endorsements

"The issue of identity has long been misunderstood and misaligned from God's original design. There is no more relevant time on earth for the restoring message found in this book, REIGN. It is a creative and powerful depiction of the hope and truth we all need by the lovely, Kat Vazquez."

Paul Crouch Jr.
American Christian Broadcaster,
Producer, CEO: PJ Video

"Discovering one's true identity is to uncover a rare hidden gem. Doing so requires biblical insight, determination and tremendous courage! Kat Vazquez hands you the necessary tools to discover fierce love and unashamed truth in her must read book: REIGN! This beautiful warrior lifts her sword in Jesus' Name, to break your chains and remove the blind folds which have kept you in the dark. You are chosen, a royal priesthood–called into His marvelous light!"

Brenda Crouch
Author, Speaker, Singer, TV Host

"Kat and Jorge Vazquez and I have been friends for many years and I have always admired their hunger for the reality of experiencing the spiritual world and to see Christs' body come into maturity.

In her new book "*Reign: Restoring Identity,*" Kat pours out a contagious measure of true passion straight onto the pages of every chapter in *Reign*.

With the perfect mix of vulnerability and much-needed boldness, Kat Vazquez has woven together a piece of work that is sure to strengthen and help the masses to see and believe who they truly are: the Bride of Christ."

Brian "Head" Welch
Co-founder of the band Korn,
New York Times best-selling Author of '*Save Me From Myself*,'
and Co-star of the *Showtime* movie *Loud Krazy Love.*

"If you are on a quest to find identity Reign is your resource. Kat Vazquez has captured the essence of our true value in Christ. This 40-day devotional will walk you through the steps of letting go of the lies you believe about your self worth and lead you into the truth of your divine destiny.

Thank you Kat for your honesty and vulnerability to help others understand their true identity."

Tammy Hotsenpiller
Executive Life Coach
Founder of Women of Influence International

"WOW. After knowing Kat for many years, I have witnessed her life be consistent and passionate about advancing God's empire on earth. Reign so simply reveals the powerful and bigger picture of God's great purpose and master plan for us as sons and daughters to take our rightful and royal authority in the Kingdom of God, in order to bring divine impact on earth. No matter who you are, after reading this your identity will be either, awakened, restored or renewed! Catch his heartbeat, see yourself the way he sees and step right into your destiny."

Beckah Shae
Speaker, Singer, Songwriter
Co-founder of Shae Shoc Records

"So many times I've traveled by interstate, scenery flying by while I focused on getting to my destination. But my most memorable journeys are when we took the time to stop where we wanted, read indicators of history, and had time to contemplate the meaning of events that had occurred. Kat Vazquez' REIGN is a journey into our personal story with signposts from our past. . . and directions toward our glorious future. Trust me. REIGN is a journey well worth the trip."

Dr. Harvey R. Brown Jr.
President,
Impact Ministries, Inc.

"Kat Vazquez has managed to write a devotional that's a step above the usual... REIGN is an interesting and thought provoking read that will get your thoughts and mindset into a power stance every day of the journey. It's clear, really relatable and packed full of overlooked and under discussed truths that will set you free from a lifetime of wrong thinking. Anyone can get some fresh revelation, some creative and thought provoking wisdom from reading this book."

Michele Hunter
Pastor and Speaker,
Illuminiate Ministries, One3Ministries

"Whether it's through her TV show, Instagram posts, and direct messages, I feel like I'm experiencing a strong woman who knows her identity and successes are found in Christ alone. In her work, Kat is not only taking her rightful place in history on earth but for all eternity, and she speaks with a boldness and authority only God himself can give. She's a woman on a mission to share the very secrets everyone is searching for in life, and I'm always inspired and motivated by how rooted and directed she is in God's word. In a world full of human opinions and empty surmising, Kat brings us back to who we are to God and the timeless truths that have been long forgotten. I can't wait to dive into her book, "REIGN.""

Lori Lara
Writer, Speaker,
Black Belt & Founder of
The Strong Girl Self-Defense Program

ACKNOWLEDGMENTS

First and foremost, I want to acknowledge my Lord and Savior, Jesus Christ, for the cross, the sacrifice, and the love that affords us the incredible opportunity to reign. Thank You!

To my husband, Jorge, thank you for loving me so well and for fully supporting my vulnerability in these pages. I am such a blessed woman to be your wife! I am devotedly your's.

To my treasures, my boys, Victor and Christian, I pray you both grasp the truths within *Reign*. You were on His mind before He formed the foundation the earth. He has marvelous plans for you both, but more importantly, He adores you both so much!

To my parents, thank you for instilling Biblical values and and always cheering us on no matter what adventure we embarked on. To my sister, Kelly, you've taught me so much about how to be brave. You're a deep well of wisdom, and I'm so honored to be your sister.

To the artists and photographers, thank you for contributing your extraordinary talent, and inspiring the *REIGN* readers through your generosity.

To my editors Lindsay Cox and Jennifer Sawyer for your feedback and helping make this book possible.

To Annie Lobert, thank you for writing the Foreword and showing His beloved daughters how to reign.

To each and everyone of you I am eternally grateful! God bless you all.

Kat

God knows who you are. Satan knows who you are. But do you know who you are?

REIGN: Restoring Identity is a 40-day journey to discover who you are as a son or daughter of God, and to find your greater purpose, collectively as part of the unified Church, The Firstborn's eternal companion, "The Bride of Christ."

Praise be to the God and Father of our Lord Jesus Christ, who has blessed us in the heavenly realms with every spiritual blessing in Christ. For he chose us in him before the creation of the world to be holy and blameless in his sight. In love he predestined us for adoption to sonship through Jesus Christ, in accordance with his pleasure and will – to the praise of his glorious grace, which he has freely given us in the One he loves.

Ephesians 1:3-7 NIV

CONTENTS

I. Foreword ... xv

II. Preface ... xvii

III. Introduction ... xxi

IV. Prologue: The Sons & Daughter's Identity: Anointed, Not Appointed ... xxxi

1. Grounded: We As Human ... 1
2. Lessons From a Kitchen in Kentucky ... 14

Part 1—The Awakening

3. The Unveiling: From Origin Stories To Warriors ... 21
4. Who is Regina? ... 27
5. The Restoration Of Regina Women's Purposes In The Church ... 34
6. Created In His Divine Greatness ... 42
7. A Brave's Reward ... 47
8. Mercy's Alliance ... 53
9. Love Is Building An Empire ... 58
10. The Model Of Love: Jesus Christ ... 64
11. Is Perfection Possible? 7 = —|—— ... 69
12. "Remind me who I am, because I need to know..." ... 74
13. A Privileged Position ... 81

14. "I'll huff and puff and blow your house down!" And Other Nonsense We Believe 90
15. Locked In His Gaze: A Union Of Spirits 98
16. The Frontline Lions 103
17. Eden's Evacuation 107
18. Unforsaken: God Is There Especially During the Hard Times 117
19. The Crown 121

Part 2—Breaking The Cycles

20. "You can have it all!" They're Selling It. We're Buying It:Perfection's Trap 129
21. Anxiety 135
22. When He Means More Than Our Own Life 143
23. Marionette: The Strings We Allow To Pull Us 152
24. Looking Like Revenge: Body Image Bondage 158
25. Captivity: Freedom From Approval Addiction 166
26. Monsters In My Head: Freedom From Anger's Grip 173
27. Braveheart: Breaking Free From Insecurity, Self-Shame and Addictive Behaviors 180
28. Identity Based on Habitation 189
29. It's all Greek to Me: The Exousia The Ecclesia Carry 196
30. Willful Sins and Their Root 206
31. Realm of Fantasy 212
32. Heartbreak and Pain 225
33. Tests and The Power of Choice 231
34. Integrity's Rebirth 240
35. The First Women's Lib Movement 246
36. We Are Ambassadors 251

37. Our Bodies: An Instrument of Worship 256
38. In Communion With Him 266
39. Community 271
40. The Church. A Bride. And Our Purposes in Establishing His Kingdom 277
41. Prayers and Promises 280

References 285

I. FOREWORD

"Slut." "Whore." "Ho." "Bitch!" These words reverbed back and forth in my mind for decades. Verbally spoken and used as a means of punishment, the lies of my father, bullies in school, and countless men that abused me for over a decade—enticed me to choose a life of searching for love in the empty cisterns of exotica dancing (stripping) escorting (prostitution). My search for peace resulted in over a decade of being sex trafficked.

Because I didn't know who I was—abuse had defined my very existence. What I need to know most was that I was loved. After years of chasing money, mirages, and pipe dreams, the love I truly needed broke through my angry, cold and callous heart. God's love intervened and filled my heart with songs of hope, peace and the knowledge that I was royalty—His daughter placed in earth for such a time as this.

When I first met Kat, her fiery eyes and warm smile beckoned me with an invitation of grace. I could see such similarities in our fashion sense, make up preferences and how we carried ourselves. Even though we were from different sides of the tracks, I knew she was my royal sister. Kat might not have sold her body for money like me, but she was looking for the same things as I was...admiration, love and acceptance. No matter what our differences, God designed us both to reign.

In REIGN, Kat lovingly describes the world's greatest story—how God came down to earth into the form of man to open our eyes to our royal worth as human beings. As you read, allow God to speak to your soul about the truth of your decree to reign in the Kingdom. I encourage you to go treasure hunting to discover your priceless value as a person—to awake to the reality that God has designed for you a unique purpose that only you can fulfill! This is truth: You are a child of the most high God!

Matthew 4:19, "Come follow me, I will teach you how to fish for people." ~Jesus

Annie Lobert

Founder of the non-profit Hookers For Jesus
& The Destiny House HookersForJesus.net
Married to Oz Fox of the band Stryper

II. PREFACE

The wonder of being a human means we have the astounding capacity to see, hear and feel, and then to think about our extraordinary reality and form judgments about it all. Out of this ability we acknowledge right and wrong, good and bad, recognizing beautiful and ugly. We feel profound emotions like love, hate or joy, discouragement, rejection, hope and thankfulness. We reason and plan our lives in ways that accomplish things. Being a human in a fallen world makes it hard to recognize that as Christians, we are spiritual beings first, made in the image of God, meant for a glorious position.

REIGN is a 40-day quest to discover your divine identity as a son or daughter of God. In a fallen world, we have stumbled into worldly patterns of behavior and understanding, patterns that can lead us down paths of confusion and wrong thinking, making it difficult to see the truth of who we really are.

REIGN is a roadmap to restoration, an awakening to the supernatural you. It's a game changer! As Christians, the Bible tells us that we are adopted into sonship, a position of divine royalty in which we carry "the Hope of Glory," the Holy Spirit, inside of us. We were created, called and Christ died for us to carry His Kingdom of love into the Earth.

That means we carry the same divine wisdom and power through which Jesus operated in His ministry on earth. It means we were created and called to a supernatural purpose, a divine invitation to continue the ministry of Christ, to continue His ministry of love and salvation, and to spread the love of Christ throughout the world.

Our lives and purposes are predestined, part of an ancient plan that God established and set in motion, even before the foundation of the Earth was knit together.

"You saw me before I was born. Every day of my life was recorded in your book. Every moment was laid out before a single day had passed." Psalm 139:16 NLT

We have been equipped for this work. To believe, to think and behave as ambassadors of Christ, we are being ruled by love to change the world.

When we shed the worldly identity we've assumed, our divine identity will emerge. Embracing your true identity and seeing yourself the way God sees you, empowers you to overcome the darkness of a fallen world. You'll still face rejection, experience insecurities and hurt, but by understanding your identity in Christ, you will take the power back from those thoughts, and make them submit them to God's truth. No longer will they control how you see your value, position or your voice as a son or daughter of Christ.

"We demolish arguments and every pretension that sets itself up against the knowledge of God, and we take captive every thought to make it obedient to Christ." *2 Corinthians 10:5 NIV*

Your divine identity aligns you with the purposes of God – purposes meant for impact and a greater awareness of your value as a key part of the unified Body of Believers, as The Bride of Christ. We are catalysts for "His Kingdom come" on earth. Are you ready to be the person God created you to be? Are you ready to do the things God created you to do? Are you ready to reign with Christ?

Reigning with Christ requires a renewed mind, an active process of learning scriptural truth, building on that truth, believing it, and consequently choosing to think and behave differently. Unlearning what we have learned from a fallen world comes through a sort of deprogramming process. We must challenge those thought and behavior patterns that aren't God's truth. And as a reminder, echoing Jeremiah 29:11, He has wonderful plans for us, He wants us to flourish, to shine bright no matter what circumstances or feelings may bring. Then reboot! By purposefully refocusing our thoughts on how God sees us through scripture reading, believing it and applying it, consequently our behaviors will change too.

We ready ourselves to reign when our heart's mission and purposes fall in line, synchronized with His Kingdom ways.

Through these devotions, I expose common ungodly beliefs and highlight the truth of what God says about them. I'll show you how to remove these blinders and see how we were created to have an impact as His children. These devotions are designed to help you work through this renewal process, to go from living in a fallen world to reigning with Christ. Are you ready to begin our quest?

III. INTRODUCTION

"Mom, I want more milk! ...Mom, my knee hurts! MOM!! He just dumped yogurt on the couuuch!" I hear a scream that sounds like a raptor from Jurassic World. It's my three-year-old retaliating against his big brother. "Okay, God, you're gonna have to help me not lose my mind with my kids, and we are gonna write this introduction this morning, because it's the only window of time I have today! Oh, and I have to get the car serviced... and I have that thing at 10am... and I really need to take a shower at some point today. Lord, can you carve out time somehow so I can get a shower today please? I love you, and I trust you!" I gulped the last of my cold, 2-hour old coffee.

This has been the past few minutes of *real* — welcome to my life! Where mom- life, work-life, and busy schedules converge with the desire to somehow be used by the Lord. With all the hats I wear, I sometimes feel I have to tap into split personalities to make it all happen! Can I get an amen out there? Thankfully, God is sovereign, isn't intimidated by my day-timer, and has some mysterious ways!

In this season, I'm learning what balance looks like for me. I'm managing a busy family schedule with a house full of boys, sponsoring my clients as a health coach which I absolutely love, all while trying to hit deadlines for a second film series and co-writing another book, oh and living at the baseball field most evenings. My husband and I are the founders of Revolution Media Ministries. We produce *The Revolution TV* and *Your Story Is Not Done*. I'm the daily admin and lead writer for both shows. I have to multitask, I have to self-start, and I have to hit network deadlines. My daily routine varies from day to day but is always nonstop.

Shoutout to all the hustlers out there with His dreams stirring in their heart!

Through the years, I have learned a critical discipline: how to hear Him. I am getting better at pressing through the noisy whirlwind of life, and I'm more quickly recognizing His still voice speaking around me, cutting through the chaos. How am I able to do that? I began praying a simple prayer a few years ago that began to change my life: I asked the Lord what was on His heart, and how I can be involved. I have paid attention to what He has been showing me, aware of even the smallest details, as if He was highlighting them for me to focus on. He has been opening my eyes up to His big picture perspective. It's almost like I'm awake for the first time. It's another level of living. I love learning how to better track with His heart! He has patiently guided me in the midst of my wild and chaotic routine, showing me some very personal, as well as, very large concept revelations that are connected to who I am as a Christian, and who we are collectively as a body of Believers.

I have started to recognize a common message emerging over the past year. God was speaking to me through dreams, visions, even hearing and seeing certain words appear over and over again in my normal routine on billboards, bumper stickers, and on the sides of semi-trucks. These were all messages that couldn't have been random or coincidental. Identity. Restoration. Impact. Sons and Daughters of God. Sonship. In fact, I have had conversations with other friends who have had similar experiences and are picking up the same messages! It's become apparent that God was talking loudly to His children. He was dropping revelation!

One verse in Romans 8 continues to stick out and haunt me, "For the creation waits in eager expectation for the children of God to be revealed." I would hear this verse spoken to me in my dreams, I would hear it like a song hook playing on repeat in my head over, and over, and over. I could almost hear the rocks crying out, nature, imagining the great cloud of heavenly witnesses in unison groaning in harmony, crying out for the Burning Ones to awaken and take their rightful places for impact in the Earth. I felt it! For the sons and daughters of God were critical to the fulfillment of a great promise: the restoration for the Earth. I started to awaken to a massive, big picture view. Christ's return was for His spotless, prepared Bride.

In our humanness, in our chaos, in our "ideas" of who God is and what He has for His creation, He is still beckoning us to listen to His heartbeat. He is preparing us for the More that's coming and what He already deposited inside of us.

As the concepts of who we really are as His children started to dawn on me, I had to write them down. It looked like freedom, purpose, and being adored by a Creator that knows us and loves us like no other human can. It's a game changer! But the key is for us to believe it and behave like it. Will you take the journey with me to awaken to your real identity as His child?

The Sons and Daughters of God Revealed

The dots were beginning to connect for me, and I was speechless at the monumental concept I was starting to see emerge. The awakening and manifesting of the sons and daughters of God was essential to the fulfillment of prophecy that was older than time. How signifiant is our role? —The promises of God require it, the teaching of Jesus Christ requires it, the testimony of the Holy Spirit requires it, the destruction of satan demands it, the vindication of Christ demands it, and the hope of the Saints demands it.

This idea was captivating! It was so much bigger than one ministry or church. It was about a collective body working uniquely together and awakening to an ancient and predestined purpose. The Bride of Christ was being prepared. And He was starting by synchronizing our heart to His. I couldn't contain my excitement to share with those who have "ears to hear!" The timeliness of this message is critical and I pray every person reading this hears the clarion call in these pages, because it's a call that was sent out before the fabric of the world was knit together. God's purposes in the earth can only be accomplished through His unified and functioning Church. His plans and people are waiting on the other side of our yes.

I believe that the living Church was predestined, existing at this exact time in history for a great purpose. God is calling deeply to our hearts to awaken to our real identity as sons and daughters of God for Kingdom purpose and impact! We will become who we were predestined to be: figures who play a critical role in the history of humankind.

The Bible calls the collective body of Believers, The Bride of Christ or Ecclesia. I wrote this book because I couldn't deny the urgency I felt inside my heart. A preparation for a unified collective of hearts and souls, predestined to become The Chosen ones who say "Yes." They will become one with God in purpose and heart. Loaded.

We see this synchronized heartbeat of Father and His people on the Earth activated in movements across worship groups, ministry outreaches, and churches all over the world, as a collective cry for His Presence and for *more*. I believe that *more* is the awakening of The Bride, the preparation and alignment of her pivotal role at this time of history. There is a predetermined outcome that is approaching as foretold in scriptures referring to the return of Christ. He's coming back to co-reign and rule alongside His Bride.

What I believe is happening right now is the Church is being made ready. Those who choose His laws of love, being unified in will and heart to the one and only rightful King of Kings, that is Jesus Christ, will undergo a restoration of identity, being made spotless and holy, and manifesting as The Bride.

The Bride of Christ, a Predestined Position

The Bride of Christ is a pivotal position. Can you imagine the scene in Heaven when God shared His plan with the angels and heavenly creatures? Imagine what the heavenly bodies thought when first hearing God's Great Plan, unpacking His vision to all the creatures in heaven. That vision caused Lucifer to shudder with fear. Humankind was the greatest threat to him. Humanity would bring forth The Firstborn. They would be created to become the fulfillment of the ages, a marriage of the Godhead's sovereign purpose, will and heart. This plan was set into motion before the creation of the world.

I believe we carry His Kingdom come. I believe we can rewrite history and rewrite headlines! Our position was a great promise spoken before time and space, before the conception of the world as we know it. Humankind was designed to fulfill the great promise of a covenant union to The Firstborn. This news triggered the eternal war for souls. It was all about the significance of the Bride of Christ arising. Even angels and demons envy the privileged position only humankind was created for: to become The Bride of Christ.

One of my favorite verses that highlights the significance of our restored identity, the relationship between God and His people can be seen in the Bible. Revelation 22:17 says, "The Spirit and the Bride say, "Come!" And let the one who hears say, "Come!" Let the one who is thirsty come; and let the one who wishes take the free gift of the water of life." We see that the desire of God and The Bride is one. We can also see that our authority is in union with the Holy Spirit, and together our purpose brings about the restoration of creation! That should blow our minds.

Gentlemen, please don't get hung up on the feminine gender of the origin word "The Bride." It is not about a gender label. The mystery is about Divinity marrying humanity. It's not about male and female. Scripture says, "There is neither Jew nor Greek, there is neither slave nor free man, there is neither male nor female; for you are all one in Christ Jesus. And if you belong to Christ, then you are Abraham's descendants, heirs according to promise." Galatians 3:28-29. What is amazing is that the personality characteristics of the Godhead encompass both masculine and feminine traits: the virtues of comforting, nurturing, and natural caregiving are just a few. These traits as well as His desire to create, were out of His nature to bestow love and be in communion with His creation. He is the totality of love.

My goal is to share a perspective that is found within the pages of the Bible. My focus is to guide you on a quest of rediscovering our identities as sons and daughters of God, and how our sonship effects how we think and behave. Once we realize the whole significance of what Jesus Christ did on Calvary, we are empowered to operate with the mind of Christ, making impact as The Bride of Christ collectively.

The Definitions and Perspectives

Growing up in church, I barely recall hearing preaching on "The Bride of Christ." Perhaps because of contextual ambiguity, or how complex the figure reads in scriptures found mainly in the mysterious book of Revelation. "The Bride of Christ" has different definitions according to various religious circles. Some see The Bride as a location such as Jerusalem, others say it's a collective voice of the saints in spirit and apostolic dominion. No matter how the role has been translated, The Bride is a pivotal role made of human believers. References to the position are found in 2 Corinthians, Ephesians, Daniel, John, and Revelation.

Revelation 21 says the position was predestined, appointed to co-rule and reign with Jesus Christ, "in a new Heaven and on a new Earth."

I believe in the Bible, every word of it is truth, cover to cover. I take its wisdom literally. I believe the Bible is logos, God's spoken word used to create. The Bible is divine instruction inspired by an all-loving God, whose desire is to be in relationship with every living soul. We are created in His image and greatness, and purposed to live as His sons and daughters on this Earth. As Christians, our new identity changes everything. We are not only assured Heaven when we profess Jesus Christ as our Lord and Savior, but the profession activates a sacred covenant that Christ's victory on Calvary afforded us: to carry out His Kingdom purposes on this Earth. Loaded right?

Ephesians 1:5-14 spells it out for us,

"For He chose us in Him before the creation of the world to be holy and blameless in his sight. In love He predestined us for adoption to sonship through Jesus Christ, in accordance with His pleasure and will — to the praise of His glorious grace, which He has freely given us in the One He loves. In Him we have redemption through His blood, the forgiveness of sins, in accordance with the riches of God's grace that He lavished on us. With all wisdom and understanding, He made known to us the mystery of His will according to his good pleasure, which He purposed in Christ, to be put into effect when the times reach their fulfillment — to bring unity to all things in Heaven and on Earth under Christ. In Him we were also chosen, having been predestined according to the plan of Him who works out everything in conformity with the purpose of His will, in order that we, who were the first to put our hope in Christ, might be for the praise of His glory. And you also were included in Christ when you heard the message of truth, the gospel of your salvation. When you believed, you were marked in Him with a seal, the promised Holy Spirit, who is a deposit guaranteeing our inheritance until the redemption of those who are God's possession — to the praise of His glory."

These are beautiful verses, but have we realized what those verses really mean? It's the restoration of a very significant identity. This role isn't just for the individual but is for a collective of sons and daughters of God, a preparation and synchronizing of will and heart will begin. I believe we are living in the times where this synchronizing is taking place, "to bring unity to all things in Heaven and on Earth under Christ." Ephesians 1:10. It is our predestined purpose.

How are we missing the mark so badly as the Western Church? Authority? Unity? We can't even agree on basics. In fact, we look more like a dysfunctional family estranged from one another. How do we do attain this identity? The answer lies in how we respond to the leading of the Holy Spirit in our daily routines. Listening for and interacting with the Holy Spirit, and allowing Him to guide us through the awakening of our true identity. Once we know Whose we are and accept the significance, training will begin to synchronize our heart and will to His, where we are ruled by love.

Christians share in the anointing that Jesus Christ carries, as the "Anointed One." Every believer fulfills the prophetic, priestly, and kingly roles that Jesus was also anointed for. In a sense, we are all prophets called to proclaim God's Word, priests ordained to offer ourselves as sacrifices of flesh and self-serving behaviors, and kings enthroned to war against the Lord's enemies to help expand His Kingdom. Yet we do not only share in Christ's kingly office, fighting against satan and the principalities of darkness, but we also reign with Jesus over creation. This identity is what Calvary's epic redemption afforded us: our legitimate identity! This redemption plan was meant to restore who the Lord made us to be. For those who answer "Yes" to Calvary's invitation, salvation restores our broken and misplaced images of identity.

I pray this book starts your inner dialogue, triggering an "aha moment" that begins a renewal process in how to see your real identity and purposes. Christ died for you to live it out! I pray the revelation forthcoming shatters the old, "familiar" faith ceilings that have limited how you see God's gift Calvary already afforded us. Finally, I want you to realize your true identity as kings and queens on this Earth. As we say "Yes," submitting to retrain our heart and will to His law of love, our thoughts and desires will synchronize with His, fulfilling the prayer, "on Earth as it is in heaven."

Photographer: Dustin Benton
Model: Beckah Shae Shocklee

Photographer: Rebecca Friedlander

IV. PROLOGUE

The Sons & Daughter's Identity: Anointed, Not Appointed

There are certain TV shows that draw us into the characters and story so well that before you know it, you become a binge watcher. Netflix's original series *The Crown* turned me into a fan girl of Queen Elizabeth II and all things British. One of my favorite scenes from the docudrama takes us back in history to 1937, giving us the fly on the wall perspective of a tender conversation between a father and his daughter.

"Princess Elizabeth is a little girl and her father is practicing for his coronation. He asks her to read the Archbishop's role as he's practicing for the big day tomorrow...he wants to respond and explain to her what giving a 'sacred promise' means. It's a promise you can never break.

You have to anoint me, he tells her, otherwise I cannot be King. "It is only when the holy oil touches me... I am transformed and brought into direct contact with the divine..." he tells her.

"I am forever changed... bound to God. It is the most important part of the ceremony," when the hands, the breast and the head are all anointed with the holy oil.

George VI takes his heir to see the crown, which weighs 5 pounds and so he has to practice walking with it on.

The scene switches to 1952 and there Elizabeth is trying it on too, remembering the ceremony and her father both now integral to the past.

In England the 'Sovereign acts as a focus for national identity, unity and pride; giving a sense of stability and continuity. Officially, the sovereign 'recognizes success and excellence; and supports the ideal of voluntary service.'

"It is not as easy as it looks," Elizabeth II says to Prince Charles and Princess Anne, who are watching their mother trying on the crown with curiosity and interest. "Can I borrow it to practice" she asks her assistant. "Well, if it is not yours Ma'am, ... who does it belong to?"[1] is his reply.

Chill bumps. In that important scene, Elizabeth turns to look into the mirror, taking in her full reflection wearing the royal crown. The camera shot captures a close up of her face as we watch her mentally connecting the dots. She realizes, in totality what the crown represents, and now sitting atop of her head, how her identity will forever be transformed from the coronation forward.

We Are Called His Royals

The picture at the opening of the chapter shows a royal figure dressed in majestic splendor, wearing a symbol of authority, a crown. The picture also captures a moment of revelation, the awareness of a transformation of identity. The coronation, or the sacred anointing of a royal makes a statement of recognition, impacting the individual's identity and also the entire kingdom.

The Bible refers to us as The Bride of Christ, a chosen and anointed collective. This position is pivotal. Ephesians 5:27 says Jesus will return for, "a radiant church, without stain or wrinkle or any other blemish, but holy and blameless." This collective Body acts in one accord with the Father, synchronized in heart to the Father's. I believe the Lord is preparing us all who have "ears to hear" for what He is saying and what is on His heart for humanity. It's about His great plan and agenda.

As the Creator of mankind, He had a predestined plan for all creation, Heaven and Earth. The Bible says when Christ, the Firstborn returns to Earth to claim His people, His Bride, they will both co-rule and co-reign in a restored Heaven and Earth. This signals the fulfillment of the ages. It is a predestined event, no matter if our minds believe it or not. He keeps His promises. We will dig into how the collective Bride works together in upcoming chapters, carrying out Father's purposes, and how I believe we carry His kingdom come on Earth.

We Are called His Warriors

The photo opening this chapter shows a sovereign, but let us also reflect on the other purposes of The Bride of Christ. In order to expand legal jurisdiction, war and conquest are inevitable to expand territory. A warrior also defines The Bride— notice the picture on the other side of the page. The Bible compares The Word of God to a double-edged sword. John 1:1-4 says, "In the beginning was the Word, and the Word was with God, and the Word was God. He was with God in the beginning. Through Him all things were made; without Him nothing was made that has been made. In Him was life, and that life was the light of all mankind."

He made all creation, in Heaven and later on Earth. By definition, "The Word of God" includes His creative breath that spoke life into existence and purpose for the restoration and fulfillment of His good will and pleasure. Scripture is the "Word of God."

The sword is just as significant as the figure holding it. If The Word of God tells us we were made in the likeness of God, then scripture, like the double-edged sword is also our identity. When we look in the mirror, we should see The Word, and The Word should define us. Hebrews 4:12 says, "The Word of God is alive and active, it's sharper than a double-edged sword, dividing soul and spirit, joint and marrow; it judges the thoughts and attitudes of the heart." Scripture is also our identity.

We are what the Bible says we are! Living in a fallen world where people hurt other people, rejection and shame can easily take root in our hearts, stealing our joy and sometimes our voice.

However, the lies we entertain are only a smoke screen to the truth of how God sees us, and how we are to think as His sons and daughters. That will affect how we see ourselves and treat others.

We are loved, worthy, capable in Him, and strong enough to hold onto the truth even in the hurricanes of life. We were made in His image, and when we ask Jesus to be the Lord of our lives, a royal adoption to sonship activates the restoring of our identity.

The Bible tells us our origin story. Humanity was created for a great purpose: to bring forth The Firstborn son, Jesus Christ, who would ransom humans back to a perfect God. Humanity would also bring forth a royal priesthood. Predestined.

Chosen and created to become sons and daughters of God. The fulfillment of the ages in Revelation tells us of an imminent event: a holy marriage between two apostolic figures: Christ and His Church, a spotless Bride. As we read the Word of God, we learn who we really are as God's adopted heirs. Our new identity was meant to advance His empire of love on the Earth. We carry and bring His kingdom ways on Earth as it is in Heaven.

In the picture, the figure is locked on, focused on the Holy Spirit dove above her head. There is peace and confidence resting on her face. She carries rightful royal authority. Believing, thinking, and behaving as a royal results only from spiritual, emotional, and mental training. The training begins with a commitment to become a carrier of conquest. A battle that always begins with your decision to accept the purpose of a warrior — to advance the kingdom.

My objective in this book is not to get caught up in the apologetics of theology, or to discuss the rapture or tribulation. My purpose is solely to share my perspective on an awakened identity as The Bride of Christ, and to embrace the *more* that's coming, as foretold in scripture. I pray we allow the Holy Spirit to lift our vision above man's perspective, and into the very heart of Christ and seek to see the Church through the eyes of Jesus.

As time moves on and we practice foundational basics as outlined in the upcoming pages of this book, we will become more aware, and confident in Whose we are and all that means.

There are so many awesome verses that back up the phenomenon of choosing to behave and think differently under His Kingdom identity. The choice to begin to renew your thoughts, and believe that you are a son or daughter of God makes all the difference. It's a game changer!

> "Greater is He that is in you than he that is in the world..." 1 John 4:4.
>
> "...with man this is impossible, but with God all things are possible," Matthew 19:26.
>
> "If God is for us, who can be against us..." Romans 8:31.

A key to walking in your authority is being in the Bible daily and quoting this scripture out loud. I personally do this in the mirror. As one of my favorite worship leaders often tells the audience, "Sing it until you believe it." — Powerful right! So that may be my next tattoo, and the perfect reminder when circumstances, emotions, or hormones contradict that truth through "feelings." And on that note, the quicker we realize we fight not against flesh and blood but principalities (Ephesians 6:12), we will start to recognize the enemy's familiar patterns that have tried to trip us up. These patterns could look like a distraction of any sort — a rabbit hole meant to keep us blinded from recognizing the truth of who we really are in Christ and God's plan for us.

In *REIGN: Restoring Identity*, we will unlearn what we have learned from a fallen world: exposing common lies the enemy uses to play mind games to desperately throw us off. He will use anything to keep us from recognizing who we were predestined to be, and from seeing how significant we are as a collective voice of believers. At the end of each devotional chapter there will be key scriptures for further study and questions for personal reflection. Additionally, there will be prayers to break off toxic thought patterns that keep recycling in our lives, possibly from outside circumstances out of our realm of control. These will serve as practical strategies that are effective when we become aware of the predestined "bigger picture" at work all around us in His divine master plan.

We were called, created, and Christ died for us to become the sons and daughters of God. The restoration of our identity is the first step. Like the anointing of a royal, it's a statement of divine authority carried not only for the individual but for a kingdom. What follows is how we reign.

CHAPTER 1

Grounded: We As Human

"Each of us tends to think we see things as they are, that we are objective," wrote Stephen Covey, "but this is not the case. We see the world, not as it is, but as we are—or, as we are conditioned to see it. When we open our mouths to describe what we see, we in effect describe ourselves, our perceptions, our paradigms."[2]

Reading *The Business of Honor* opened my eyes to why we as humans are constantly on a search for purpose. The author described our perceptions and paradigms as the stories we tell about our lives. As human beings we are always looking for meaning in our experiences, and tying those meanings together in a narrative that makes sense to us. We are each driven to look for meaning, the meaning of us in our lives, families, communities, nation and world. We are looking for identity.

The truth is that the only one who can tell us with final authority who we really are, is our Creator. Because of the fall with Adam and Eve, we have all grown up searching for identity in a world of painful experiences, confusing messages, unhealthy relational dynamics, and by the apparent silence of any "authority" figure in our life who might set it all straight. We feel like the lost character in a novel searching for ourselves.

God's people are living in a society that is trapped in "grounded" cycles of chasing the proverbial white rabbit. We subconsciously chase platforms, recognition, status, money, and people's approval.

What inadvertently happens is that we start living under our own set of standards that we feel will secure love. We even sometimes allow ourselves to be objectified, and our bodies hijacked for temporary "cheap love."

Will attaining these feelings of acceptance by another human make us complete? Our definitions of identity have evolved from our society's search for purpose.

The false identities we chase are not automatically corrected the moment we come to know God and accept Him as our Lord and Savior. In that moment we enter a new identity, being adopted into sonship, and a new relationship with our Creator unfolds. However, to enter into the story, living in this new identity and relationship we must "unlearn what we have learned," as Yoda says. We all have struggled, searching for our identity in what we have, what we do or the people we choose to be around. These are not true identities, they are distractions and counterfeits. We must recognize and break false identities, and accept the truth of what the Bible says about who we really are.

Identity is "*the fact of being who or what a person is.*"S Once we ask Jesus to become the Lord of our lives, we take on a new identity, we become royal heirs as the Bible tells us. The next natural development is to learn to walk in our new identity as sons or daughters of God. This is relational identity.

Misplaced Identity

How difficult this fallen world has made it for us to find our value in our real identity. Our skew for identity comes from our own perspectives, past experiences and those "authority" figures who did or didn't leave us secure in who the Bible tells us that we really are. Perhaps those figures were present in our life, building us up as children under their care, or not present at all, leaving us vulnerable to rely on ourselves to figure out the universal questions: "Who am I and why am I here".

How easy it is to allow the residue of a broken world filled with rejection, misguided messages, other hurting people, and the absence of God's truth regularly spoken into our life shape our thoughts, emotions, behaviors, responses, and the perception of our own identity. We search relentlessly for "our place," and can easily get side-tracked into orphan-cycles of chasing our security, our value, and our identity in other people and positions. In that cycle, we will never really be "found."

Victim Identity

A lie we can mistakenly make definitive to our identity is victimism. A victim mentality is defined as, "an acquired personality trait in which a person tends to recognize themselves as a victim of the wrong actions of others, and to behave as if this were the case in the face of contrary evidence of such circumstances."

[4]In some situations, those with a victim mentality have been the victim of wrong actions by others, even though they may be entirely innocent. I'm not saying anyone who suffers through tragedies doesn't necessarily mean they will develop a universal victim mentality, constantly believing to be a victim. Victim mentality is mainly developed from relational dynamics between family members and situations experienced during childhood. Victims of abuse and manipulation often get trapped into a self-image of victimization. Some people suffer with a constant sense of feeling helpless, loss of control, negative thinking, along with strong feelings of guilt, shame, self-blame, and depression.

Specifically, I want to look at shame and guilt, and show you how an experience from the seeds of shame can impact our identity, if not recognized and corrected against the Word of God. Guilt is associated with an action; shame is tied to identity. When shame twists, sets root, and becomes our identity, it fuels the sense that we are unworthy. The truth is that we were made for connection with our Creator!

We live in a world filled with humans who make decisions out of their God-given free will. Decisions that impact others positively or negatively. No human should hold the power of our identity or value. The significance of recognizing our real identity created in God's likeness is a game changer, and embracing what our Creator says about us in the Bible is the most freeing and healing feeling. No one knows best like the One who knew what He was doing when He made us. "For from Him and through Him and for Him are all things." Romans 11:36. If only we would come to Him, our Creator, for our healing, setting our anxious minds and weary hearts right from the misdeeds done to us that resulted in our wounds, emotional trauma, reactions, and search for worth. We don't have to define ourselves from our experiences, heartbreak, or feelings. The Bible's definition of how we were designed tells us the Uncreated One had a magnificent plan. Psalm 139:13-14 says, "You created my inmost being, you knit me together in my mother's womb. I will give thanks to you because I am fearfully and wonderfully made..."

We were created in the likeness and greatness of God. Those who profess Jesus Christ as their Lord, and begin a relationship with Him are offered a new identity in Christ, a new perspective and new way to live on Earth! We take on Christ, and are ruled by His law of love. We were predestined as humankind to fulfill prophecies spoken before the creation of the world. We are The Elect, The Beloved, heirs with Jesus Christ, children of God. This is who we are!

*If this section spoke to your heart, or you've experienced abuse and trauma, or struggle with thoughts of depression, self-harm and suicide, I urge you to contact a Christian counselor or your local church and seek out a respectful and humane counseling practice.

Sexuality as Identity

Growing up one of my favorite movies was Dumbo. I was taken with the adorable, baby pachyderm and fascinated by the life of the circus, where Dumbo the "flying elephant" was the main attraction. Years later, I remember watching a documentary about the real life situation of circus animals and trainers. The elephant act caught my attention. In the footage, I remember seeing a mighty and incredibly strong mammoth being restrained, a chain around its leg, held only by a stake in the ground. I was amazed by that: how could a simple binding tethered to a peg actually hold such an animal? But au contraire! It did hold. It was as if the elephant was resigned to "staying put." Was this some kind of Jedi mind trick?

Come to find out, this is how circus elephants are trained to "stay put."

In an interview with a trainer he shared, "When they are young they tie a chain around their leg and attach it to a concrete block that was anchored deep into the ground and for the first few months they will tug and tug on the chain." Over the next few months of pulling on the chain they realize it is useless because they are never going to get free. As soon as the elephant gives up they can replace it with the rope tied to the stake. The elephant will feel the resistance and they will not attempt to escape. Now does the elephant have the ability to get away? Of course he does, but he doesn't know that does he?

A lot of us struggle with feeling tethered to the ground, unable to realize our full God-given potential. How difficult this fallen world has made it for us to find our value in our real identity. Sadly, there are many reasons why people question the legitimacy of their gender. The idolized celebrities tell them, "I was born this way..." feeding into the narrative that sexuality, defines our identity.

The issue of gender preference has become almost prioritized in our Western culture: to where the role has redefined the purpose of family: which is natural procreation.

Gender confusion runs counter to how God designed our bodies. Ramming a round peg into a square hole: it just won't fit... no amount of surgeries, hormone injections and empowerment talks defending why you were "born that way" will fill what God designed originally. It's undeniable. You are perfectly and wonderfully made. You are made in the image of God. Some say, God has no gender, that He is a spirit only. But in multitudes of ancient books across cultures, the names of God all carry masculine traits. He is commonly referred to as God the Father.

So gender is intentional, allocated by the Divine Creator Himself, and purposeful. Without gender there would be no procreation to make the generations...for the purpose of God to lavish his infinite love on.

Jackie Hill Perry is the author of "Gay Girl, Good God: The Story of Who I Was and Who God Has Always Been" and shares her personal story and perspective.

> "In Genesis, we all know that in the beginning it was God who created the heavens and the Earth. Him being God means he is all-authoritative. Him being God means that he is eternal. Him being God also means that he's good. And he creates these people, Adam and Eve. He makes them in his image. Them being image bearers of the living God, is a sign post of who they are to serve, who they are to belong to.
>
> In Genesis three, it says that Eve looked at the tree and it was desired to make one wise. That's an affection. That's a passion. And so, now I come inside of this lineage of people who are ruled by passions. This lineage of people who, when they look at something that God has told them not to handle or not to eat from, they don't think he's right in his estimation of what will happen if they disobeyed. I was born in St. Louis, Missouri to a single mother. She loved me well. My daddy loved me sometimes. I think my daddy loving me occasionally kind of gave me an early skepticism towards men. A skepticism that meant, or to me said, that they are not to be trusted. That they are not to be believed. As well as, I wasn't only just fatherless, but I also was molested. And so, not only am I abandoned and rejected by my dad, but I am also objectified by another male figure.

Now, I think many people might think that is the reason behind same-sex attraction. I don't think molestation and fatherlessness cause the same- sex attraction to exist. I think if anything, it gave me reason for why I should pursue it. I think it existed before that because I was born in sin and shaped in iniquity. But if anything, it affirmed that this is really what I should do because all of the evidence of doing the opposite doesn't seem that safe."

This is senior year, I'm 17, and a friend of mine, she walks up to me and she said, she didn't say, "Hi." She was like the devil...she comes up to me and she said, "Hey Jackie, when you (wanna go out) you should be my girlfriend." I said, "Wait, that's a real gay." Because I had to act real straight. I said, "That's gay. You gotta chill out with that." But she didn't know that her question actually gave me now calls for who I could act out these passions with.

And so, I got in a relationship with her.

I enjoyed it. But even in my enjoyment of the women that I was with, even in my enjoyment and all of the other sins that I persisted in, I did not have peace. There was this weird kind of awareness that me and God were at odds. I think that that's owed to Sunday school.

I say that because, that's just a caveat of encouragement that the little small but heavy big truths that we give to our children might very well be the thing that God uses to convert them later in life. And so, I think what Sunday school taught me was just the simplicity of the gospel, which is that Jesus has come to die for sinners so that they might live. That's all I needed to know. I didn't need to know Leviticus and justification and torment and propitiation. I didn't need all that. I just needed, "Jesus loves sinners, so he died for them." In this time, I have this conviction that I don't know what to do with.

And so, what happened was, I had a conversation with my cousin, Keysha. Keisha was the one Christian that I could call that would actually talk to me. What I mean by talk to me is, I could call her and she wouldn't immediately go to, "You know you're going to hell, right?" She didn't feel this pressure to have a evangelistic conversation with me every time we talked. To me, it felt like she loved me like Jackie, the image bearer, and not just Jackie, the gay girl. She loved me in a way where I knew she wasn't trying to fix me, she was just trying to love me. That's not to say that we don't have specific conversations, but it is to say that how we love people has to be a holistic kind of love.

And so, I called her and I said, "You know what, I feel like God is calling me. I really do feel that way. I feel like God wants me, but I don't want him. I'm good. I'm enjoying myself. I'm enjoying my life. I ain't going no peace. That's why I'm scared to die, but other than that, I'm enjoying myself." And she told me, she said, "You know what, Jackie? I'm not worried about you, because I know that God is going to show you how much you need him." I'm a sinner, that didn't make no sense to me. I'm like, "Okay. Amen. I echo that." That was way more funnier to me than it was to y'all.

She was right though because, what began to happen is that my life got a little difficult. I got arrested and went to jail for like two hours. My father passed away in a motorcycle accident, which was hard. Because to me it meant that the hopes that I had that our relationship might one day be normal, would never be, would never happen. And I started to think, "Does

God really want me this much that he would make my life difficult?" I think that's the beauty of Providence and suffering in it, because I feel like God was allowing my life to become a little messy so I had to look up. all of you is messed up. And if all of

> you was messed up, that means that all of you needs me." God is saying, "I don't want a section, I want all of it for myself."
>
> God wasn't calling me to a temptationless Christianity, but God was calling me to love him and walk with him so even in light of whatever temptations may persist and consist, that he would give me the power to flee every time if I trusted him.
>
> I just saw my sin for what it was. I just saw that if God is calling me away from these things, then they must not be worth it. And if they aren't worth it, then he must be the worthy one. Then he must be the one who I was created to love and enjoy and know, which is still terrifying. Because it's terrifying to let go of all that you know, that has been keeping you comfortable, that you think has been keeping you safe, and to fling yourself on the mercies of God not knowing what it is to be with him. When you persist in unbelief so long, it's hard to actually trust that God will be there to catch you when you fall." (July 11, 2020) "Jackie Hill Perry on Gay Girl, Good God." https://www.thegospelcoalition.org/podcasts/tgc- podcast/jackie-hill-perry-on-gay-girl-good-god/

When we repent, we start the transformation process of conforming to His image. Therefore if anyone is in Christ, old has passed away, behold the new has come (2 Corinthians 5:17).

Our skew for identity comes from our own perspectives, past experiences and those "authority" figures who didn't leave us secure in who the Bible tells us that we really are. I believe because we search in all the wrong places for "our place," we easily get sidetracked into orphan-cycles of chasing affirmation, our value, and our identity in other people and positions. In that cycle, we will never really feel "found." It's undeniable, the ache will remain to search out Whose we really are: that is relational identity.

Jackie mentioned because of witnessing other "authority" male figures in her early life who didn't model good character, it drove her away from wanting a man at all. From her experience men were unstable, untrustworthy, and unkind.

Here I want to highlight a critical point. People are by nature sinful. We often look to people and throw God into the same box, making it nearly impossible to wrap our heads around trusting a "Good Father." Because half of us don't even have a grid for that. On top of that and even more shameful, God the Father has been grossly misrepresented by people in "the church" throughout history. It makes so hard to humbly yield our hearts and come to God with our will and even attempt to look to God who you may or may not believe exists at all.

But friend, there is proof He loves you more than anything, because the Bible tells us so. The Bible, against what most think, isn't a book of rules or a book of legends. The Bible is a true story... it is a daring rescue story...it's an epic love story...The Best part about this story is that it's true! There are lots of stories in the Bible, but all the stories are telling one main story—the story of how God loves His children and comes to rescue them.

So let's put to rest how God has been misrepresented as a good father and totally trustworthy. Allow me to build this case through His Love Letters.

> *My Child, you may not know me, but I know everything about you (Psalm 139:1). I know when you sit down and when you rise up (Psalm 139:2). I am familiar with all your ways (Psalm 139:3). Even the very hard on your head are numbered (Matthew 10:29-31). For you were made in my image (Genesis 1:27). In me you live and move and have your being (Acts 17:28). I knew you been before you were conceived (Jeremiah 1:4-5). I chose you when I planned creation (Ephesians 1:11-12). You were not a mistake, for all your days are written in my book (Psalm 139:15-16). You are fearfully and wonderfully made (Psalm 139:14). And I brought you forth on the day you were born (Psalm 71:6). I have been misrepresented by those who don't know*

me (John 8:41-44). I am not distant and angry, but am the complete expression of love (1John 4:16). And it is my desire to lavish my love on you (1John 3:1). Simply because you are my child and I am your Father (1John 3:1). I offer you more than your earthly father ever could (Matthew 7:1). For I am your provider and I meet all your needs (Matthew 6:31-33). My plan for your future has always been filled with hope (Jeremiah 29:11). Because I love you with an everlasting love (Jeremiah 31:3). For in Jesus my love for you is revealed (John 17:26). He is the exact representation of my being (Hebrews 1:3). He came to demonstrate that I am for you, not against you (Roman 8:31). And to tell you that I am not counting your sins (2 Corinthians 5:18-19). Jesus died so that you and I could be reconciled (2 Corinthians 5:18-19). His death was the ultimate expression of my love for you (1John 4:10).I gave up everything I loved that I might gain your love (Romans 8:31-32). If you receive the gift of my son Jesus, you receive me (1John 2:23). And nothing will ever separate you from my love again (Romans 8:38-39). I have always been Father, and will always be Father (Ephesians 3:14-15).

The question is...Will you be my chid? (John 1:12-13). I am waiting for you (Luke 15:12-13).

Love,

your Dad, Almighty God

Adams,Barry.(1999).FatherHeartCommunications-https:// www.fathersloveletter.com

Now do you believe His love for you is more than your love for you?

He is a good Father and desires us to be at peace, be whole, and walk in heart and emotional health. Since we live in a broken world where rejection is rampant, our wounds impact how we see ourselves, and sometimes who we think we are supposed to be. It's easy to listen to noise around us. But the only true place to find the truth about who we are is with the one who has the ultimate authority, our Creator.

Let's just put the sexual identity issue aside for a moment: We are all sinners, born into iniquity. At the most costly gift of Calvary's Cross, God made provision for us, to be made holy as He is holy. It is God's ultimate desire for you to be found by Him, know true peace and receive healing into areas you may have kept in the closet for years. It is part of human nature as a sinner, there will be things that come out of us that we didn't choose, that we don't know what to do with.

But guess what? We do have a God who gives us a spirit, if we would choose to repent and believe in him. Who will empower us to have self-control: a fruit of the spirit!

If you are feeling conviction of any sort, please be courageous and capture this moment with the Lord. Ask Him to forgive you of listening to the wrong voices, of believing the noise. He wants all of you...He wants to take the trauma, the confusion out of your head and heart, to help build back trust, not just in other people but in a God who really is *for you*, has your best at heart and is wildly in love with you. He wants you to believe even for the possibility of a healthy, consistent, compassionate relationship with the opposite sex. It's not only possible, it may be part of a bigger purpose than just you and your experiences to date. Dare you to dream outside of the box? Because He is able to accomplish more than you could ever ask or imagine!

Artist: Melissa Burch

CHAPTER 2

Lessons From a Kitchen in Kentucky

I grew up in a very close knit family in Kentucky. Family tradition was almost religious. Over the river and through the woods to Grandmother's house we go, in our case it was my aunt's. Every holiday was an occasion to get the bunch together. Easter, Fourth of July, Thanksgiving, Christmas, and New Year's, we would all congregate. All the cousins would show up, the mothers toting in aluminum-wrapped casserole dishes, and happiness electrified the air. There would always be singing and lots of praying when everyone got settled into my aunt's family room. Memories of eating sweet potato casserole with gooey marshmallows, sneaking fancy cookies from the tower of colorful treats stacked carefully on top of paper doilies, and my sister's and my favorite tradition: dancing to my aunt's Beach Boys "Summer Days" tape. She had the raddest 8- track floor console! It had stereo sound and was huge, complete with disco lights that flashed to the beat. We got that thing rattling! My sister and I would dance for hours, getting totally dizzy and sweaty, but we had the best time! Those days shaped how I saw family, enjoyed being silly me, felt safety, and learned how to trust.

Throughout the years of family gatherings, some very important conversations would come up around my aunt's kitchen table. My aunt counseled us, helping us conquer fears, get summer jobs, figure out guy problems, and general teen issues.

One particular summer sticks out for me. We had been attending church meetings a lot. My Mom found an awesome lady evangelist who was really ministering to where her heart was at the time. She had taken me to some of the evening meetings. Her prayers were being answered, because I can remember breaking down and crying out of the blue. I was trying to explain to my cousin this unfamiliar yet acute void I was feeling in my heart. I felt so wretched, and aware of how selfish I was. I adored my cousin, she was just like my aunt, bold in her faith. She lead me in a prayer asking Jesus to come into my heart. And there on the floor, a snotty-nosed mess, I found a peace I had never experienced before. The Lord used my family to speak into my life at very impressionable stages.

Being Robbie Lynn's and Terry's daughter I learned how to "do family well". Thanks to the matriarchs of the family, we saw early on what that looked like, and the impact it had. It was evident when it was time to leave but no one wanted to. The amazing women in our family had grown up in a large family all under the same roof, and experienced the same type of family strength. If it wasn't for their hard work behind the scenes getting the house ready, food made, and care given to the details, the generations of cousins wouldn't have passed those characteristics on to their kids. We are two generations deep now, we have 3rd and 4th cousins crawling around underfoot at the Christmas gathering!

A few years ago, my husband and I decided to follow his career moving us to Florida. I hadn't realized the scope of how things would be different for us, especially missing my close-knit family. Our year round, large family get-togethers were reduced to one special trip: Christmas in Kentucky. Now as a Mom, I was learning how important the feeling of "family" was, and for my boys, I wanted them to recognize the same value. We started our own traditions in Florida opening our home up for prayer gatherings, get togethers, and always having lots of food around. I even still make some of my Kentucky matriarch's famous southern recipes. God was filling my heart's need for family as a Florida transplant.

I realize a lot of what I learned about family came from the strong women who loved us all unconditionally, not only giving us endearing memories or shaping how I make our own family traditions, but how we reach out to others. Women by nature possess a unique God-given gift that affects how we see ourselves, including our natural need to nurture and encourage others. And when you add in the power of prayer in that group, oh my! Half a dozen praying sisters (and brothers) will put 10,000 angels to flight!

Even though my precious grandmothers and aunt are in Heaven now, their prayers and encouraging counsel are alive in me. Those prayers kept me alive. Their love, which was sometimes tough, challenging me to rethink my decisions, more often than not got me back on track over the years. Hearty. Their love and affirmation was so stick-to-the-ribs hearty it seemed like it should be served with a side of sweet potato casserole. And it changed me.

"Family" is a foundational dynamic that shapes us. But its intimacy with a Father that brings real heart-filling wholeness. And what better way to understand Family than with the ultimate Papa. And what does the Creator of the Universe say about His children? I feel He wants to lovingly affirm us, even closer than a mother or grandmother can, meeting our heart's deepest needs. I feel He wants to encourage his sons and daughters out of ambiguity and uncertainty, and love on us, coming just as we are.

Guys, the strength and wisdom God naturally downloaded to men, scare the crap out of satan when aligned for Kingdom purposes. My husband attends a men's Bible study group regularly and every time he comes back more energized in spirit, inspired and confident. Brothers contending for each other in prayer, challenging each other through accountability and God's truth. Godly bros uniting to pray for their families, jobs, struggles, spheres of influence and communities can inspire and light the fires for God's sons to inspire, be activated in their unique callings, and literally bringing heaven to earth! Agreement in prayer is powerful!

And ladies, the enemy of our soul will use whatever means necessary to silence the natural God-given combo that only you possess: maternal compassion and natural intuition, because by nature we are caregivers. This combo of genuine care and intuition is a lethal threat to the enemy's agenda which is to steal, kill, and destroy. The enemy desires to mock, sabotage, create divisions and abort the God-ordained promises that we carry. So family, take up your crowns as His royal children who have amazing and predestined purposes to fulfill as the collective Church, the Ecclesia, His Beloved.

The crescendo is building. The crying out of the spirits of those who are called and chosen, are entering into a sort of birthing pain season, where our heart and will are being prepared and unified to bring His purposes to the Earth. The preparation of the Bride is happening. Individuals wanting to have an active relationship with Jesus, depends on one simple factor: free will. It is a decision to pursue His presence and pursue the things on His heart.

After professing and surrendering your soul to Jesus Christ in salvation, a great contention ensues of being a human meant for supernatural impact in God's realm that is unseen, yet very much alive! We will be taking on the internal struggles of the human that contend with the royal heir of God you really are. We will learn how to walk out and, more importantly, *believe* who you really are: a sovereign who is under the influence of the Holy Spirit for His Kingdom impact on the Earth.

PART 1

The Awakening

Artist: Eric Samuel Timm

CHAPTER 3

The Unveiling: From Origin Stories To Warriors

In 2017, Warner Bros. Pictures released a highly anticipated film about Wonder Woman, based off the comic book superhero in the DC Comics universe. My respect for the character grew as I watched the retelling of her origin story, her realization of who she was, and finally realizing her unique purpose. She was a daughter of the Queen of the Amazons, a tribe of fierce women warriors.

Watching the movie, I was captivated. I had never seen anything like an entire tribe of female warriors, just as fearless and strong yet filled with compassion that influenced how Diana Prince (Wonder Woman) ultimately made her choices. In a follow up movie, where she worked with a team of other Justice League superheroes to save the world, Batman confronted her after she told him to "... move on from mourning" his parent's death. He turns to her and says, "You're one to talk, you ran away for a hundred years because your boyfriend died!"[5]

Batman was addressing Wonder Woman. I loved seeing the respect come to life on screen. Balls-to-the-wall banter ignited between two superheroes, both with equal clout from accomplishments and their origin stories. Yet they both admitted to their frailty, succumbing to human emotion, and the pain of loss that rocked both their personal worlds so severely that Wonder Woman went MIA for "a hundred years."

However in this particular scene of reckoning, they both realized they were needed for purposes greater than themselves, and their time to step up was *now*. It was a choice. And in that conversation, they both were persuaded to let go of reflecting backward and inward, and start opening their eyes again to their greater purposes that would impact all human-kind. They realized who they really were: super creations, with god-like strengths, and because of the losses they experienced, a deeper empathy for the people it was all for. A compassion and resolve was building inside them to keep going even after experiencing a few temporary defeats, because they saw a greater vision: to bring peace, protection, truth, and justice for humankind.

In writing this book, the Lord was gently revealing to me that I had lived way below my pay grade. I was bought with a great price: the price of the blood of God's only Son, Jesus Christ. With that sacrifice, which was voluntary, a perfect God wrapped in human skin became sin and died on Calvary's cross. However, that was just the 'Introduction' to the book! Jesus, the perfect son of God was the sacrificial lamb, and if you study out "the making of a covenant" in ancient books and especially the Bible, it was a cutting of a sacred promise. The covenant would be made to restore humankind to God's ultimate plan.

That plan was for the fulfillment of the ages: humanity would bring forth the immaculately conceived Firstborn son of God. He was predestined to be crucified, cutting a covenant with humankind, and because of the cross, human hearts could hear the call and choose to become one with the Father in will and heart. This union of heart would bring the awakening of the Bride of Christ. The Godhead's plan was envisioned, and put into effect with the creation of humankind before space and time.

At the appointed time, the perfect Son of God was sent down to Earth, to show humans His ways, demonstrating what love really looked like to a broken world, and how to walk with the Father.

"Blessed *be* the God and Father of our Lord Jesus Christ, who has blessed us with every spiritual blessing in the heavenly *places* in Christ, just as He chose us in Him before the foundation of the world, that we would be holy and blameless before Him. In love He predestined us to adoption as sons through Jesus Christ to Himself, according to the kind intention of His will," Ephesians 1:3-5. Is that loaded or what?!

Let's jump back to my favorite fictional character, Wonder Woman. In the comic book, the writers share Wonder Woman's origin story as Diana Prince. As a child, Diana was aware that she was the Queen's daughter, and eventually realized and embraced her purpose. It was pivotal to humankind: she was called to save them, and re-establish truth and justice. She fought against the villains who wanted to selfishly make it all about them, striving to control the world (cue Wolfenstein and Lex Luther, among others.) Once she realized her purposes as a royal and a savior, she was trained to develop her physical strength as a warrior. This training began in the battlefield of her mind. Like any child born into a royal family, at the appropriate time they will be able to handle the reality of who they are and their destined purposes. The birthright is realized, and a decision is made to become who you are born to be.

It is so easy to be lulled into society's "grounded" cycles, chasing approval from people or status. That's pretty generalized, but it's the truth. I feel God gave me a big sister heart to rally the troops, share truth, and cheer the royals on in their real identities. If we could only recognize the divine authority we carry. If then we could only break away from society's distracting "matrix" of chasing accomplishments, and the approval and acceptance from other humans. Ephesians 1:3-5 talks about sonship. The verses say that, because of Christ's sacrifice on Calvary, we are offered adoption and every spiritual blessing in Christ. It was God the Father's pleasure to ransom His own divine Son, the Firstborn, to fulfill a predestined position, and to prepare His Bride.

How would we live differently knowing we were sons and daughters of God? I imagine a culture of Believers fearlessly speaking up for the weak, and seeking more opportunities to give to outreaches who are being the hands and feet of Jesus. This is what the first church looked like. They did life with others, showed them what discipleship looked like. They weren't just followers of Jesus Christ, some had literally walked on the Earth next to Jesus as his friend. They knew Him.

Even Christ's closest friends didn't grasp the full scope of Jesus's identity and their part in birthing the first Church, until they saw Him ascend into Heaven. He left! Their moment of reckoning had come. It was a choice not just to believe everything Jesus taught and lived out, but to think and behave like Him, from His laws of love. They probably didn't feel much like superheroes, but they had known the One who had defied death and the grave. They knew He lived inside of them. That realization was the game changer.

DIGGING DEEPER

Promises and Reflection

1. Read Ephesians 1

2. How does being adopted into royalty change everything?

3. How would you live differently knowing you were already approved of, and had "every spiritual blessing in Christ?"

4. Creative Gush: The space below is designated for you to unleash the creative you! Feel free to doodle, draw, write poetry, song lyrics...whatever this chapter has revealed to you.

CHAPTER 4

Who is Regina?

"Women, if the soul of the nation is to be saved, I believe that you must become its soul,"[6] Coretta Scott King was an author, activist, civil rights leader and the wife of Martin Luther King Jr. I couldn't imagine the daily struggles she faced in the 1960's and the conversations she had with her children explaining to them why it was all worth it: to change hearts and strive to end civil injustice once and for all. A woman of great faith, like her husband, Coretta walked out with dignity and stood up for truth in front of her children every day in a tremendously volatile time in history. I admire everything about her life and sometimes think about how deeply she hurt for her children and their friends as daily they faced bullying, heard hateful words yelled at them, and experienced physical assault at impressionable ages, just because of the color of their skin.

Her mother's heart of strength, compassion, and dignity made her a trusted voice for civil equality. By example, she embodied the word "mother," standing up for all minorities living in the United States.

The word "mother" probably gets you thinking about your own mom. But the definition I want to land on for a second, is the verb context of the word mother, meaning to treat someone with great care and affection.[7] Empathy, compassion, sensitivity, and courage to stand up for someone you feel responsible for are naturally what a mother's heart is wired to do. Nine times out of ten, a mother's radar isn't just for her own kids — just ask all the mothers I pass at Walmart who have given me "the evil eye" of judgement, or the eye of "I get you Mom, I have been there," when I wheel my kids out bickering as they kick their shoes off or scream for a free cookie at the bakery. Nevertheless, Moms have a heart-radar that aches deeper and holds on longer. There is science to back this up!

Women have a different set of chromosomes and a maternal structure that men don't. A woman has a built-in compassion button for nurturing, care-giving, and empathy. Certain neurons in the brain explain why females naturally behave as the "nurturer." Another interesting scientific fact about females, is that because of a "mirror neuron," we mimic emotion we see in others, and because of the compassion we naturally feel, are affected by it quicker than the "logic" signals connect in our head. This makes us natural advocates because of empathy.

Props to my ladies! And guys, I get that compassion or empathy may not come to you naturally, you really have to be aware, search it out and choose that perspective but it's very effective once mastered!

Here's an example: if we are given the gift of eyesight, but we don't see and notice things, then how can the *purpose* in our eyesight affect the world around us? Our destiny can also be engaged when we address something that may need repair or attention. Taking this to our spiritual purposes, we may take notice of something that digs at our hearts —that's compassion! And maybe that "unction" is for us to bring heaven down to earth and pray for that situation!

I love praying for individual situations. I also believe in the power of praying from a "big picture" view. We can intercede for, "His kingdom come on earth as it is in heaven." This perspective will revolutionize how you see God's plan at work in the earth. How God specifically designed female's brains and emotional structure for compassion is on purpose! Living in this world but not of it, we can pray for God's perfect will to be done on the earth from a perspective of genuine care, wholeness, restoration and freedom. It's all about people, and that natural compassion we carry inside our hearts will affect our prayers for others.

When we yield and are receptive to God's plan for our day, we will start to notice how He purposefully places people in our path for His reasons. We are His ambassadors on the Earth, thus we are carriers of His message of love and hope. Just like a photo filter can be applied to a picture, changing the color, lighting and resolution of the image, we can apply a sort of filter of perspective when seeing others. The filter Jesus wants us to start applying more frequently is how to start seeing others as Christ sees them, and that He died for them too. Once we start seeing through that filter of unconditional love, that's how His empire of love will advance, one kind gesture at a time. Through this perspective, we will start to recognize "Heaven coming down to Earth," because we are motivated by His heart for people. That's how God uses us to change the world!

Shining Bright

Every one of us has a unique story. Our struggles, exposed in a climax, can be turned over in a decision to overcome circumstances from a fallen world or even negative emotions, to capturing victory and trusting in a good Heavenly Father to walk with us through it all. It is a choice. It's God's intention that we let our lights shine through our thoughts, attitudes, choices, behavior, and outreach, reflecting His character and plans. If not, we are prone to become miserable, self-aware beings, stuck in that rut waving a white flag of resignation, and all owing circumstances to silence our voice and faith. According to Jesus, the heart really matters: "For out of the overflow of the heart the mouth speaks." Matthew 12:34. Complaining and grumbling reaps a harvest of toxic weeds from seeds coming out of our own murmuring mouths.

I was never a so-called social "follower," and that was built into my backbone. I couldn't accept it if I felt something deep down was wrong or off. I have always had an active and real relationship with the Holy Spirit so I would talk about it with the Lord, and later I understood that I was to be a voice for His ways. On some occasions I wouldn't participate in a situation, or if I was meant to affect and infect the situation, my heart would feel engaged, and I would pray for the situation to turn towards redemption and into a testimony. I would feel the Lord's heart was saddened by the hurt of people's choices.

That's who I am and why I am writing this devotional. It's a candid presentation from my perspective, and a conversation for us to read some truths we may normally miss in our fast-paced routines. I hope to bring in another perspective and realign what we see as truth, how we see ourselves, and how critical our voice of faith, our presence carrying Holy Spirit, and prayers can be. That view should make all the difference: that we are free to reign in this life, making impact for His Kingdom purposes. The Bible brings this point home reminding us that we were bought with a great price for His goodwill, and we are not our own.

It's time to pull the sheet off that has covered our true identity, revealing the image that the finished work of Calvary afforded us: to be the resplendent warrior Bride. That means all professing Believers in Jesus collectively will be carrying out His purposes in the Earth. Just as a body has many parts and purposes, so does the royal Bride of Christ. We are unique in reach and function, meant to touch all of creation for His kingdom impact.

Another beautiful analogy of this can be seen in a marriage. Just as husband and wife become one in the flesh, spiritually unified in a sacred covenant bond, the Ecclesia, or Bride, will become unified with Him in holy marriage, in will and in heart. Their purpose is to rule and reign together when He returns, which is imminent. Scriptures say in that age, there will be a new Heaven and Earth. Future generations of believers will make apostolic impact on the Earth.

It's a vision greater than any comic superhero's origin story can duplicate, because "The Bride of Christ" was already on the Lord's radar before the foundation of the Earth! To build on the foundation we read in yesterday's devotion, we begin to see the bigger picture chosen for us to be involved in:

> "Praise be to the God and Father of our Lord Jesus Christ, who has blessed us in the heavenly realms with every spiritual blessing in Christ. For He chose us in Him before the creation of the world to be holy and blameless in His sight. In love He predestined us for adoption to sonship through Jesus Christ, in accordance with His pleasure and will."
> Ephesians 1:3-5.

DIGGING DEEPER

Promises

1. Read Revelation 21:1-5

2. Creative Gush: The space below is designated for you to unleash the creative you! Feel free to doodle, draw, write poetry, song lyrics...whatever this chapter has revealed to you.

CHAPTER 5

The Restoration Of Regina Women's Purposes In The Church

"There is no such thing as a Junior Holy Spirit!" I remember hearing a minister emphatically preach this truth and it was revolutionary! The message of Scripture is clear, God has called all His children to prophesy, minister, and preach. Women, minorities, children: we all receive and carry the same Hope of Glory! It's unBiblical to say that women are not equipped to assume leadership roles in the church. Cultural norms as well as religious mindsets have helped spread and given credence to this lie, but in spite of arguments to the contrary, it is not supported by Scripture.

Bible verses have been contextually mis-preached because of the historical culture in which the scriptures were written, hence "submission" being the infamous word we normally associate with women in the church. But let's rewind about two thousand years ago and look at how Jesus, in his God-character, actually treated and viewed women.

Jesus was a huge advocate of women and their voices, and He was quite the rebel for the time. In fact, He taught the disciples well, and the writers of The Gospel followed His example, making it a point to include women and children in scripture, equally acknowledging women in a time of cultural sexism and suppression. He called them to be His disciples during a time when religious leaders instructed that it was disgraceful even to teach a woman.

As a woman, naturally I wanted to know how Jesus endorsed this suppressed people group. Ancient writings were sacred, as were the names worthy enough to be counted in ink on papyrus. Hundreds of women were highlighted, and their names featured in great appearance throughout scripture. Stories of strong women leaders reel from the Bible. Miriam led the Israelites in worship, and she was a protector and provider. Deborah the judge, Esther the Queen, Abigail, Ruth, Naomi, the Proverbs 31 women—were all women who made judgment calls and acted to benefit God's purposes.

In the New Testament, we read of the endorsement of the ministry, teaching and leadership of Priscilla, Lydia, Dorcas, Tryphena, Euodia, Syntyche, Junia, and Phoebe among others. God endowed these women with unique gifts for handling what came their way as they built God's realm.

Most of these were ordinary women living in their society, paying their dues as citizens when divine purpose chose them! And today we can read in one the oldest historical texts, the Bible, how these women's voices were highlighted and used during a time of great gender suppression.

I want to briefly land on how amazing one particular woman was named in the Bible as Mary of Magdalene. She was mentioned by name 14 times in the scriptures, a noteworthy woman for that unique culture and historical time. Most people immediately typecast her as the scandalous one, and Mary certainly did have a story, but not in the way most Christendom portrays. She was from a town called Magdala, known for its corruption and violence. Years and years of art and books haven't helped the cause, but she was most referenced in the New Testament as "the other Mary", signifying a loyal bond had developed with a restored Mary. Her story arc swings to leading other faithful sisters to financing the Lord's work out of their own means and following Jesus wherever He went. She was also the first person Jesus appeared to in His resurrected form. Here I want to address something that's become seed for scandal, but is false.

Some movies and fictional works have said she was the wife of Jesus. Upon seeing Him for the first time resurrected, her gut reaction was not, "Sweetheart!!" She addressed him as "Rabbonai" which is a formal term meaning "great teacher." The relationship was teacher to student or follower. I love allowing my imagination to read between the lines of scripture, and becoming aware of just how groundbreaking Jesus's presence was in Mary's life.

Mary Magdalene is just one example but let the truth of her story sink deep as you read in between the lines. Jesus desired women to be completely free from judgement and suppression. In fact, He definitely wanted them operating in influential positions. In fact scripture supports that He commissioned them to minister in His name. When Jesus sent Holy Spirit upon the church, as read in the book of Acts, many of these same women were in the upper room and received empowerment on the day of Pentecost.

> "They all joined together constantly in prayer, along with the women and Mary the mother of Jesus, and with his brothers." Acts 1:14.

> "When the day of Pentecost came, they were all together in one place. Suddenly a sound like the blowing of a violent wind came from heaven and filled the whole house where they were sitting. They saw what seemed to be tongues of fire that separated and came to rest on each of them. All of them were filled with the Holy Spirit and began to speak in other tongues as the Spirit enabled them." Acts 2:1-4.

Those who were Christ's disciples had been commissioned to go into all the Earth as witnesses, but they had been instructed to wait until the Holy Spirit came upon them to empower them to fulfill this commission. You can read about what that would actually looked and how it changed everything in the book of Acts.

To drive it home just how revolutionary Jesus actually was in that society during that time in history, we can look at another woman's story. In John 8 the scriptures tell us this lady was about to be stoned to death for being caught in the act of adultery. It was just the woman who was sought out to be punished, stoned to death, not the guy. Isn't that messed up? In this story, Jesus steps up and intervenes not only on the woman's behalf, but makes a bold statement about the dangers of judgement. Jesus turns to the crowd and asks them who was without sin to throw the first stone. With that one powerful challenge, the self-righteous filled with angry judgement were the ones publicly shamed. The crowd began lowering their stones, dropping their "weapons."

Jesus never saw the woman as an object like the rest of the crowd did, he saw right through to her soul. What was happening was fascinating and revolutionary! Check this out, it was the religious crowd who actually hyped the drama. They were just trying to use her as bait to frame Jesus! In spite of all the dynamics happening in those seconds, the fevered rage mounting among the crowd screaming for her blood, Jesus froze time and space. He saw her. He saw her past, heard her racing heartbeat, and saw her redemption story, filled with hope and joy. This is how Jesus *saw* people.

The crowd kept demanding an answer, so he turned to address them and said, "All right, but let the one who has never sinned throw the first stone!" John 8:7 (NLT) "Then Jesus stood up again and said to the woman, "Where are your accusers? Didn't even one of them condemn you?" "No, Lord," she said. And Jesus said, "Neither do I. Go and sin no more," John 8:10-11.

Jesus was one of the first women's lib advocates! He challenged women to think for themselves, to make positive choices that would lead to fresh starts, wholeness from adultery, that only leads to torment. Jesus saw all people as restored, set free, and purpose. The fact that his destiny as a man was picked to live on Earth in a very suppressive culture and time period, clearly implies that Jesus came to set all humans free from bondage and to share with them how God sees them! Jesus literally saved the woman's life, publicly trumping a religious law, and gave her an epic second-chance story!

He loved using taboo situations especially to demonstrate what God's love looked like, highlighting lessons for everyone from less than perfect people. He was into restoration stories that had ripple effects, championing those needing unconditional love the most.

The Bible is filled with stories of how God powerfully used women. It clearly says that women will preach. They will lead. They will be on the front lines of ministry. Like Deborah, they will take the church into enemy territory and watch as the Lord gives victory. Like Esther, they will not keep silent. Like Phoebe, they will co- labor with apostles to establish churches in regions that have never heard name of Jesus.

By His very life and teaching Jesus demonstrated that all believers, regardless of gender, ethnicity or social status, would have full access to the graces of the Spirit, and be anointed to share the message of The Great Commission to all the earth!

DIGGING DEEPER

Promises

1. Jesus was an advocate for women. Read Luke 8:3
   John 20:1,16-18
   John 8:1-11
   Acts 2:17-18

2. Have you judged certain people groups through a different lens? If so, have you noticed this bias play out in your culture? What would it look like to address this situation and include those overlooked in your personal world?

3. To church leaders, I ask the same question: what would it look like for you to address and include those in your church or ministry?

4. Creative Gush: The space below is designated for you to unleash the creative you! Feel free to doodle, draw, write poetry, song lyrics...whatever this chapter has revealed to you.

CHAPTER 6

Created In His Divine Greatness

God created us for greatness, and we are meant to use our greatness. Greatness. Another favorite word of mine. Genesis even says that humans were created in the image and likeness of God. If we could acknowledge that we carry God's likeness, then we would certainly treat each other differently! Genders and cultures would be celebrated! He came that all of us would be saved, unified, and included. People who value each other, can more easily recognize the beauty of diversity, and the richness in our differences. This type of respecting beyond "borders" demonstrates the heart's capacity to love beyond what we are familiar with. We can start seeing people with this type of respect, that our friend circles are added to, believe in and even start encouraging what they bring uniquely to the table. It becomes a celebration of diversity in relationships, ideas as the family of God does what we are meant to do best: shine bright!

We are all meant to bring divine impact to the earth. Each one of us is attracting another who may have a similar style, or share in our tastes for certain music or art. Respecting each other's greatness would be the filter in how we see others. No one would be viewed as second class or more deserving. To see each other through the eyes of God's love, means to see that He came and died for each one of us, every one.

If we were all created in God's likeness and greatness, and that Jesus Christ died on the cross for every one of us, then we are filled with purpose! That purpose activates when we accept Him into our hearts, becoming the sons and daughters of God by divine adoption. That is heavy! Let those words sink in a minute. So we have access to whatever is in his realm because we are His family. We were made in his likeness, so we are royals! Wow! But our society does a fantastic job, keeping us distracted into the rat race of chasing counterfeit greatness.

There are several definitions for *greatness:*

- "Unusual or considerable in degree, power, or intensity."
- "Wonderful; first-rate; very good."
- "Notable; remarkable; exceptionally good."[8]

It's popular to define greatness as perceived success. If you have power, money, and status, then the world calls you great. Sometimes it's chance; sometimes it's not. *"Some are born great, some achieve greatness, and some have greatness thrust upon them,"* says *William Shakespeare.*[9] Greatness, by the world's standards, is about material possessions and accomplishments. Achieving a gazillion followers on social media and attaining mass influence is great; there's nothing wrong with any of that. But is this the correct definition?

The world's messages of greatness can keep us in a ravenous cycle of chasing the next "standard." And often are like the dog who spots a squirrel— it's all over and off we go, totally distracted and running hard after the next level of accomplishment. So what's true greatness?

C.J. Mahaney explains the stark differences in the world's definition versus God's definition of *Humility: True Greatness, "As sinfully and culturally defined, pursuing greatness looks like this: Individuals motivated by self-interest, self-indulgence, and a false sense of self-sufficiency to pursue selfish ambition for the purpose of self-glorification. Contrast that with the pursuit of true greatness as biblically defined: Serving others for the glory of God. This is the genuine expression of humility; this is true greatness as the Savior defined it."*[10]

Jesus completely redefines what greatness is: serving others to the glory of God. In a word it's about humility. Knowing we were made in His divine likeness signifies that we were made for the glory of God while being a catalyst of humility for others. So children of God, how does that affect how we think and act? #RedefiningGreatness

DIVING DEEPER

Promises

1. Jot down some words that come to mind when you say the word "greatness", how does our culture define it?

____

____

____

____

____

____

2. Read Read Mark 10:43 and Phil. 2:6-7

3. Using the example of Jesus, what are some character traits of "being great" according to these scriptures?

____

____

____

____

____

____

4. Practically, how would you implement these characteristics in your relationships at home/school/work?

____

____

____

____

____

____

Reflection

1. Ask the Father to show you why He made you in greatness and how He sees you:

____

____

____

____

____

____

2. Pay attention throughout the day and even tonight, perhaps He'll show you in a dream. Write down what He shows you, or if you're feeling creative, sketch it out, write a poem, lyrics, etc...

CHAPTER 7

A Brave's Reward

Sometimes we travel through dark valleys so chilling and lonely, it shakes the core of who we are. Feelings of betrayal, rejection, and division squeeze the life out of us, and our heart feels like it's bleeding. And yet. Though the hurt feels fundamental, the deeper magic is waiting, pulsing. It consumes the sadness, bears it, transforms it and then restores it. Life has a way of testing what we're really made of.

Years ago I was struggling in a long test of my will. I was very aware and weary from the conviction I was feeling. I was desperately praying for answers, freedom and peace during a season in my life that felt confusing and on a professional level, down right disappointing. I had looked back at years of what seemed like sacrifice, laying down my dreams for others in critical seasons for them. How did the seed of discontentment and "wanderlust" get planted in my own heart? Years of comparing myself to other's lives played a big role.

When we pray, the Lord answers. He earnestly wants to expose the lie that had snowballed into discontentment and resentment. The Lord wanted me to release a misconception that had tainted my decisions, and consequently my resignations. When I started becoming aware of how I had squandered years of constant blessings, rest and fun to pursue "an identity" I was driven to achieve most of my life, I became withdrawn and angry. Years of chasing the white rabbit were wasted. Life situations beyond our control had stolen the luster from what my husband and I had always planned for and pursued in our "mission lives".

Even further, I was disappointed, I felt abandoned, and forgotten about. I wanted to feel worthy, to be heard...and everything in our situations felt like we were being buried alive. I was suffocating. I am being illusive for a reason, there are some stories I'm just not ready to share in detail, nevertheless, the pain and confusion I felt was real.

How I responded in that "crucible" season was dangerous. I began to dream outside my boundaries. I would imagine starting my life over. I wanted to feel valued, my professional experiences, and résumé recognized, the opposite of what I felt at the time: forgotten and buried. Those feelings of disappointment felt like a light exposing on the so-called "voids" I felt in my professional life. It was a low-frequency buzz of disappointment starting to resonate further and further, deeper and deeper into how I perceived just about everything in my personal life. In my inward-cannibalistic mess, I allowed my imagination to run wild. Fantasized possibilities quickly spawned into hope and desire! It's possible that the ground of our imaginations can be so alluring and deceptive that if left unchecked, we will throw all caution to the wind succumbing to wanderlust. My imagination was persuading my "good girl" willpower to give up.

I had convinced myself I was at a crossroad. I was so confused and hurting. I prayed. In my heart I knew He was exposing the ugly truth of my derailment plan. I had held onto it for years, keeping it a real option in my mind. The secret plan always brewing in the back of my imagination, it was altering my personality in a negative way. I had even changed how I dressed, disgusted by the good girl demeanor that got me nowhere. Resentment and anger were settling in, not good!

In exhaustion from struggling with an internal torment kept alive by my own imagination for years, I cried out to the Father. I literally felt like I was suffocating. I needed total freedom from this stronghold. I knew one scripture that contradicted everything I was feeling. It was the double-edged sword of truth in my situation, Jeremiah 29:11. "For I know the plans I have for you," declares the LORD, "plans to prosper you and not to harm you, plans to give you hope and a future."

I let myself drop under the weight of the conviction. I was finally waking up. I remember the day I broke under the power of the truth. He sees me as worthy. He has hope and a future for me, and not a dead end that I had felt. I crashed in a heap on the floor balling my eyes out. I wanted peace and to know that He would make beauty even for the ash heap I saw of my life. I realized I had been the arsonist in my own imagination.

The Lord then showed me very clearly a vision of an eagle's feather. I began a study of the significance of the eagle feather and immediately I knew He was speaking to me about my situation.

In many cultures throughout history feathers have been used as adornments on clothing, in the hair, or on ceremonial display that are very significant. In the African, Egyptian, Asian, Polynesian and American Indian cultures for thousands of years, artifacts have been found with feathers, specifically connected with royalty or as an award. In the American Indian culture, the eagle feather typically is given to a warrior or "a brave," person who has demonstrated honorable characteristics in battle. The feather symbolizes trust, honor, strength, wisdom, power, freedom and other attributes. Indians believe that eagles have a special connection with the heavens since they fly so high.[11] Some tribes today will not let individuals wear the eagle feather unless they are from royal blood.

What an incredible analogy! The character attributes of courage can only be developed while going through a hard battle. They are champion-worthy! Remarkably, He was telling me that He had already awarded me, calling me *brave* in my personal test that had lasted years. I was wrecked at that revelation. And in the same moment of revelation, I hear Him tell me that I could be trusted! He showed me He was honoring me because He heard my heart's real cry for the wisdom and God's perfect will to be done in the midst of my painful test. The Holy Spirit exposed the lies and gave me power to overcome and conquer the battle once and for all. He met me on the battlefield of my mind. He saw me as victorious already! That humbled me to tears because the fact was, I had struggled with shame for so long. But His banner over me was love, and consequently freedom because of Calvary's Cross.

I used to get buried in shame and guilt over struggles. Thankfully now I recognize the inner struggle quicker. That struggle is actually an internal war of conviction. The fact is that there is an active and opposite view loudly calling us above our circumstances, not only to have self-control in the face of temptations but also to stand up and war with the truth of scriptures. Jeremiah 29:11 is a great weapon of choice! This verse is proof that tests are meant to make us stronger, not bury us. The harder the battle, the greater our impact on the earth I believe. We will carry the overcomer's reward.

In spite of the dark lonely times or whatever our circumstances may look like, those who choose to reign in their imaginations, declaring the truth of what scripture promises say, will soar high above any situation. Those tests make us stronger, they make us warriors, reigning in this life for His Kingdom impact.

Embracing life's paradox of the bittersweet is where we discover our mettle. To struggle in a test is not shameful, but how we regain truth and reign through it brings about the manifestation of our real identity. Let us always remember whose we are, and that we are royal heirs by God's divine adoption. We are called sons and daughters of God. Let the motives of our heart be yielded to His heart, let the trust in a good God and His grace bequeathed to us from sacrificing our self-serving nature, exposed in testing seasons, give way to His loving and higher ways. Let the fragrance of our offering of praise be our adornment as His royals on this Earth. We have already been counted war-decorated braves! Let it ring to our core: we are children of the Living God!

God knew what he was doing when he created the eagle, one of the most noble, and majestic animals throughout history. The eagle is brought up 33 times in the Bible. Just as other cultures have used eagle feathers as sacred adornments, the characteristics the eagle represents are noble, very much a reward to those who choose to fly higher, seeing from God's perspective. Can I go one step further with this? Eagles' feathers cover their wings. The significance of wings denote strength to soar to heights no other bird can. Wings also symbolize protection throughout scripture.

Just as the Lord gave me a personal message saying he saw me as a victorious brave, He also protects us as we seek to do the right thing in the face of our personal battles and tests of character. Scriptures tell us we have the strength of the mighty as believers in Jesus. Just as Isaiah 40:31 says, trusting and waiting on Jesus in our trying times, our strength will be renewed. This is our heritage and promise as children of God!

> "Yet those who wait for the Lord will gain new strength; they will mount up with wings like eagles, they will run and not get tired, they will walk and not become weary," Isaiah 40:31.

We may enter into dark valleys for a season, where the quiet coldness of rejection and lies are deafening, shaking us to our core. It feels like winter and death, sorrow and pain. All half-truths. But God's deeper truth persists, refusing to be overwhelmed. It is older than death and wiser than time. The truth knows that there is more. There is hope. And in that hope we reign.

DIVING DEEPER

Reflection:

1. Ask the Father to show you where an experience from your past was actually a test to grow your faith and deepen your trust in Him. Write briefly about that test and what He showed you.

____

____

____

____

____

____

2. Memorize Jeremiah 29:11

CHAPTER 8

Mercy's Alliance

One of my favorite stories comes from Mark Twain's, *The Prince and the Pauper*. The historical fiction story unfolds on the upbringing of a poor young man raised by an abusive father and grandmother. And one day has a run in with fate. In an opening scene, the boy named Tom is daydreaming about what living in the lap of royal luxury might look like. Consumed by his imagination, the street beggar Tom began wandering toward Buckingham palace, where at that particular time some pomp and formality was going on just outside the royal grounds. Tom forgot himself for a moment, getting "too close to the palace gates" where England's Prince Edward VI was standing during a royal processional. This was a major no- no. Tom was seized by guards and imprisoned.

The Pauper and the King meet and are struck by how much they look alike. The two start to strike up a friendship. They devise a plan to switch roles for a little while. In a nutshell, the true King has the experience walking in the pauper's shoes, and is abrasively met with the garish reality of class inequality in England during the 16th century. People are burned at the stake, branded, and hanged for petty offenses like stealing a loaf of bread. Wild gangs wreak havoc in the streets fueling an atmosphere of danger and fear. Everyone is desperate to just survive one day at a time. And the King gets a real life taste of life outside the royal palace.[12]

The pauper, as one might imagine, enjoys the luxury of kingly living but has to learn the basics of royal manners and making laws. His manners are not consistent in the court, and that tips off a member of staff that starts the chain reaction to expose the imposter wearing the king's crown. In a turn of events, right before the official coronation of the imposter "Prince Edward VI" the real prince returns to the royal scene. The pauper learns what a king's rightful authority affords him, and the prince learns the lessons of mercy and compassion having barely survived London's streets. In *The Prince and the Pauper*, the experiment affects the newly coronated king and laws are changed, making life more humane in England. Wasn't Mark Twain brilliant?

The story telling talent of the author can trigger self-reflection, where we relate to a particular character. For me, I noted that our society today can be compared to the behavior of the pauper, just trying to survive in the wild streets of our own choices. But the tragedy here is not to realize the truth that we were purposefully created in the very image of the Godhead! Colossians 2:9 says the fullness of the Deity lives inside those who ask Jesus to be the Lord of their lives, surrendering their will to a heavenly Father's loving plan. When we submit our individual will, we take on the identity of a rightful royal, with lawful authority to impact the Earth with a unified will connected to the King of the universe! Our heartbeats synchronize as one with His heartbeat. Isn't that mind blowing?! His heartbeat is all love. He desires everyone to be saved and return to their Father as read in 1 Timothy 2:3-4, "For this *is* good and acceptable in the sight of God our Savior, who desires all men to be saved and to come to the knowledge of the truth."

The story of mercy is key. As we advance in our understanding and acceptance of one another as created equal in His likeness and greatness, not only will mercy grow in us, but an awakening to the truth: that in Him and through Him all things were created equal in His greatness! Cultures, heritage bloodlines have a common thread having been created in His likeness. Celebrating, encouraging others to discover and share all God has put inside them creatively to make impact is critical for believers to demonstrate. Our backgrounds and unique cultural stories of overcoming can birth the very seeds of compassion, a sense of family, respect, and human value. In His kingdom, hate and disunity were defeated at The Cross of Calvary.

To be made in His image also means we carry His heartbeat. Science proves that when two people hold hands, their heartbeats synchronize. I believe that is what is happening right now with God's people who are tracking with the Father's heartbeat for humanity. Mercy and compassion surge life-giving oxygen to God's heart, because He desires every soul's restoration. That same surge is pulsating louder. Can you feel his heartbeat? Our will and desires are being synchronized with God's love story for humanity. We can see this already happening across the world in prayer groups, worship events, movements of revival sweeping areas wherever God's people are unified in prayer, prophetically calling down heaven to earth. I believe the *more* the voices of the Burning Ones are crying out for is actually the synchronization of humanity's heartbeat to the Father's, we are wanting what He wants! The prayers we pray from how He unconditionally loves and desires all people to be in relationship with Him will sound like a declaration in the earth. We can get a glimpse that the collective body of Believers praying are actually the pivotal figure the Bible calls "The Bride of Christ". The Bride's heartbeat is syncing with His. The sound is building into crescendo, signaling a fulfillment of the ages.

DIVING DEEPER

Promises and Reflection

1. Read Genesis 1:26-27
   1 Peter 2:9
   Galatians 2:20
   John 3:16
   Romans 8:28-30

2. Creative Gush: The space below is designated for you to unleash the creative you! Feel free to doodle, draw, write poetry, song lyrics...whatever this chapter has revealed to you.

CHAPTER 9

Love Is Building An Empire

Soldier. General. Emperor. French military leader Napoleon Bonaparte was a giant of history and conquered much of Europe in the early 1800's. Near the end of his life, the exiled Emperor Napoleon came to the following conclusion about Jesus: *"I know men, and I tell you Jesus Christ was not a man. Superficial minds see a resemblance between Christ and the founders of empires and the gods of other religions. That resemblance does not exist. There is between Christianity and other religions the distance of infinity. Alexander, Cæsar, Charlemagne and myself founded empires. But on what did we rest the creations of our genius?*

Upon sheer force. Jesus Christ alone founded His empire upon love; and at this hour millions of men will die for Him.

From the first day to the last He is the same; majestic and simple; infinitely firm and infinitely gentle...The more I consider the Gospel, the more I am assured that there is nothing there which is not beyond the march of events and above the human mind. What happiness that Book procures for those who believe it!"[1]*S*

So said Napoleon Bonaparte. Love changes everything.

An empire built on love suggests governing from the heart. The scriptures say God is love. He created humankind to bestow his love and compassion on. God's grand capacity to love people is also seen in the intriguing life of Jesus Christ when He walked as a man on the Earth. The personality of Jesus is fascinating to me.

I get caught up reading in between the red-letter lines. He was a master at storytelling, driving a divine point home. His social circle was very fascinating. He hung out with people who needed love and they knew it, most of them were outcasts or misfits. He championed those who were suppressed like women, minorities, and loved it when children showed up. And he didn't just preach, he knew those precious people traveled a distance in the heat, and he fed them—miraculously in their thousands. Jesus valued people, and after all, wasn't that what the plan was all about?

How does this capacity to love translate to today's me, me, me society? Selflessly giving your time, and investing in someone else's life. This will impact their purpose! Do you see how this would advance a culture of love? How do we do that? Simply by reaching out! Do life, encourage others in multiplication of spreading His light on the Earth. The best way to teach that is by demonstration. Some label this discipleship or mentoring, no matter what it's called, the most effective way is to model Christ's characteristics as outlined in the Gospels chronicling his life.

The twelve disciples learned from "doing life" with Jesus on Earth. They watched as He led as a servant, locking eyes with the most overlooked citizens of Jewish society. He hung out with the culture's "unsavory," being called a drunkard by the religious leaders plotting to trap him because of jealousy. But what was He doing? The apostles knew. He was loving unconditionally. He was even referred to as a "friend of sinners," talking, laughing, and making conversations intentionally, diving into the personal lives of drunks, prostitutes, and tax collectors. He saw past their broken lives filled with dead-ends, rough-around-the-edges jokes, and loved every second He had with them. He hung out with what the church folk of that time called "the worst offenders". He saw them as Mary, Peter, Paul, and Nicodemus, their lives were all turned inside out and upside down once they encountered this man Jesus Christ. They got to hang with Almighty God wrapped in flesh, standing in front of them, and probably sharing a beer with them! They *received* Him. He not only paid attention to but the perfect son of God stopped life to zero-in on the sick, crippled, demon-possessed, deceased literally, and hopeless.

It was all about people and his mission was to model it all out in 33 years and make a sacred sacrifice. Feeling the all-consuming, fiery love His perfect heavenly Father had for humankind, He humbled his flesh to the point of being murdered on a Roman cross. Why did he do this? For love.

The red-letters in the scriptures show us how Jesus Christ himself "did life" with others, God wrapped in flesh and dwelling among humanity. He was sent as the love offering because God himself loved humanity that much. Jesus recklessly loved people. Do you think any belief kept him from reaching out to people and reading their hearts? I didn't hear of Jesus vetting people, for who deserved a miracle or not. He never asked what political party they were or who they voted for before he "read their mail" and healed them. Do you think he was intimidated if someone was drunk or unruly in his presence? Hello, Peter, the salty seaman! I mean do you get a picture of how Jesus valued other people? He was the most captivating personality that ever lived! Speaking of Peter, Jesus gives him a hint on how to build the empire of love in Matthew 4:19. Addressing the salty fishermen brothers, he calls out Peter and his brother saying "Come follow after me, and I will make you fishers of men." The next verse says, they dropped everything that instant and followed him. Wow!

To advance the empire of love, what Jesus Christ came and died for, we must reach across political divides, keep communication lines open no matter what agenda someone may stand for. We are called to be the ambassadors of unconditional love.

We are the only barometer another human has for God, when we call ourselves Believers. Strike up friendships with someone you normally wouldn't reach out to. Invite them to church, a prayer group, and continue reaching out. Get creative!

Invite them to your house for dinner, bring them a homemade meal, include them at your Thanksgiving table. As Christians I believe we are to do "family" well and that means extending what family looks like in our hearts. The greatest influence we have is the testimony of our life. Let's rewrite the headlines and advance the kingdom of love, starting by adding a leaf to our dining tables.

Even the mightiest of emperors can acknowledge that there is no power more influential and transforming than God's love.

"Love the Lord your God with all your heart and with all your soul and with all your mind and with all your strength.' The second is this: 'Love your neighbor as yourself.' There is no commandment greater than these." Matthew 12:30-31

DIVING DEEPER

Promises and A Challenge

1. Read Hebrews 4:15, Hebrews 2:5-18, Matthew 16:24-25, Isaiah 53 What characteristics about love stick out to you after reading these passages?

____

____

____

____

____

____

____

____

2. Challenge: "Add a leaf" to your dining table:
   In your prayer time today, ask the Lord to highlight someone He wants you to encourage. Perhaps this is someone he wants you to start "doing life with." Invite them to church or a prayer group, or just out for coffee, and let the Holy Spirit speak through you.

3. Creative Gush: The space below is designated for you to unleash the creative you! Feel free to doodle, draw, write poetry, song lyrics...whatever this chapter has revealed to you.

CHAPTER 10

The Model Of Love: Jesus Christ

The disciples had seen Jesus blow everyone's mind for three years. He was the ultimate! No one left his presence unchanged. He turned water into wine, brought a dead man back to life, healed people who were permeant street-side figures as begging cripples. The society knew who this man was. His disciples had seen him break society's social rules; He was a Jewish rabbi who told an angry crowd to consider their own sins before stoning a woman to death. She had been caught in adultery and drug into the street. His friends heard the tender kindness and masterful way He accepted requests of healing from toughened Roman soldiers on behalf of their families. Who did that in politically corrupt Judea at that time?

The disciples also witnessed the unthinkable. In the middle of a silent night, catching their Zzz's while Jesus was praying in a garden, Roman soldiers charged into the space with swords drawn demanding for Jesus. How did they react?

They were brothers protecting their own! But how Jesus responded in the middle of a fight baffled them all. He reached out to heal the soldier's ear Peter had sliced off in violent defense. Who did that? And what was going on? Was the miracle worker walking into a trap? Jesus wasn't caught off guard, as his band of brothers thought. It was hardly a trap, in fact, it was part of The Plan.

Jesus was about to be charged for religious treason, and executed as a criminal on a Roman cross. Throughout the Old

Testament, scriptures foretold of a Messiah coming that would cut a blood covenant oath affording humans who accepted Jesus as their Savior, the eternal promise of reigning with Him in heaven. "I am the way, the truth and the life. No one comes to the Father except through me." John 14:6. And all are welcome to accept this life-changing gift!

Anyone who comes to me will be saved. "For God so loved the world that he gave his one and only Son, that whoever believes in him shall not perish but have eternal life." John 3:16. The disciples were also going to witness the most horrific injustice in all of human history. They knew him and yet in this moment they clearly didn't; they were taken off guard, scared, overwhelmed, and then they bailed! His friends totally abandoned Him. Within three days, creation groaned, the Earth convulsed with earthquakes, nature was giving testament to a divine covenant being cut. Jesus the man received His most important mission: to die and take death on. But death had no power over him.

Scriptures tell us Jesus took up our pain, bore our suffering, took on our sicknesses and brokenness—every misdeed, everyone's, multiplied by all of human history—and yet His soul was not abandoned! Oh can we let our mind even go there? Hang on, because it gets even more epic! The Bible says He ascended (from the depths) a conqueror of death! "I am the Living One; I was dead, and now look, I am alive for ever and ever! And I hold the keys of death and Hades." Revelation 1:18.

Then true to his amazingness, He appeared in his resurrected body to his friends on earth. He told them what it was all about: The Great Commission. "Then the eleven disciples went to Galilee, to the mountain where Jesus had told them to go. "When they saw him, they worshiped him; but some doubted. Then Jesus came to them and said, "All authority in heaven and on earth has been given to me. Therefore, go and make disciples of all nations, baptizing them in the name of the Father and of the Son and of the Holy Spirit, and teaching them to obey everything I have commanded you. And surely I am with you always, to the very end of the age," Matthew 28:16-20.

He left his friends with a clear directive: to advance His empire of love! How do we do this practically? Through our compassion. Jesus was the perfect example. We see Him time and time again responding to those suffering in his society, we read about the accounts throughout the Gospels. The sick were made well and the blind given sight. He liberated those who were bound by social injustice and prejudice. Those bound by demonic powers were set free. He was led by the Father, making time for people even in the most chaotic circumstances.

Christ's empire of love will spread through how we treat one another in respect. Jesus respected people, especially the overlooked in society. He repeatedly gave voice and valued women – an attitude largely unexpected and unknown in his culture and time. He respected the downtrodden and poor. It's the purpose for which He came according to Luke 4:18-19 "The Spirit of the Lord is on me, because he has anointed me to proclaim good news to the poor. He has sent me to proclaim freedom for the prisoners and recovery of sight for the blind, to set the oppressed free, to proclaim the year of the Lord's favor."

I have noticed that the gift of listening really makes me feel valued. Jesus was an extraordinary listener. Whether it be his enemies or his disciples, Jesus valued people by listening to them, and He always responded thoughtfully and with patience.

Finally through encouragement, people will notice when we see them through God's perspective. Jesus spent a great deal of time encouraging people in love.

The Beatitudes in Luke 6 serve as a call to be responsive to God, and to love others as Jesus taught throughout His life. He challenged us to be peacemakers, humble, pure in heart and merciful in times of difficulty. Throughout the Gospels that recorded Jesus's life, it can be seen that He accepted and loved all people, especially those at the bottom of the social pyramid – the poor, women, outcasts, lepers, children, prostitutes, and tax collectors. Jesus is the perfect model of loving your neighbor as yourself.

The Bible tells us God's very purpose in creation and redemption was to have a family of children conformed to the image of His Son. Jesus was the model of love, our perfect standard. Out of the overflow of Jesus's love for the Father was a life in constant service to others; this is how His empire of love will spread through us, one person at a time.

DIVING DEEPER

Promises and Reflection:

1. Read 1 John 2:6, Matthew 5:1-12, Luke 4:18-19, John 13:34

____

____

____

____

____

____

2. In reading Matthew 5:1-12, in what ways do you see the Beatitudes challenging and conforming our own attitudes to Christ's? Can you give a recent example?

____

____

____

____

____

____

3. Ask the Lord to show you how to be a model of love to someone today.

CHAPTER 11

Is Perfection Possible? 7 = —|——

The person I want to emulate is Jesus Christ. He knew no sin, and the Bible said even though he was tested like any man, He was perfect! The Word also gives us instruction implying that this is possible for us! "Be perfect as your Father is perfect," Matthew 5:48.

Now I know what you must be thinking right now, "Yea right?! Me, I could never be perfect!" Well, let's look closer at what Jesus actually meant by that.

He was telling us that God is the standard against which everything else is measured. Specifically, we are to love our enemies so "that you may be children of your Father in heaven," Matthew 5:45a.

You all know I love word studies, so track with me as we unpack this. The use of "perfect" here means complete. God loves everyone, even evil people. This is how we can be perfect like God. Our love for our fellow human beings needs to grow, maturing to even include loving our enemies. If we do not love our enemies, we are not behaving as the sons and daughters of God should. So can humans who are believers in Jesus be perfect? This is kind of a trick question. We've all heard the sayings, "Nobody's perfect," and "Christians aren't perfect, just forgiven."

God doesn't expect us to be perfect in the sense that we never sin. He knows we sin and has made provision for us through Jesus. "My dear children, I write this to you so that you will not sin. But if anybody does sin, we have an advocate with the Father—Jesus Christ, the Righteous One," 1 John 2:1.

"If we claim to be without sin, we deceive ourselves and the truth is not in us," 1 John 1:8.

We commit sins of commission—doing that which we shouldn't, and sins of omission—not doing that which we should. God sees and knows our weaknesses. And that is why in daily life we need His undeserved grace.

In spite of us, His infinite love is unconditional. Our relationship to God is not based on our perfection, but on Christ's. His perfect obedience is accredited to us so when God looks at us, He sees us as perfect. If we could be perfect by our own strength, Christ's death would have been unnecessary.

As His ambassadors, we are to live by Father's higher standards of love. He loves completely. Perfectly. Jesus instructed us that we must show love to all people, no matter what faith, nationality, or personality. If you love your enemies, you then truly are perfect and complete, like your heavenly Father.

Will we ever attain loving perfectly like our Father loves? This should be our goal! And we are to pursue it with our whole heart! Perfect love is a standard impossible for us to attain by our own efforts but what is impossible for man is possible with God. It's only through the power of God's Spirit His people can truly love and pray for those who intend to do harm.

I will get nowhere if I trust in my own abilities. That which God demands, only He can accomplish, including the demand to love our enemies. What is impossible for man, becomes possible for those who give their lives to Jesus Christ through the power of the Holy Spirit who lives in our hearts. For "I have been crucified with Christ and I no longer live, but Christ lives in me. The life I now live in the body, I live by faith in the Son of God..." Galatians 2:20.

Reading between the lines of the red letters in the Gospels, I am so intrigued at the man Jesus! I am fascinated at how he blew everyone's mind especially in that culture at that time. He is who I want to be like. His standard constantly challenges me to see, and treat others with complete love. His personality was all-God perfection, all-loving, and all-holy. Because of His love, the mercy and grace consumed and overpowered every other characteristic. This in turn made other humans who came in contact with Him want to be with Him all the time— they even left their homes and families to follow Him wherever He went! This wasn't charisma... it was Love! A love that spoke truth and no one was left the same after being in His presence. He genuinely wanted them free and He wanted them restored. He shared this wisdom in his parables while living a human life on Earth, and He was totally filled with compassion for people and that oozed out of Him. Love's effects on a society can change the world, one person at a time. This is how we are to do life with others God puts in our paths. They will encounter the God inside us.

Grace is mind blowing to me, making it possible to even love our enemies! Want to hear something else mind blowing? The Bible says when we ask the Lord to become Savior of our life, renouncing our sins He comes inside us changing us from the inside out! I believe this literally. That's also why we hear so many stories of people feeling conviction or turmoil over former lifestyle choices that just don't "fit" anymore. It just won't because we gave the reins over to an all-loving Savior who wants to steer us into total freedom, and loving people as He does. The Holy Spirit takes up real residency inside us, and things just feel different from then on.

Do you see what He sees? Do you hear what He hears? Do you want what He wants? Proof is in the convictions you feel when "trespassing." Mind-blowing right? So if He's literally taking up space in the temple of our body, we have access to everything He is! #ChangesEverything

The other side of this coin is that we feel his heartbeat, feeling what hurts him, feeling what affects him, and feel what He wants: a restored relationship with all His creation. Accepting the call to partner with Heaven transforms us into His ambassadors on the Earth.

DIVING DEEPER

Promises and An Experiment:

1. Read Romans 12:14-21

2. Experiment: For a fun experiment, ask Him to reveal to you that He literally takes up residency inside your heart. And in turn, ask to feel his heartbeat for people. What you will experience will feel like an encounter and is key for you to grasp as we read the pages ahead. This is a huge step, one because He wants to rebuild on a corrected foundation, two because He is restoring identities so we think and behave as He does!
   What is He showing you?

3. Creative Gush: The space below is designated for you to unleash the creative you! Feel free to doodle, draw, write poetry, song lyrics...whatever this chapter has revealed to you.

CHAPTER 12

"Remind me who I am, because I need to know..."

Actor and country music star Tim McGraw is one of my favorites. His knack for honest song writing really highlights where he's come from and where he stands. In an interview with Larry King on CNN, Tim shared a story when he was an eleven-year-old child, when he accidentally came across his birth certificate tucked away in his mother's closet. What he read on the paper changed everything for Tim. There was a different last name on his birth certificate, a very recognizable last name. His father was the major league baseball player Tug McGraw.

> *"The thing that I got from Tug more than anything is, coming from where I came from, and some of the situations that our family was in growing up that, you know, something about finding out that a major league baseball player, who's successful is your father, I think it instilled something in me that I didn't have, and it made me feel like I could go out and accomplish some things."*[4]

For McGraw, the discovery of who his biological father switched a light on, highlighting his real identity. The revelation inspired him to embrace a "skies the limit" mentality, enabling him to dream big, show up and go for it—all because he realized that what his real dad carried, and Tim had that in him too. It was life changing!

The same revelation holds true for every believer but on a cataclysmic level. We are called sons and daughters of God! Discovering what our heavenly Father says about us is the game changer: it will open our eyes to our real identities and our purposes. The Bible says we were on his mind before the creation of the world, we were called His family for great purpose!

"For He chose us in Him before the foundation of the world to be holy and blameless in His presence. In love He predestined us for adoption as His sons through Jesus Christ, according to the good pleasure of His will," Ephesians 1:4-5.

Facts are not the same as truth. A *fact* is a reality, like a stray piece of a puzzle. It's an object, or a bit of trivia. *Truth*, on the other hand, is all about *meaning*.

There are so many beautiful scriptures that explain our identity in truth. We are His ambassadors, His city on a hill, meant to carry the Hope of Glory into the world. He went to the cross for us to walk, talk, think, behave, forgive and love as our Father does. It's our royal lineage! Have you ever stopped to ask, "What does God think about me? Who does He say that I am?"

He sees us as valuable

> "I am the Creator and you are my creation. I breathed into your nostrils the breath of life, Genesis 2:7. I created you in my own image, Genesis 1:27. My eyes saw your unformed substance, Psalm 139:16. I knit you together in your mother's womb, Psalm 139:13. I know the number of hairs on your head, and before a word is on your tongue I know it, Matthew 10:30. You are fearfully and wonderfully made, Psalm 139:14."

> "You are more valuable than many sparrows, Matthew 10:31. I have given you dominion over all sheep and oxen and all beasts of the field and birds of the heavens and fish of the sea, Psalm 8:6–8. I have crowned you with glory and honor as the pinnacle and final act of the six days of creation, Psalm 8:5."

"However, from the very beginning, you exchanged the truth about me for a lie. You worshiped and served created things rather than me, the Creator, Romans 1:25. You have sinned and fallen short of my glory, Romans 3:23. You were children of wrath, living as enemies to me, Ephesians 2:3. You turned aside from me. You became corrupt. There is none who does good, not even one, Psalm 14:2–3. What you deserve is my righteous judgment, Psalm 7:11–12."

"And yet, in my great love, I gave my unique Son, that all those who believe in him will not perish but have everlasting life, John 3:16. While you were still sinners, Christ died for you... While you were still hostile toward me, you were reconciled to me by the death of my Son, Romans 5:8, 10. Sin doesn't have the last word.

Grace does, Romans 5:20."

"Now everyone who calls on the name of Jesus will be saved, Romans 10:13. You who have believed are born again, 1 Peter 1:3. I have adopted you, Ephesians 1:5. You are children of God, heirs of God, 1 John 3:2; Romans 8:16–17. You are no longer orphans. You belong to me, John 14:18; 1 Corinthians 6:19. And I love you as a perfect Father," 1 John 3:1; Luke 15:20–24."

He sees us as made new!

"In my eyes, you are a brand new creation. The old has passed away; the new has come, 2 Corinthians 5:17. Sin is no longer your master, for you died to sin and are now alive to me, Romans 6:11; Ephesians 2:4–5."

You are finally free from the slavery of sin and death. There is now no condemnation for you, Romans 8:1–2. All your sins are forgiven, 1 John 1:9. All your unrighteousness has been cleansed by the blood of Jesus, 1 John 1:7, 9. You are now righteous in my sight with the very righteousness of my perfect Son, Romans 4:5."

"You've been saved by grace, Ephesians 2:8. You've been justified by faith, Romans 5:1. You are utterly secure in me; nothing will be able to separate you from my love in Christ Jesus, Romans 8:39. "No one is able to snatch you out of my hand," John 10:29. "And I will never leave you nor forsake you," Hebrews 13:5.

He gives us His Spirit.

"You not only have a new Father, but also a new family of brothers and sisters, Luke 8:21. You are now part of the people of God, 1 Peter 2:9. And together the life you now live is by faith in my Son," Galatians 2:20." Look to Jesus. Keep your eyes on him. He is the author and perfecter of your faith, Hebrews 12:2. Christ is in you by my Spirit, and you are in Christ, John 15:5; Colossians 1:27. Stay close to Jesus. Abide in him, John 15:4. For your life is found in him, John 14:6; Colossians 3:3–4. "To live is Christ, and to die is gain," Philippians 1:21.

Don't live by your own power or understanding. No, live by my Spirit within you, Zechariah 4:6; Proverbs 3:5. Remember, I have given you the Holy Spirit to be with you and in you, Romans 5:5; John 14:17. The Spirit will guide you into all truth, help you to obey me, and empower you to do my work, John 16:7, 13; Acts 1:8; Galatians 5:16."

He sees us as transformed!

"As you seek me and see more of my glory, I am transforming you into the image of my Son, 2 Corinthians 3:18; Exodus 33:18. One day you will be changed, in a moment, in the twinkling of an eye, at the last trumpet sound, 1 Corinthians 15:52. When Jesus appears, you will be like him, because you shall see him as he is, 1 John 3:2; Romans 8:29."

"You will be delivered from your body of death through Jesus Christ, and your dwelling place will be with me, Romans 7:24–25; John 14:3. And I will wipe away every tear from your eyes, and death shall be no more, neither shall there be mourning, nor crying, nor pain anymore," Revelation 21:3–4.

"You will drink from the spring of the water of life without payment, and I myself will make for you a feast of rich food and well-aged wine, Revelation 21:6; Isaiah 25:6. You will enter my rest, inherit the kingdom I've prepared for you, and step into fullness of joy and pleasures forevermore, Hebrews 4:9–11; Matthew 25:34; Psalm 16:11). But most of all, you will see my face and be with me where I am," Revelation 22:4; John 14:3.

He sees us as ambassadors, representatives of Him on the Earth.

"Therefore, walk in a manner worthy of your calling, Ephesians 4:1. You are no longer darkness, but light in my Son. Walk as children of light, Ephesians 5:8. You are the light of the world, a city set on a hill, Matthew 5:14. I have called you, 2 Peter 1:3. I have chosen you, Revelation 17:14. You are now a saint, a servant, a steward, and a soldier, Romans 1:7, Acts 26:16, 1 Peter 4:10, and 2 Timothy 2:3.

You are a witness and a worker, Acts 1:8 and Ephesians 2:10. Through Jesus you are victorious, 1 Corinthians 15:57. You have a glorious future, Romans 8:18. You are a citizen of heaven, Philippians 3:20. You are an ambassador for my Son," 2 Corinthians 5:20.

When you receive Jesus into your heart, your identity is found, you're adopted into royal sonship. Colossians says the fullness of the Deity takes up residency inside of us! This should impact how we see our identity as a citizen of Heaven living on Earth.

Let's not be responsive, defensive, reactionary, or even copy the ways of the world. For we are aliens, we are in it but not of it. The mold was broken with us. We are royals, purchased with a blood covenant that conquered death and hell. Let that soak down to our core. He did that for You! This revelation is the ultimate life changer, it can impact our faith levels and our destinies! Our faith will be a place where hope is birthed, we start to dream again, and we show up, making impact for His kingdom.

American Idol contestant turned Grammy-winning worship artist Lauren Daigle wrote a song that shares the same revelation of how discovering our real identities in Him changes everything.

"You say I am loved when I can't feel a thing
You say I am strong when I think I am weak
You say I am held when I am falling short
When I don't belong, oh You say that I am Yours
And I believe, oh I believe
What You say of me
I believe
The only thing that matters now is everything You think of me
In You I find my worth, in You I find my identity,"[15]

DIVING DEEPER

Scripture Memorization and Reflection

1. Memorize this verse, "For in Christ all the fullness of the Deity lives in bodily form, and in Christ you have been brought to fullness. He is the head over every power and authority." Colossians 2:9-10.

2. Reflection: How will the revelation of being a son or daughter of God impact your faith? Share your insights here:

3. Declaring powerful truths out loud, and even sometimes in repetition, reminds our ears and in time, with continuous practice, starts an awakening in our minds and hearts of its chain-breaking, powerful truth. It can change how we think and ultimately behave.

Please join me in saying this Declaration out loud: "*I am loved by the Father. I am adored by the Father. I am approved of by the Father. He finds pleasure in me. He calls me capable. He calls me worthy. I am His desire. I am beautiful. I am indispensable. Today I receive His great love for me.*"

CHAPTER 13

A Privileged Position

In car rides, my oldest son sometimes instigates a game called *Would You Rather.* As you could imagine it gets interesting when a question is posed like: would you rather puke in public or pee your pants in public? It makes for some lively debate among our crew. So, readers, want to play? Would you rather — have power or authority? They're not the same. My guess is most people have never thought about it, and neither did I, until I started watching a documentary piece about the British monarchy.

Queen Elizabeth has authority without power, she is only a figurehead. Parliament has the authority to make laws. I love studying the origin of words. I am about to unpack for you a concept that can change everything for us as children of God if we receive this. It starts with comparing the differences between two words: power and authority.

Dunamis means power.[16] Exousia is a Greek word that means authority.[16] As children of God we were given both! Mark tells us in chapter 16 that we have been given power to cast out demons, lay hands on people and see them recover, and "read people's mail" prophetically. Those miraculous acts are *powerful* tools used like a hook God uses to show people how much He loves them and in turn for them to be receptive to Jesus Christ becoming their Savior. When we ask Him to become our Lord, we are adopted into royal sonship with the Deity. This affords us the authority to be counted as a joint heir with Jesus Christ! What a privilege that humanity was offered this gift because of conquered Calvary! However, when it comes to realizing our identities and this book's purpose we must compare the definitions of authority versus power. How do these two words pertain to our identity functioning as The Bride of Christ?

Exousia is a Greek word that means the sovereign, legitimate, legal use of power. Now don't start to yawn on me yet! To break this down here's an example to drive home how this applies to our identities. A police officer has a handgun, that means he has the 'power', but it's the police officer's badge that symbolizes that he has the legitimate, legal authority to exercise the power. How does this apply to our identity? Christ took away satan's authority and defeated it. "I am the Living One; I was dead, and now look, I am alive for ever and ever! And I hold the keys of death and hades," Revelation 1:18.

So there is no contest, family! There is no power struggle. Christ defeated him. Sure he roars around like a lion on the Earth, huffing and puffing, but we carry a rightful and privileged position of ruling and reigning with Christ Jesus. That should shock your faith back to life! When we want what the Holy Spirit wants for His purposes, we are as sovereign as He is.

Want to know the true purposes that comes with our authority as His children? His predestined purposes for us to be involved in are unshakeable. Incorruptible. Unmovable. Promises fulfilled. Meant for expanding and taking back areas of influence that rightfully originated from His Kingdom. No stronghold in hell has entitlement to souls and ideas meant for His Kingdom flourish. Love is building this empire! The Bride carries His Kingdom come to this Earth. We as The Church must recognize how this changes everything. The Great Commission explains "the how," spoken by Jesus himself before he ascended into heaven, "Go and make disciples of all nations, baptizing them in the name of the Father and of the Son and of the Holy Spirit, and teaching them to obey everything I have commanded you..." Matthew 28:19-20a. After all, what was the Cross for?

Recognizing what the Cross afforded us, to become joint heirs with Jesus, and carry the authority of Jesus indwelling inside us, we virtually carry the Hope of Glory! We carry Holy Spirit, who has all the answers not only for personal growth in Him, abundant living with relationships and family, but we also have creative access for strategies to make impact in the world around us practically. The Bible talks about asking for wisdom, this includes people God created to imagine and create inventions, find solutions and strategies, and artistically influence culture to be applied in all areas of the seven mountains of societal influence. Those areas of impact are: business, religion, family, education, government, media, arts, and entertainment.

If we are God's ambassadors, and God dwells inside us, the very God who designed and spoke all of creation into being, then we must have access to make impact on the Earth. I'm not talking about only wisdom but Holy Spirit insight, heavenly revelation of pioneering ideas, we bring to the Earth.

Business

Ingenuity, enterprise, creativity, and effort is a God-given gift, as well as a universal impulse. The markets and economic systems are the backbone of a nation. It makes sense that Believers called into these significant roles of influence, recognize that their presence in these arenas can usher in heaven's kingdom, all while pursuing leadership and excellence with integrity.

My husband lives by a code of honor to others. How do we do that? In my humble opinion, he embodies excellence and leadership skills. Where Jorge has experienced promotion, unmerited favor and opportunities has come from praying daily and walking in integrity. God honors faithfulness. By honoring others, not being motivated by greed or corruption, but being moved by a mindset of honor, character and integrity, the Lord will always reward. The Lord always sees our hearts and will give them more room for growth. And the fruit of honor reaps a harvest that continues to multiply into others lives. Jorge's business philosophy is "leaders make leaders."[17] His goal is to see others succeed in their areas of influence, cultivating an awareness to "pay it forward." The awareness then grows into a culture, a system of honoring other colleagues and clients alike.

At home, Jorge and I pray specifics around his business, our finances, and dreams for the future. God loves planting seeds for outrageous dreams. The more incredible, the more glory He gets when it is realized! Praying those specific outrageous dreams, and hearing what He shows you for next steps to realize those ideas is a lot of fun! That's how Jorge has gone from sitting behind a pink desk, answering phone calls for a bank, to becoming a senior leader for one of the largest communication firms in the world, managing roughly half a billion dollars of revenue a year! Our lives changed, and it all happened within a relatively short amount of time.

We credit God totally but none of it would have happened without a lot of prayer. Praying without a faith ceiling can be applied to any area of influence. Our God is limitless, his resources are infinite. He has no beginning or end so provision to become what He created you to bring to the earth uniquely is all there!

Religion

On the website for prayer organization Generals International, Christian speaker and author Cindy Jacobs describes the role religion plays shaping culture. "*Every society has some type of belief in a superior being or beings. In the east, religions tend to be polytheistic (many gods) or outright idolatrous (such as Hinduism and Buddhism). Although these religions are thousands of years old, they nonetheless continue to thrive today. In the west, Christianity and Catholicism are predominant, but postmodern views are increasingly being accepted and the concept of God is being rejected. This is especially true in Europe...* The Christian Church is described in the Greek language as the Ecclesia. *Literally translated, the word Ecclesia means "governing body." Although we don't condone theocracies, this translation suggests that the Church should have great influence in all other spheres that make up a society."* 1[8]

With over 4,200 religions estimated around the world, it's the Church's role to reach the lost with the love and truth of Jesus Christ, and expand His Kingdom through ministry efforts around the world.

Family

Family is the building block of societies. Family also symbolizes how we ought to live our lives as Christians. God desires that men, women, and children within a family be united in His love. After all, He is the ultimate Father. "For those who are led by the Spirit of God are the children of God. The Spirit you received does not make you slaves, so that you live in fear again; rather, the Spirit you received brought about your adoption to sonship. And by Him we cry, "*Abba,* Father." The Spirit himself testifies with our spirit that we are God's children. Now if we are children, then we are heirs—heirs of God and co-heirs with Christ, if indeed we share in his sufferings in order that we may also share in his glory." Romans 8:14-17.

Sadly, the beautiful dynamic that should be family is under constant attack.

Fatherlessness is on the rise, where the divorce rate is up to 50% in marriages, abuse, homosexual marriage, pornography, and other negative influences bring dysfunction into our lives.1[9] God is calling out fathers and mothers, both spiritual and biological, to bring order to the chaos and hurt that satan has unleashed. He also wants to bring healing to marriages and relationships within families in order to maintain a solid foundation for children and future generations to stand upon.

What is your definition of family? I started chewing on my own definition, perception, and challenging it. The beautiful dynamic of family is what God's Plan is all about! Rethinking it through His lense has made all the difference in understanding how we are to live as family. Adoption, fostering children, starting a process to open an orphanage...the idea of family is near and dear to the Father's heart! The Father desires us to reign on the Earth, stepping up and strengthening the family foundation. This will impact our children and future generations, giving them moral foundations.

Education

Decades ago, the Bible and Biblical values were incorporated in daily school life. Now, kids are inundated with atheistic teaching, ideologies and anti-God principles in our public schools and in most universities. In a nutshell, students are being indoctrinated with biased and anti-Biblical information. Reinstituting Biblical truth and Bible-based values is the key to renewal, and restoration in our educational system.

Government

> "Righteousness exalts a nation, but sin condemns any people," Proverbs 14:34.

Many times, as read in the Old Testament, a nation's moral standards are linked to those exhibited by its leaders or a political party. While each person is responsible for his or her own actions; the fact sticks that people are definitely influenced by the morals (or lack thereof) that popular leaders hold to. In fact, many political groups, seek to remove anything related to God or Christianity from the governmental and educational systems because of a misapplied interpretation of "separation of church and state."

In America, our nation was founded on Biblical principles. As Christians we should be aware of the laws impacting our families and let our voices be heard by voting in primaries and general elections. Also as Christians our prayers are for righteous political leaders to arise and positively affect all aspects of government.

Media

I was a long time member of the press. I've written for newspapers, reported for radio news programs, and worked as an on-air TV reporter for news stations. I knew firsthand about the power of words, and I saw their effects on families and communities.

The influential sphere of media includes radio, TV news stations, newspapers, published works, internet news and opinion (blog) sites among others. The media has powerful potential to sway popular opinion on current issues based upon its reporting of "the facts," which is not always truthful or accurate. In the 2016 U.S. Presidential election, a new term was added to dictionaries defining the fabrication and biased reporting practices of noise makers in the media. Fake news. The words producers write, and what reporters and anchors speak out on the air waves are generally received as "truth," and it impacts the masses. Media outlets play a vital role in shaping public opinion.[20]

In order to bring transformation in the sphere of media, Christians who are God- wired for and called into this industry must be willing to report righteously and truthfully, even if it's not popular.

Art and Entertainment

"Art, freedom and creativity will change society faster than politics."[21] Influential business man *Victor Pinchuk* recognizes the powerful impact the arts have on society, and has been sighted among other influential forces like George Soros.

Music, filmmaking, television, social media, and the performing arts steer cultural drive, values and standards of society, especially its youth. Primarily relying on the "sales" appeal of sex, drugs and alcohol, the arts and entertainment industries hold significant influence. The body of Christ needs powerful, righteous sons and daughters of God who are not afraid to take their God-given talent into the arts and entertainment industry. Those given the God-created talent and the call into that massively dark world will glow in the dark. They are God's Burning Ones, ready to further His purposes, while impacting those who are lost in darkness and would not otherwise be interested in any kind of Christian message in traditional forms.

Great hope abounds when we realize our identity as sons and daughters of God and our purposes to carry The Hope of Glory into our culture. We are fully backed and equipped by the Father to bring solutions and breakthroughs into the world, and demonstrate that nothing is impossible with Him.

As God's ambassadors on the earth, we are all wired with unique skill sets to make impact on society. How do we get started? It starts with a simple prayer:

> "Father, show me the purposes you have for me to uniquely bring to the Earth. I want to share them with excellence, impacting souls for your Kingdom purposes. Begin to highlight those big dreams I'm meant to carry out, and show me the next steps to accomplishing them. I ask you to prove to me that you are limitless. Your Word says that You are the source of life itself, and you hold everything together. I pray to have your vision, creativity, concepts to bring healing and revelations that pioneer! Teach me how to honor others and remain faithful to the call you have on my life. Guard me from greed and the pride of life. Thank you, in Jesus Name, amen!"

The Lord will answer your prayer, positioning you to make impact in your God- ordained purposes. As the Lord begins to spark new ideas, give you dreams, and show you the next steps, I encourage you to journal what He shows you.

DIVING DEEPER

Reflection:

1. How does recognizing your authority in Christ Jesus change your identity?

2. How could this personal revelation be used to make impact at work, school, to your friends, family or anyone that comes into your path?

3. Ask the Father how He wants to you use to make impact for His Kingdom. Take note of any ideas He shows you, including dreams, interests He may highlight here. Jot them down here.

CHAPTER 14

"I'll huff and puff and blow your house down!" And Other Nonsense We Believe

As a child I remember a big colorful storybook filled with fantastic pictures, nursery rhymes and fables. One that always carried a bit of suspense was the story of the Three Little Pigs. The story opens with the title characters being sent out into the world by their mother, to "seek out their fortune." So the three pigs begin building three houses, each made of different materials. A big bad wolf comes along terrorizing the pigs at each of their homes with hopes for a pork dinner, and a theatrical exchange begins:

"Little pig, little pig, let me come in."

"No, no, by the hair on my chiny chin chin."

"Then I'll huff, and I'll puff, and I'll blow your house in."[22]

The big bad wolf starts his huffing and puffing, blowing down the first two pigs' houses. Construction materials were straw and sticks respectively. The practical third little pig had a house made of bricks. The wolf fails to blow down the house. In his desperation for a barbecue dinner, he attempts to trick the pig out of the house by asking to meet him at various places, but he is outwitted each time.

Finally, the wolf resolves to come down the chimney, where practical pig catches the wolf in a cauldron of boiling water, and slams the lid over top of him. Who had the last laugh in that fable?

Like the devious and desperate big bad wolf, satan may exert power here on earth, but he does not have authority! The enemy can still cause destruction, sow seeds of devastation, and plant twisted lies in people's minds, but when it comes to the Bride, a collective voice of God's people, we were given authority and power. Our identity is where we get our authority. We can't work that up in our life! It's simply a realized understanding of Whose we are, and because of that, what we have a right to is the game changer. I am in Christ. Christ is in me.

Colossians 2:10 brings home a mind blowing truth, "...the fullness of the Godhead dwells in me."

To break this down again let's go back to the thief and the police analogy talked about in yesterday's reading. Power is the gun and authority is the one holding the legitimate authority representing justice, a characteristic of Christ. Now let's notice the difference of power's limits visualizing the cop on the scene confronting the thief with a gun. It's the cop who has the authority to say to the thief, also holding "power" (aka a gun), to stop and he must. Even those the enemy uses, throwing his power around on earth that sows seeds of discord and hate violently sometimes, but in the scenario, it's God's people who have the advantage. How? Because we have the rightful authority and Colossians 2 affirms it. There is no power struggle.

That should make all the difference in our faith life and in our thought life. We hold a position of rightful authority. Even if we feel like the enemy is huffing and puffing in our circumstances, he has no ground, in fact he is trespassing! If we get that into our spirits, we can pray and declare from that position of authority scriptures around our situations that feel out of control and terrorizing. Nothing can deny an encounter with the Living God. Prayers from His Elect (that's us) are the weapons of our warfare. "For our struggle is not against flesh and blood, but against the rulers, against the authorities, against the powers of this dark world and against the spiritual forces of evil in the heavenly realms," Ephesians 6:12.

Once you realize your identity dwells inside Christ, the conqueror of hell and the grave, spiritual warfare takes on a whole new perspective. We fight from the victory, there is no power struggle. We are reigning with Him; we shouldn't receive fear in a test because our exousia is set. We can now take care of business!

Asking the Lord what His thoughts are toward x-situation. This is how we are to war in intercession, and also to rest knowing we carry the presence of the Lord with us wherever we go. This is abundant living folks!

Do you now recognize the crazy matrix the enemy wants us to believe and blindly follow? Let's wake up from being under the influence of the enemy's "little-red pill", and see we already have the authority to bring His kingdom purposes to the earth! So roar in confidence on those front lines! Charge forward, shine brighter, bolder in all His resplendent glory, as God's ambassadors. Pray for people outside grocery stores, outside your classroom, at work. Your expectancy will be fueled by the truth of the finished work of Calvary's cross.

Allow Him to position you perfectly in His timing. Pray to be intentional with every soul He trusts you with and puts in your path. Do what you do best, with your skill, your ideas, sharpening your craft to launch those seeds of impact with excellence! Ever thought that He placed those in you uniquely to plant "seeds" that will point the way back to Him? Mic drop! Shake up the status quo, because in Him and through Him all creation moves and has their being. This is our Father! To hit this concept home here's one of my favorite translations, "He existed before anything else, and he holds all creation together," Colossians 1:17 (EST).

So we were graciously chosen to exist on earth for such a time as this for a reason, family! We are being built into the radiant Bride He is returning for!

Knowing that we rightfully carry authority to pray from the victory and continue to until there's a shift, renounce the plans of the enemy, and believe for redemption and healing in situations and hearts that need Father's perfect love, is why we hold this position, saints. We are co-reigning with Him to take back families, communities, cultures and laws that have been influenced by a terrorizing enemy. But his destruction is imminent and he knows it.

One of my favorite true stories comes from the book of Esther. As for her backstory, Esther's was an orphan who was raised by her righteous Jewish cousin, Mordecai. When the Persian king came looking for young virgins to possibly fill the role of his new queen, she appeared in the lineup. She wins favor with the people in the harem and eventually with the king himself, becoming queen. But all is not well in the king's courts—treachery is afoot. The plot basically involves the king's right-hand man, Haman going to the king and saying, "I think we should kill all the Jews in the Persian Empire." And the king says, "Alright." The king doesn't know that his own queen is Jewish, because Esther's been keeping it secret. But the threat of the Jews' imminent demise kicks Esther and Mordecai into action. Because Esther and Mordecai were God-fearing, they put a word out to a community of Jews to begin praying and fasting fervently for the queen. The dots were beginning to connect for Esther, and why God placed her in the palace. Her day of reckoning had come:

"For if you remain silent at this time, relief and deliverance for the Jews will arise from another place, but you and your father's family will perish. And who knows but that you have come to your royal position for such a time as this?" Esther 4:14.

Recognizing who she had become in Persia's royal palace, a royal who would be the only one to turn the situation around, Esther accepted the responsibility that would impact a nation. Her faith and courage highlighted in Esther 4:16, "I will go to the king, even though it is against the law. And if I perish, I perish." She was remarkable, willing to put others' lives ahead of her own. Esther exposes Haman's plan and motives. The Jews were saved, cousin Mordecai was even promoted into the royal palace, and Esther's goes down in history as being mentioned more times in the Bible than any other woman.

God maneuvers every aspect of life to position people, governments, and situations for His plan and purpose. Just like Esther, she was at the right place at the right time and given her royal authority as Queen of Persia, saved the Jewish people, exposing a devious plan to take God out of that society.

Queen Esther knew that prayer accompanied by fasting was a way to get closer to God and boy did she need Him more than ever! In times of spiritual warfare, fasting can be a way to focus our spirits to hear God clearer. The literal meaning of the Hebrew word for "fast" is "to cover the mouth." Personally I have fasted not just from eating food for a time period, but abstained from other activities during a fast, like being on my phone or watching TV. But traditionally the definition of fasting means abstaining from food. It's a level of sacrifice coupled with prayer focus that becomes like a powerful weapon. On top of the spiritual power fasting brings, and realizing our identity as sons and daughters of God carrying Him inside, things shift in the supernatural, it moves the hearts of kings!

During times when the enemy is huffing and puffing on our door, we must stop to recognize the authority God gave us—the truth that we are His. Even heated battles, He may be calling you to fast as Esther did for breakthrough. This spiritual discipline helps us to hear God's voice even clearer, and experience a deeper level of spiritual power. In that awareness that we have the Father on our side, we can enter into spiritual battle equipped, knowing we fight from the victory. Declaring in prayer His promises over the situations in our life, we will undoubtedly see how faithful and good Father is: all the dots will connect "for such a time as this."

DIVING DEEPER

Promises and Reflection:

1. Read Colossians 2:9-10 Esther 4

2. Reflection: What does the story of Esther show you about God's sovereignty?

3. How does knowing that God gave you authority affect how you see your purposes?

4. How does recognizing your authority affect your faith when it comes to your prayer life and how you view spiritual warfare?

5. Creative Gush: The space below is designated for you to unleash the creative you! Feel free to doodle, draw, write poetry, song lyrics...whatever this chapter has revealed to you.

CHAPTER 15

Locked In His Gaze: A Union Of Spirits

The great mystery of The Bride of Christ can be explained as a believer's identity that is grounded in dwelling *inside* Jesus. The finished work of the cross made our identity possible. Grace, forgiveness, and our deepest heart needs are all met inside Jesus.

Colossians 2:6-15:

"So then, just as you received Christ Jesus as Lord, continue to live your lives in him, rooted and built up in him, strengthened in the faith as you were taught, and overflowing with thankfulness. See to it that no one takes you captive through hollow and deceptive philosophy, which depends on human tradition and the elemental spiritual forces of this world rather than on Christ. For in Christ all the fullness of the Deity lives in bodily form, and in Christ you have been brought to fullness. He is the head over every power and authority. In him you were also circumcised with a circumcision not performed by human hands. Your whole self ruled by the flesh was put off when you were circumcised by Christ, having been buried with him in baptism, in which you were also raised with him through your faith in the working of God, who raised him from the dead. When you were dead in your sins and in the uncircumcision of your flesh, God made you alive with Christ. He forgave us all our sins, having canceled the charge of our legal indebtedness, which stood against us and condemned us; he has taken it away, nailing it to the cross. And having disarmed the powers and authorities, he made a public spectacle of them, triumphing over them by the cross."

Thanks to what Jesus did on Calvary's Cross, those that invite Him into their hearts become one with him in spirit, thought and truth. Think about it like this: we invite him to move in with us literally...so when he takes up residency in our hearts, there's no room for our past crutches, broken dependencies, or bondages—feelings of conviction start because those old things just don't fit like they used to! Literally they don't fit, there's no room for them when we've been made new and the indwelling of the Holy Spirit sets up room in our hearts. The Hope of Glory now lives inside of us!

Calvary's cross made all this possible! In Christ Jesus you were given grace before the world was created. "He gave us grace *in Christ Jesus* before the ages began," 2 Timothy 1:9. In Christ we were chosen by God before time and space. "God chose us *in Christ* before the foundation of the world," Ephesians 1:4.

In Christ Jesus we are loved by God with an unconditional, unending love. "I am sure that neither death nor life, nor angels nor rulers, nor things present nor things to come, nor powers, nor height nor depth, nor anything else in all creation, will be able to separate us from the love of God *in Christ Jesus our Lord,*" Romans 8:38–39.

In Christ Jesus we are justified before God and the righteousness of God in Christ granted to all believers because of Calvary's cross. "For our sake God made Christ to be sin who knew no sin, so that *in him* we might become the righteousness of God," 2 Corinthians 5:21.

In Christ Jesus we have become a new creation and a son of God. "If anyone is *in Christ*, he is a new creation. The old has passed away; behold, the new has come," 2 Corinthians 5:17. "*In Christ Jesus* you are all sons of God, through faith," Galatians 3:26.

In Christ Jesus we have been seated in the heavenly places. "God raised us up with Christ and seated us with him in the heavenly places *in Christ Jesus,*" Ephesians 2:6.

In Christ Jesus everything we really need will be supplied. "My God will supply every need of yours according to his riches in glory *in Christ Jesus,*" Philippians 4:19. In Christ Jesus the peace of God will protect our heart and mind. "The peace of God, which surpasses all understanding, will guard your hearts and your minds *in Christ Jesus,*" Philippians 4:7.

In Christ Jesus we have eternal life. "For the wages of sin is death, but the free gift of God is eternal life *in Christ Jesus our Lord,*" Romans 6:23.

By faith and consciously by our own actions we demonstrate this incredible union of the Holy Spirit's divine presence in our soul. Christ dwells in our hearts "through faith," Ephesians 3:17. The life we live in union with his death and resurrection reflects our trust and dependence on Him to meet our deepest needs. Being inside of Christ, as He is dwelling inside of our hearts means a synchronization will start. Our heartbeat will sync up and we will begin to want what He wants! When you want what God wants for God's purposes, we are unstoppable! This restored identity is for us to carry and bring His Kingdom purposes to the earth for impact. So dream! Let your faith be led by His thoughts and purposes. Allow your faith to believe. Allow your faith to trust. Let your faith depend and finally let your faith soar!

DIVING DEEPER:

Promises and Reflection

1. Read Matthew 28:16-20

2. Allow yourself to reflect on the finished work of Calvary's cross and all that means. After reading the verses from Matthew 28, think about Jesus' final instruction as he was ascending to Heaven.

   Let's position our hearts in thankfulness for the eternal provisions made that gave humankind the heart-capacity to fulfill the Great Commission. Such a vast and great plan is unfolding, a role, reserved for the sons and daughters of God who hear Him. Do you hear the call of "there's more"?

   Add your insights here.

3. *Exercise:* Talk to him from this place of gratitude and ask how Him how he wants to use you to spread his empire of love. Jot down what He shares with you here.

CHAPTER 16

The Frontline Lions

The Lord has been speaking not just to me but so many others about the significance of who and what a lion represents in creation. They are the rightful "kings of the jungle". Let's dissect that name.

A king holds lawful authority. In their habitat, all other creatures know who the lion is and comply! The jungle is the lion's domain; they carry natural authority wherever they move into. They are a great example of knowing who they are created to be. The Lord also uses his majestic creation the lion as a description of Jesus and other people in the Bible. It should be a hint for us too!

Jesus was referred to in scripture as the Lion of the Tribe of Judah. I like word studies. Check this out, in the Biblical book of Judges the Lord instructs his people to put the "The Tribe of Judah" first, at the front lines heading into battle. Do you know why he picked them specifically? The scriptures tell us something significant to what breaks down war: praise and worship. Yep, they were the worshippers and musicians singing declarations and the promises of God Almighty! They won those battles. Do you see a key here in how we are to walk through difficult times? The antithesis of fear is celebrating the foreshadowed victory—that's faith!

Further, what is the purpose of a battle? Battles are meant to expand a "kingdom" or a culture of belonging. The seeds of declaration, grow into belief, and we start to adopt a victorious mindset! That belief in God's promises and victory give way to a natural feeling of gratitude which positions our faith to confidently sing and declare that the victory is our's for His Kingdom impact.

The frontline can be lonely, scary, and challenging. Those chosen to be positioned there were the first to step onto ground that was foreign, but could soon be their new homeland. The Tribe of Judah was worshipping and declaring as they charged into confrontation—a key for this season as His Kingdom confronts the enemy's territories. However, we were made for this time in history and those who have ears to hear, and feel this message resonating, are receiving his mandate to go through the process of being made worthy to stand on the frontlines. We are the answer to Jesus's prayer as read in Matthew 6, "His kingdom come, his will be done on earth as it is in heaven." We were made to carry His purposes and restore the earth's kingdom to make way for Jesus Christ's reign on earth. Loaded. These truths are found in scriptures in Revelation 21 and backed up further with Romans 8:19-23, "For the creation waits in eager expectation for the children of God to be revealed. For the creation was subjected to frustration, not by its own choice, but by the will of the one who subjected it, in hope that the creation itself will be liberated from its bondage to decay and brought into the freedom and glory of the children of God. We know that the whole creation has been groaning as in the pains of childbirth right up to the present time. Not only so, but we ourselves, who have the firstfruits of the Spirit, groaning inwardly as we wait eagerly for our adoption to sonship, the redemption of our bodies."

Those called to the frontlines are meant to breakthrough, counted as trustworthy, and be the first to step onto new ground, which advances a kingdom culture.

Going first isn't easy. In fact, it normally means you will go through tests that develop perseverance, self-control, patience, and an unwavering trust in the goodness of the Lord's ways. That's pretty loaded, and not everyone will say "yes" to that call to the frontline. There is always a process of heart-conditioning in order to be counted worthy and chosen to be on the frontline. Deep down we all want to be that person.

How do you do that? It starts with going through a sort of heart and soul "boot camp" training. Disciplining the mind is key to becoming a soldier, to be trusted to carry through The General's plan of advancement. In order to fully grasp how critical it is to choose to surrender an individual's will to the will of the empire of love, self has to take a back seat. The power of choice makes or breaks this opportunity. Free will and acting on choice set into motion the evacuation of Eden.

What helps me get a better understanding of this concept is the idea that we are not our own. The Bible says in 1 Peter 2 that we are citizens of heaven living on earth. We have a spiritual identity first. This fallen world is waiting on us to bring unity and restoration to all things in heaven and on earth. It all depends on accepting who we really are as sons and daughters of God meant to manifest His Kingdom come to the Earth through our God-given skills, moved by His heart and purposes.

To know we are loved, will affect how we see ourselves and treat others. This is huge! Walking and behaving in integrity, honor, and trust will impact other relationships. I'll explain how we do this while living in a fallen world in upcoming sections. This is how the Lord will use his human sons and daughters, filled with compassion for others, on earth to advance his empire of love on the frontlines.

DIVING DEEPER

Promises and Reflection

1. Read Matthew 6:9-13 Matthew 16:24

2. Reflection:
   How does knowing God reflect on your choice to trust Him even with things we feel are crutches?
   And if I press a bit further, how would knowing Him effect surrendering our individual will, plans, and future to Him? If you honestly can't answer this, and feel you should recommit your life in pursuing a real relationship with Jesus Christ, who is very much alive please pray this prayer with me right now:

   > "Dear Father,
   >
   > I admit I have strayed from my first love, Jesus, I want to recommit my life, my will to you. Help me to become the person you created me to be, I want you to be the Lord of my life, renew my heart, renew my passion to walk more closely to you, restore the joy of my salvation. Help me to fulfill the unique purposes you have for me. Thank you for the Cross and your shed blood on Calvary that cleansed me and made me whole, restoring my identity as your son/daughter.
   >
   > In Jesus Name I pray, amen!"

CHAPTER 17

Eden's Evacuation

With the Earth still brand new, the deceiver wasted no time trying to sabotage the trust relationship between God and the first humans. He approached the female, in desperation to derail the co-existence between creation and The Divine. A bait was set, and the first lie was told by a miserable antagonist, satan disguised as a snake.

Adam and Eve really did muck it up for all of us. In Genesis 3:16-17, existing in complete freedom, in paradise, having no emotional or physical need, literally walking in personal contact with God himself, the first humans both fell to a lie baited by a talking serpent. The lie was twisted just enough to make them experience the first taste of doubt, a feeling of heavy self-awareness. And therein is where the battle always is waged: within, internalized from a thought spoken out loud and meant to trap us. The same strong pull of a twisted idea that caused the angel of worship, lucifer, to turn his back on Love. In his decision he exchanged his heavenly identity for the devil, and consequently became totally consumed with himself, and ultimately tormented for eternity. It was his choice.

The serpent presented an alternative and false viewpoint. He sold the perspective that the fruit from the tree of wisdom wasn't meant to be eaten in order to keep humans "in the dark ages," so they wouldn't attain God's wisdom. So a tree's fruit contained the secrets of the universe apparently.

I believe, the truth of why that tree was in the garden at all was to test Adam and Eve's trust in God's goodness, as a loving Father. I believe God purposefully planted the tree, and placed Adam and Eve there as caregivers knowing they would be faced with a choice, based off the only rule given. I mean think about it, the only rule given was not to eat fruit from a tree? It was a kind of weird rule, but satan spun the idea of knowledge as a "hot selling" commodity in Eden. Even though the humans had everything they could ever need, because they were the created children of Father God, Who was literally abiding in His full, glorious presence alongside them. The all-knowing One had created out of His great capacity for love, to love, bestowing his protection, hovering over, and guiding His own children in a real relationship of doing life together. Nonetheless, the humans bought what the deceiver was selling them, spinning the need to strive and harness wisdom, as the gift of wisdom was elevated to idolatrous desire. Thus the devil's plan was devised through a major mind game of manipulation.

Was God blindsided by the humans' betrayal of the rules? No way. But humanity didn't make it any easier on themselves. They not only ate the fruit, but later Adam also side-stepped the truth and blamed Eve, introducing a landslide of self- preservation characteristics! The mess was made because they made a choice.

They trusted a good God but chose to listen to a talking snake, which resulted in an acute awareness of self-doubt, and their eyes were opened to their nakedness. Enter shame, guilt, and toil on the Earth. You never know what you got till it's gone!

The freedom and the beautiful abiding presence of God left them. They were alone, entering into self-conscious bondage, and striving from then on.

Mucked up. However, God knew it would go down like that because that's how real love works, after all. Reciprocation of that love is a choice. God, whose great capacity to love meant he created beings to bestow his love on, and waited to receive that love back from His creation in the first test. It meant the decision of the heart to be genuine would be left up to the created. He gave them the great gift of free will.

It came down to a choice. God allows us to choose our alliance from an all-loving good Father or what our selfishness desires in the moment. Consequently for Adam and Eve, their choice affected history. They chose to disobey God, God removed His covering, allowing pain for the first time. But even though humanity had to leave an earthly paradise where they shared dominion with God Himself, I believe it was all a divine setup, and we haven't really read between the lines of scripture to see Act 2. I will connect the dots in a moment. Even though Eden was evacuated because of sin, there is unfinished business awaiting His children. I believe we are meant to return and restore creation to its original form, and co-exist with the returned King of Kings!

Romans 8:14-17 says, "For those who are led by the Spirit of God are the children of God. The Spirit you received does not make you slaves, so that you live in fear again; rather, the Spirit you received brought about your adoption to sonship. And by him we cry, "*Abba,* Father." The Spirit himself testifies with our spirit that we are God's children. Now if we are children, then we are heirs—heirs of God and co-heirs with Christ, if indeed we share in his sufferings in order that we may also share in his glory." Further into the chapter it says that creation is awaiting the sons and daughters of God to be revealed, to liberate them from their bondage into freedom.

If we share in His glory because of this amazing position of sonship, scripture says we are meant to restore creation! We carry His resurrection life inside our hearts. What the disciples experienced in Acts 2 not only birthed the first church but the Holy Spirit's power was activated in them. They went on to travel from town to town, spreading Jesus's truth, setting people free from disease, life-long physical issues, and torment. Can I get an amen?

If Christians would get as excited about *growing up* in unified heart and walking in their authority as they do about *going up,* the Body of Christ would reach its maturity much sooner. What would happen? They would fulfill all Scriptures, restore all things and thereby "bring back King Jesus."

All of creation is waiting for the manifesting of the sons and daughters of God to be released from their torment. But how does this overwhelming promise happen on our watch? Since the Church is called more than a conqueror I believe it will not only reclaim scriptural truths that were lost after the historic "dark ages" but also reclaim and restore what satan stole from Adam. Intimate fellowship with God was broken, rebellion and physical death entered the human race. Slowly restoration of all scriptural truths are being reactivated.

It's taken us over a thousand years for the restoration of truth, which looks like the swinging pendulum of a clock. Swinging way to the right, then leaning back to surge to the left, and finally hanging in the middle of two extremes. It has taken all of us: The Catholics, Protestants, Evangelical, Pentecostal, Charismatic and Prophetic to receive ordained revelation over time. In his book *The Eternal Church*, Dr. Bill Hamon lists the the truths that have been restored throughout Church history : Faith, water baptism, sanctification, the Second Coming of Christ, divine faith healing, Holy Spirit baptism, prophecy and the laying on of hands, worship and praise, discipleship, faith messages on abundance, Kingdom now dominion, ministers in the marketplace, and sons and daughters recognizing their full purpose being positioned to co-reign as the Church-Bride, in preparation for Christ's return. (Hamon, Dr. Bill. *The Eternal Church*. Shippensburg, PA: Destiny Image, 1981. Print.)

What satan stole from Adam, the Church has been reestablishing over time. God is setting up His Saints in the marketplace, who function outside the walls of the local church to arise, take and possess the wealth of the world. This will put them in powerful roles of influence providing resources for travel, communication, building and establishing the Church throughout the world. They will do their work with favor and success just like Daniel and Joseph in the Bible, but also operate as modern-day prophets and ministers in the marketplace.

I believe supernatural health is the next truth to be restored. As God's children step out in bold faith, living above the world system, live in divine health, get and stay out of debt, and practice principles that bring about physical and material prosperity for the advancing and establishing of the Church age on earth. The Body is finally waking up to the truth in Psalm 24:1 "the earth is the Lord's, and all its fullness." I believe the world's wealth, including means of transporting and communicating the Gospel belongs to the Church for His Kingdom promises coming to pass.

According Acts 3:21 Jesus must remain in heaven until the final recovery of all things from sin as prospered in ancient times. All that the fall of man and sin has taken away from humanity, Jesus, through His Church, will restore...a symbolic "return to Eden" if you will.

Jesus, through His death, burial and resurrection, provided all things necessary in order for His Church to bring about the recovery of all things. Jesus through his death and resurrection came back in the power of His Holy Spirit, and is now living and working within His corporate children, the Church! Jesus has identified Himself with the Church, they are One. 1 Cor. 6:17 says Jesus and His Church are one in spirit and ministry, and everything He will do will be in, through and with His Church-Bride, being a part of its fulfillment. Nothing can stop Jesus Christ from fulfilling His purpose in His Church.

What does that look like on the ground? We will see a return to what the Church originally looked like in Acts. Rewind two thousand years and the disciples and early Church saw the impossible become possible. Miracles were part of the Church's job description, and the children encountered the Holy Spirit continuously leaving no one the same. Blinded eyes were opened and cold hearts instantly softened in the Presence of Holy Spirit.

The Saints are Christ's living letters! "Since we have such a hope, we are bold." 2 Cor. 3:12. Family, I must ask, is this scripture a living experience in your life? If it is not active in the Church, then begin to pray and believe for it to be activated and fulfilled.

" I have given you authority to trample on snakes and scorpions and to overcome all the power of the enemy; nothing will harm you." Luke 10:19. I believe that to be physically true as well as spiritually.

"As you go, proclaim this message: 'The kingdom of heaven has come near.' Heal the sick, raise the dead, cleanse those who have leprosy, drive out demons. Freely you have received; freely give." Matthew 10:7-8.

"As you sent me into the world, I have sent them into the world." (with the same commission, power, and authority) John 17:18.

"Very truly I tell you, whoever believes in me will do the works I have been doing, and they will do even greater things than these... "John 14:12.

I believe this is how the real Church should look today. Shining bright and bringing healing and hope of Jesus into the real world situations, the hard, desperate and dire places. It's what Christ died for us to become, His Ambassadors on earth sharing the hope of Glory to humankind in their daily routines, bus routes, and zip codes. Showing up and stepping in when the Holy Spirit highlights a person or situation, is all we have to do, then watch Him do what only God can, through your obedience.

The Church has been operating on flickering candlelight power and not using the Holy Spirit's mega watt authoritative power, which is capable of world-changing ministry. All things yet to be revealed, restored or fulfilled will be accomplished in, by and through His Church. The Church-Bride is now functioning as co-executor of His Word and will continue in that role more fully united and eternally magnified in its ministry with King Jesus! What the Lord is doing on the earth now to prepare and position His Bride will capture you, because it was all part of the glorious fulfillment of the ages foretold in scripture. All the fruit and gifts of the Spirit will be activated in The Church, signaling the restoration of creation.

Search the scriptures for more examples of what God has planned. It will help you build your faith and position you to participate in God's purposes and Scripture promises coming to pass through His Church.

A Return to Eden

I do believe Eden will be redeemed. At the earth's beginning, all of creation was unwillingly contaminated by the pride, rebellion, and fall of lucifer. Natural creation fell into bondage of decay and death when Adam sinned, however scripture tells us a New Heaven and New Earth is promised. Revelation 21:5, "He who sat on the throne said, 'Behold, I make all things new'".

2 Peter 3:10-13, "But the day of the Lord will come like a thief. The heavens will disappear with a roar; the elements will be destroyed by fire, and the earth and everything done in it will be laid bare. Since everything will be destroyed in this way, what kind of people ought you to be? You ought to live holy and godly lives as you look forward to the day of God and speed its coming. That day will bring about the destruction of the heavens by fire, and the elements will melt in the heat. But in keeping with his promise we are looking forward to a new heaven and a new earth, where righteousness dwells."

Scripture promises tell us that all of creation is anxiously waiting for the manifestation of the sons and daughters of God when they come into their maturity and oneness with Christ. The Phillips translation of Romans 8:19 describes the scene, "The whole of creation is on tiptoe to see the wonderful sight of the sons of God coming into their own." Doesn't that verse stir excitement in you?

Manifestation, to most of us it's a word that conjures up images of mystical scenes normally seen in creepy horror movies. So what does that verse, and specifically the word "manifestation" mean? Paul explains to the church in Corinth that every person in their membership was given a supernatural ability to bless others. 1 Cor. 12:7 references this, "Now to each one the manifestation of the Spirit is given for the common good."

If the Lord is restoring the purposes of the Church, the manifestations of the Holy Spirit through His People will become more common to bless His Church and help restore others to Jesus. We need to expect more! Church leaders reading this, I pray you catch this. It will take *every* person in your congregation to be reminded, and encouraged of how valuable they are, and how crucial their unique and supernatural giftings are to the Body of Christ. Further, they are indispensable to God's plans on earth to advance His kingdom. To every reader, please pray to be equipped and activated in your supernatural abilities. He wants to use us to display His power, because certainly more is coming for His Promises to be fulfilled!

The More That's Coming

In his book, Dr. Bill Hamon prefaces, once the Church receives its full redemption and inheritance then creation will be redeemed from its cursed conditions of decay and death. "The destiny of the overcoming Church is to rule and reign over God's redeemed earth." (Hamon, Dr. Bill. *The Eternal Church.* Shippensburg, PA: Destiny Image, 1981. Print.)

The mysterious scriptures in Isaiah 65:17-25 describing the literal coming of the Kingdom of God during the millennial age, have been open for interpretation and application. I am no theologian but I believe in the Word of God cover to cover. I have had to ask the Lord to supernaturally open my eyes to His vision, praying for understanding as I read about the age to come. He is so faithful to shed light on His Word, which has changed everything for me, and radically boosted my faith.

With that one simple prayer, Jesus's famous prayer in Matthew 6:10 took on a new reality for me: "Your kingdom come. Your will be done on earth as it is in heaven." Chillbumps! Whenever I read that verse I can't help but feel the Father's beaming smile, and with a twinkle in his eye, feel Him give me a little wink-wink of the Promises to come.

DIVING DEEPER:

Promises and Reflection

1. Read Acts 2:1-4
   Acts 2:17
   Romans 8

2. After reading these scriptures, what is the Lord showing you about what it means to *be* the Church? Write down your thoughts here.

____

____

____

____

____

____

3. Experiment: Ask the Lord to use you today, shining His love, hope and truth through you to someone desperate for The Answer.

____

____

____

____

____

4. Creative Gush: The space below is designated for you to unleash the creative you! Feel free to doodle, draw, write poetry, song lyrics...whatever this chapter has revealed to you.

CHAPTER 18

Unforsaken: God Is There Especially During the Hard Times

Sometimes when I haven't had my coffee in the morning, or I step barefooted on an invisible Lego piece on the floor, or I get a heart-wrenching phone call, my thoughts start to tank. I can feel overwhelmed and alone. God are you there?

What pattern of thinking do your thoughts take? Do we realign our thoughts to what God says or let our own fears or frustration take over? Are we learning to truly hear Him, and *then* respond after we've heard what He says? "For He Himself has said, 'I will never leave you nor forsake you.' So we may boldly say: 'The Lord is my helper; I will not fear. What can man do to me?'" Hebrews 13:5-6.

"I will never leave you..."— not for any reason; not my sin, selfishness, stubbornness, or intentional waywardness. "I will never... forsake you." Sometimes it is not the one-off hard times of life that get me but the drain of it that makes me think God will forsake me, that He forgot me. Even in the silent seasons when we can't especially feel His closeness or there's no vision from Him, just the everyday routine of fast-paced life— do we know God's assurance even then? But as we grow in maturity in His grace and goodness, we learn that God is glorifying Himself here and now, in all these moments.

Our God sees right where we are; his love is strong. That's why I can't blame Adam and Eve harshly, they were allowed free will, the same right we have. I believe just as Ephesians 1:4 says, "For he chose us in him before the creation of the world to be holy and blameless in his sight." Did you catch that? So the Deity already had a plan to send Jesus to make it right, to ransom humanity back from being separated from a perfect God as seen when Eden was evacuated. So all is not lost, no matter how far away from home we may feel, our story is never done!

God is all love and all about redemption stories. He's waiting on us to turn around to meet His gaze! That realization changes everything. No matter how hard we may try to fix it, in order to really receive healing, it starts with total humility.

Humility isn't weakness, in fact it's bravery to face your truth. Then when we have enough confidence to let it fall apart, letting it go, coming to the end, that's when God's incredible redemption kicks in. A submission, a yielding to a Father's love that will change us. The ability to love our enemies, to see ourselves completely free from any human's opinion of us, free from anxiety, and to trust is where "second chance" is realized. Let this realization settle deep: there's a God who sees right where you are. His love makes it possible for you never to lack for anything. His love won't let go, He holds us with His heart. Even when we are far from home. He sees.

It's time to awaken out of our slumber and arise as the sons and daughters of God. God was about to prove that point to me, coming down eye level, in the middle of my ordinary, busy routine. It was a Friday and I had just dropped the kids off to school and was rushing to meet Jorge at an appointment with a photographer friend for a book he had just written. Little did I know that day would bring a deluge of emotions, becoming the day a spark was lit inside me, starting an unquenchable fire.

DIVING DEEPER

Promises and Reflection

1. Read Deuteronomy 31:6
   Isaiah 41:10-13
   Psalm 55:22
   1Peter 5:7
   Philippians 4:6-7
   Romans 8:28

2. Reflection: What does it mean to you knowing the scripture promise that He will never leave or forsake you? Share your thoughts here.

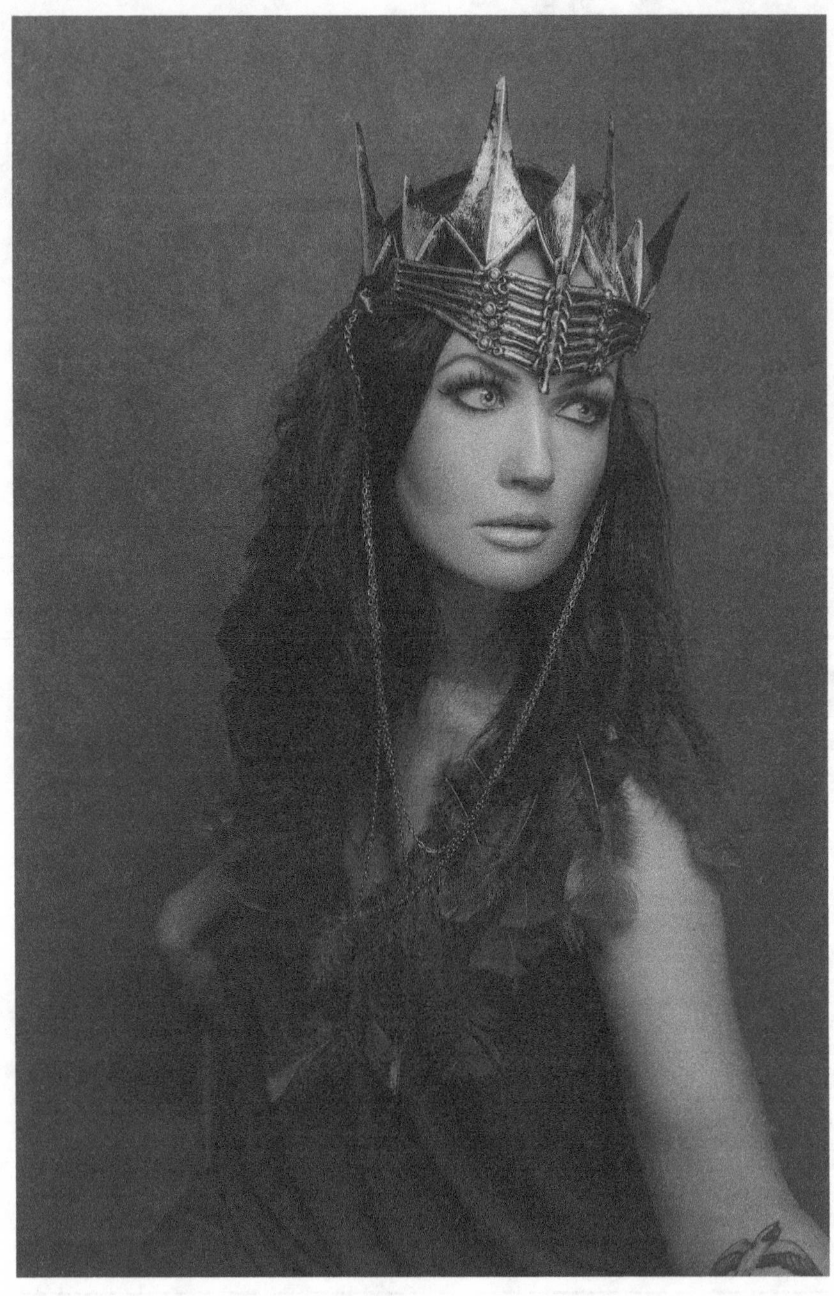

Photographer: Antonio Pantoja
Model: Kat Vazquez

CHAPTER 19

The Crown

My husband and I had a photoshoot scheduled with a very talented photographer friend. I don't know if it was the awesome Pandora station he had playing on surround sound, but creativity kicked into a new gear at that shoot. I asked if he had any props and the first one he pulled out of his box was a really sick looking crown with chains dripping off the front of it. He was a master at his craft behind that camera, and knew exactly how to capture classy yet "other-worldly" at the same time.

After getting that dramatic, crowned image back from our photographer friend, it triggered a deep, rooted unraveling of how I saw myself. I was shocked at how I was reacting! I felt unworthy and like I should be nowhere near a crown. That image started a journey that was the seed for this very book. A few years later, I now believe the absolute truth of what it means to be a child of God. I feel so much freedom to be able to look at that same picture now, and celebrate that this is how my Father really does see me—as well as every one of His elect children.

As followers of Jesus, we take on a new identity by relation. We are His chosen children, royals, elect saints in the Earth, and we are all wearing a crown. Now let's look at this image and specifically the crown, I want to share some encouraging revelation!

A crown is placed on top of the head, a symbol of birth-right authority and honor. The crown is an adornment worn on the head, where the mind is, where thoughts are created to distract or drive you toward your already given jurisdiction. Are you

getting the message behind the imagery? When you become a Christian, you are adopted into sonship. You are royalty!

Now let's go back to the battlefield of the mind. Certain thoughts can make or break your purpose right? We can line up with the Lord's promises for us or we can allow lies to take root, and eventually sabotage you. Sabotage is anything that can render you ineffective for His kingdom purposes that He has for you; it's the impact only *you* can make. Thoughts can only be healed through the presence of Jesus, and a renewed mind's fruit comes from hearing the word of God and trusting it.

The finished work of Calvary afforded us this incredible position. This glorious plan was already envisioned, it had a determined outcome, and effectually was put into place before the foundations of the world were fabricated. When Lucifer fell, 1/3 of the angels followed him. But the Trinity was never thrown off by this. There was an amazing plan to ransom humanity back, and that was put into activation. I wanted to share a bit of Lucifer's backstory only to highlight how time, space, and even supernatural creatures' decisions don't have a hold on God's ultimate plan. His empire of love will become reality on the Earth as it is in heaven.

Lucifer's Backstory

Ezekiel 28:12-18, "Your heart was lifted up because of your beauty. You corrupted your wisdom by reason of your splendor. I cast you to the ground; I put you before kings, that they may see you. "By the multitude of your iniquities, in the unrighteousness of your trade you profaned your sanctuaries. Therefore I have brought fire from the midst of you; It has consumed you, and I have turned you to ashes on the Earth in the eyes of all who see you."

That was the story of how fame corrupted an immortal being, but it didn't catch the divine Trinity off guard, oh no! In fact, it activated the advancement of God's empire upon the Earth. It didn't slow anything down, it just activated it.

The amazing part of this story to me is that the Godhead, the Trinity, decided that Jesus, God's perfect son would come to Earth as a frail human baby. They decided He would live out 33 years as a man on Earth, a perfect human experiencing everything you and I experience, feelings, doubts, struggles, but not once sinning against Father's laws of love. Jesus would willfully align His heart to the Father's as He would be brutally tortured, and killed on a Roman cross. The Romans at that time in history were masters of killing people, and Jesus did die. But on day three, proving the ancient prophecies true, He defeated hell and the grave.

This is how we have the hope of eternal life and when we ask Him to be our Lord and Savior, it gives us access to align our thoughts up to His! I heard an evangelist recently explain that prophecy is actually "staying awake" for what the Father is awake to, and resting in what He is resting in. When we start to see how in union we actually are with Him, we can start to train our human thinking, emotions even, to line up with His as seen through love.

Our real identity as sons and daughters of God is sovereign. Nothing the enemy can do can take that away from us. Scriptures say collectively, the unified church operating as followers of Jesus, is The Bride of Christ, who Christ is returning for. The Bible also says Christ's return is imminent, and if you reflect on the basics of Christianity, it proves why our identity is set, because His return must happen.

"Above all, you must understand that in the last days scoffers will come, scoffing and following their own evil desires. They will say, "Where is this 'coming' he promised? Ever since our ancestors died, everything goes on as it has since the beginning of creation." But they deliberately forget that long ago by God's word the heavens came into being and the Earth was formed out of water and by water. By these waters also the world of that time was deluged and destroyed. By the same word the present heavens and Earth are reserved for fire, being kept for the day of judgment and destruction of the ungodly. But do not forget this one thing, dear friends: with the Lord a day is like a thousand years, and a thousand years are like a day. The Lord is not slow in keeping his promise, as some understand slowness. Instead he is patient with you, not wanting anyone to perish, but everyone to come to repentance. But the day of the Lord will come like a thief.

The heavens will disappear with a roar; the elements will be destroyed by fire, and the Earth and everything done in it will be laid bare," 2 Peter 3:3-10.

"Then I saw "a new Heaven and a new Earth," for the first Heaven and the first Earth had passed away, and there was no longer any sea. "He will wipe every tear from their eyes. There will be no more death or mourning or crying or pain, for the old order of things has passed away." He who was seated on the throne said, "I am making everything new!" Then he said, "Write this down, for these words are trustworthy and true," Revelation 21:1,4-5.

Christ is coming again. The very promise of God demands it. The teachings of Jesus demand it. The testimony of the Holy Spirit demands it. The vindication of Christ demands it. The destruction of satan demands it, and the hope of the saints demands it. He is returning for a collective Bride submitted, unified with His heart, holy and blameless.

"...Just as Christ loved the church and gave himself up for her to make her holy, cleansing her by the washing with water through the word, and to present her to himself as a radiant church, without stain or wrinkle or any other blemish, but holy and blameless," Ephesians 5:25b-27.

Our position was a great promise spoken before time and space. We were made in His image, and for a great purpose. It's time we look in the mirror of His Word that defines us, and straighten our crowns.

DIVING DEEPER

Reflection and an Experiment

I love a good romance movie! The kind that makes your toes curl and heart flutter, well are you ready to be romanced by your heavenly Father? The Bible says not only does our Creator meet our heart's deepest needs, but his entire plan to send Jesus Christ to Earth was for us. He is the ultimate romantic!

1. Experiment: Ask the Father how He sees you. He may show you in a dream, maybe through song lyrics He pricks your spirit to, or some other creative way. But He will show you and you will know He's answering that prayer. It may be an image, a trigger word, or He may whisper in your ear for real, like audibly. One of my favorite ways to ask this question is, "What were you thinking when you formed me in my mom's womb?" Write down anything He shows you. If He shows you in a dream, don't forget to write it down!

With that revelation of how He sees you, perfectly designed, filled with purpose and meant for impact, then we can start to live as we were created to! We were made in His likeness and in His greatness. As born-again Believers, we were given the mind of Christ.

Artist: Rebecca Friedlander

PART 2

Breaking The Cycles

CHAPTER 20

"You can have it all!" They're Selling It. We're Buying It: Perfection's Trap

"You can have it all!" This popular buzz phrase has been floating around for the past few years and is just now having its real effects on our society, with the number of counseling sessions on the rise. Kinda like the FDA results that come out later saying the weight loss pills can cause organ failure. But the pill company sales representatives keep peddling unrealistic promises to get paid until the first lawsuits are filed. The "you can have it all" ideal is fueled in part by consumerism and sadly, has been passionately adopted into daily lifestyles across America.

Perfectionism

There is a difference between striving for personal excellence, and being driven by perfection. According to the dictionary, perfectionism is the refusal to accept any standard short of perfection.[23] Psychologists and counselors are recognizing perfectionism as being fear-based. Dr. Brene Brown notes that, "perfectionism is not about healthy striving, it is a thought process that says if I do these things perfectly, I can avoid shame, blame, and judgment."[24]

Perfectionism is a place we cannot and are not meant to arrive. This way of thinking can lead to comparing ourselves to others or even self-loathing when we can't meet our goal or complete a task. Our society has even made perfectionism into a healthy attribute – we convince ourselves that this way of functioning is a positive form of "motivation." The perfectionism way of thinking can also give us a sense of control or power, making this cycle pretty attractive, as many of us want to feel accomplished and "on top of our game."

Christian counselor, Erik Meldes has heard the stories first hand and seen the negative effects perfectionism can have, *"It has been my experience that individuals with perfectionistic thinking are in fact less likely to truly be motivated or healthily functioning human beings. This is largely due to the reality that their goals quickly become greater, and in the process, less attainable or even impossible. Individuals can become depressed or anxious when goals are not attained or standards not met. Inevitably, the cycle continues if these thought patterns go unrecognized, causing more stress, anxiety, and low self-esteem."*

Perfectionism can set us up to be in performance-based relationships, which will not be genuine or life-giving because they set us at odds with others and with ourselves. Dr. Brown gives an example about a very common effect perfectionism has on body image. Perfectionism would say, *"I'm ugly and ashamed of how I look. I need to be different in order to fit in."*

This is completely different from healthy striving, which says, *"I want to do this for myself to feel better. I am not given by worth or love by the number on a scale because I believe I am worthy of love. I am motivated by how I feel, and will give myself compassion in the process."*[25] Do you see the difference in those thought processes?

Growing up in a pageant family, I admit I struggled with the damaging thought patterns of perfectionism. When you see "perfection" on stage and being crowned, "Miss Name Your State," that becomes the standard. The other contestants notice. The audience notices, and so do all the impressionable little eyeballs searching for their identity and value.

Perfectionism is tied closely to our self-esteem and identity. Christian counselor Erik Mildes sheds some light, *"There tends to be somewhat of a lesser view of one's self with individuals exhibiting needs to be perfect. I have found this to be an interesting parallel because society believes striving for the best is a positive trait when in truth perfectionists may be striving for anything they can control because they view themselves in such a negative light."*[26]

In the aftermath of feeling so insecure, perfectionism can even drive us seeking affirmation anywhere. Sometimes we even allow ourselves to become objectified, a cheap prize, just to feel a moment of being "enough," desired, or feeling valued.

We all are constantly searching for meaning in our life's experiences. From our unique set of experiences, we develop perspectives and paradigms, tying those experiences together as a narrative that makes sense to us. We search for our meaning from those moments. We search for our identity. We search for our worth and identity in other imperfect people, in positions, or things we feel will complete us once attained. This cycle of defining our value in another human or something this fallen world offers, will set us up for disappointment every time.

To shed some light on this subject, I want to share an interesting conversation we had on camera. Our friend was a highly successful R&B artist. In an interview for our show *The Revolution TV*, he shared the insider perspective of what happens when you're considered idol status in the music industry. He disclosed that once an artist reaches a certain number of sales, the recording label's image consultants step in. They allegedly would advise their clients on how to become an "attractive" artist in their "product line," an icon. Our friend shared a line he remembered being told by one such consultant, "You need to be the person who every woman wants to get with and every man wants to be like."

No offense to anyone in the music industry but the idea of having a salaried position with the primary purpose to change someone's image to the public, just to sell more albums is pretty eye opening. Clearly, society values certain standards built on attraction in order to sell more units. Are you buying what I'm selling? I know I'm generalizing right now but how often do we get caught up in sizing ourselves up next to someone younger, more clever, or has a gazillion followers on social media? We have stories playing around in our mind on how we perceive ourselves coming across to others. We can easily fall into presumptions, and with the comparison filter always up, we tend to view ourselves in a negative light. It becomes our ceiling, to a room we believe we are to live in.

Genesis tells us we were created in the very image of God. If we sit in that truth for a moment, it should settle any insecurity and need to compare ourselves against any other human. We were created in his divine likeness and greatness. We were created to receive His love and nothing will satisfy us, but that wholeness only our Creator can fill. After all, we were created by and for Him. We are not meant to be self-satisfying, self-preservers, everything our hearts could ever need is found in Him and His perfect love. Once we see and believe how He sees us, our insecurities will dissipate like a smoke screen. We are meant to shine, uniquely created for His kingdom purposes and maintained by His perfect love. The purpose of *REIGN: Restoring Identity* is to reinforce the truths of Whose we are and *believing* it, where our need and value will never be determined by what another human acknowledges about our image, it simply will never matter. Because It only matters what He thinks of us.

Our thoughts influence our behaviors. Taking back our own thoughts of ourselves and lining them up to what God's promises say about us will feel like a deprogramming, however, the freedom on the other side of walking out truth will feel so right! Through our thoughts, we have influence over ourselves. Our thoughts not only affect how we see ourselves and others, but they also influence the goals to go after.

Grace. We need more of that for ourselves! Counselor Eric Meldes suggests, "*Try speaking kindly to yourself. It may feel strange at first, but if we can be our own worst critic, we can also be our own greatest cheerleader! Give yourself permission to fail. It is inevitable, and may become extremely freeing from a life of always having to work harder and be "better". These small changes in your life can ease the anxiety if you find yourself in comparison with others or putting yourself down.*"[26]

Tongues Like Swords

What makes the comparison game even more tormenting is that we fall victim to our own judgments of others. An "idea crop" starts growing in our subconscious levels based on how we judge other's responses to our actions or conversations. So it's a false perception of judgement thrown on others that sets a bar of how we see ourselves presented to the world. And once we have this judgmental view of ourselves we start to speak it inadvertently, slipping out in nervous chatter, or feeling like we missed the mark in a situation, living under a cloud of disappointment.

My Mom grew up in the country, and she used to bring up life lessons based on what she learned about happening through nature on the family's farm. One story she told me that I recount a lot is how powerful our thoughts and speech are. She told me about seedtime and harvest on the farm. You may have heard the term, "you reap what you sow..." this is true! If you plant bean seeds, you'll get a bean crop. If you plant watermelon seeds, watermelons form on the vine. Same is true for your mouth, it will attract the same toxic results of judgement, gossip, any dishonoring speech you allow to come out of your own mouth. And out of the heart, the mouth speaks. So what are we believing to be truth, are we putting up walls, and defenses because of past hurts?

The Bible says, "The tongue has the power of life and death," Proverbs 18:21. That's why correcting our self-image starts with aligning and being more proactive in our thought life. It takes persistence and a commitment to fight against the negative thought patterns and personal burdens we lay on ourselves.

What stories are we "making up" in our own heads about ourselves? So how do we start being more proactive in our thought life? By being grateful. The truths of blessings and gratefulness grounds us in peace!

DIVING DEEPER

Prayer

If this is you, I encourage you to join with me in a prayer, breaking the chains of rejection once and for all!

> "Father, I am coming to you just as I am, tired of living in this bondage of negativity. Help me to forgive those who have wronged me, who planted that seed a long time ago that broke my trust, where it felt like a betrayal. I release them to you, they may not have realized how badly it hurt me. In turn, forgive me for not even knowing that I was busy sowing a crop of judgement and rejection back onto myself. Please take those words that I have spoken, and erase their power. I speak a crop failure over that. I ask forgiveness for sowing those very same 'rejection' seeds in judgement back on others through distrust, jealous thoughts, words spoken in gossip, or straight rejecting them. And Father, please show me how you see me...Thank you. It's done in Jesus Name, Amen."

Prayer of declaration:

> *"I am loved by the Father. I am adored by the Father. I am approved of by the Father. He finds pleasure in me. He calls me capable. He calls me worthy. I am His desire. I am beautiful. I am indispensable. Today I receive His great love for me."*

CHAPTER 21

Anxiety

I started struggling with panic attacks and crippling anxiety during my thirties. The symptoms of trauma didn't hit me until after a 2-year series of devastating events. I lost a baby, we lost our house, a very close person in our life lashed out, and attacked my husband. It resulted in a visit to the emergency room. All within months, I lost our first baby, my husband and I had to figure out where to live, carry the shame and uncertainty of bankruptcy, and still put on a "God's got this" face when we showed up on camera.

The events had ripple effects impacting all areas of our life: our family, our friends, our jobs, and our ministry. My husband and I felt abandoned. It was just him and me in that season of desolation. I have a high pain tolerance, but that particular year had knocked all the stuffing out of me. I was hurting pretty badly. Since everything had happened within months, I started manifesting PTSD symptoms. I dug deep and clicked into performance mode daily, smile was on, positivity coming out of my mouth, but silently my heart was crushed and barely beating.

That year had robbed us of so much. I needed a fresh start, so Jorge supported me as I auditioned for a network hosting gig in Atlanta. It came down to me and another. I didn't get the part, so my husband and I drove 16 hours straight back to Kentucky that night, speechless. I just felt empty. So when we got back home, with my thread-bare resolve, I jumped at the first opportunity I saw. My coffee run turned into filling out an application at Starbucks. I just needed a revamp, a new start...from anywhere.

Since we had experienced some traumatic changes in our life, all within a matter of a year, my body and emotions were finally catching up. I began processing the stress, the changes, the loneliness, trying so hard to contain them while pushing forward to just do life. I started having PTSD symptoms.

I felt numb. I wanted to avoid certain places and people that were reminders of our losses. Since we lost a baby, our house, and what had been an inner circle of close friends, I became a hermit, wanting to withdraw inside my house every time I got out of work. I couldn't sleep. I was on edge and becoming more and more resentful as time went on. I was depressed. The constant incurrent of anxiety was escalating.

Many of us experience difficulties and struggle with crippling anxiety. Even pop super star Beyoncé admits to creating alter ego Sasha Fierce to overcome her anxiety of performing. But with the rise of school shootings, and other traumatic events of loss, it's healthy to not only acknowledge our feelings, but also bring them into the healing light of what God says, starting down a path of total healing and freedom.

When it feels as if no one can understand what you have been through, remember that Jesus Himself endured traumatic events and even died on the cross. He knows about suffering and trauma and He promises to be there for His people. "...casting all your anxieties on him, because he cares for you," 1 Peter 5:7.

Founder of Hope For The Heart, counselor Jane Hunt shares some starting steps for healing from the emotional toll trauma in our lives has taken.

"Acknowledge the reality of your trauma. Admit to yourself, to God and to at least one other person that you are hurting and in need of healing. Identify the symptoms you are experiencing, their frequency and their impact on your life."[27] "Trust in him at all times, you people; pour out your hearts to him, for God is our refuge." Psalm 62:8

Jane also suggests, "recognizing the source of your trauma." To do this start exploring the source of your pain, then share what you experienced with a trusted, mature friend. Think about connected experiences that have been spin- offs or repercussions from the original trauma.

Please seek counseling for any severe symptoms you may experience. This journey can include processing flashbacks, dreams, nightmares and other troubling experiences with a licensed Christian counselor. Always reach out and share with a medical doctor if depression becomes overwhelming and severe. "The prudent see danger and take refuge, but the simple keep going and pay the penalty." Proverbs 22:3.

Jane Hunt also brings to light the value of examining self-shaming thoughts or behavioral patterns. Honestly evaluate how negative thoughts are resulting in negative behavior, and deliberately replace them with loving, encouraging thoughts based on God's heart for us found in the scriptures. Another valuable perspective is to pinpoint ways we could be sabotaging ourselves personally or professionally, and explore the reasons why with a person who understands PTSD or other complex trauma effects.

"We all, like sheep, have gone astray, each of us has turned to our own way; and the LORD has laid on him the iniquity of us all," Isaiah 53:6.

Jane Hunt further shares an eye-opening suggestion bringing light to the bondage of crippling fear can have. She says in total honesty to self-reflect on any "emotional and psychological walls you may have erected, and self- protective tools you may have employed. Enlist close family and friends to help you consider the illegitimate ways you have tried to meet your God-given needs for *love, significance and security.* Explore all defense mechanisms designed to keep relationships superficial or separate from your past traumas like isolation, anger, a critical spirit, or the like."[27]

"Nothing in all creation is hidden from God's sight. Everything is uncovered and laid bare before the eyes of him to whom we must give account," Hebrews 4:13. Dealing with painful experiences is painful, but it is critical to healing and to the hope of a promising future. Pain held captive in silence is pain never freed.

Remember that pain expressed is pain released.

" Then you will know the truth, and the truth will set you free," John 8:32. Anxiety is one of the biggest deceptive patterns we fall into.

When we ask Jesus to be Lord of our life, it's not only a ticket to get into Heaven one day, it's a profession of belief that He *is,* and *has* all the love we could ever need!

We were created with a God-shaped hole in our heart that only He can fill. Just because we feel nervous from uncertainty or impending dread over something, doesn't mean we are doomed to fail. It means that feeling of uncertainty can be cognitively and intentionally laid at the feet of Jesus who came to earth to conquer all fear, and He has your rest and answers in His love. He's got everything you need. Just switch over your perspective to *that* truth.

"Do not be anxious about anything, but in every situation, by prayer and petition, with thanksgiving, present your requests to God," Philippians 4:6.

Learning to pray right by, asking God to supply our needs and trusting Him to do that according to His will and wisdom, will bring victory over anxiety.

Inevitably, praying and trusting Him will bring an attitude of gratitude, thanking Him for His provision even if it is different from what we originally wanted. This right attitude stabilizes our hearts with peace and joy. When we feel an overwhelming tide of anxiety start to rush in, that's the perfect time to capture them.

"Finally, brothers and sisters, whatever is true, whatever is noble, whatever is right, whatever is pure, whatever is lovely, whatever is admirable—if anything is excellent or praiseworthy—think about such things," Philippians 4:8.

We are commanded to think on what is true. Anxious thoughts speculate on what might be true but in reality might *not* be! An example is we may suspect someone has cheated us, or been unfair. We begin to believe the worst about someone– sure, they have betrayed us–yet no facts to back the speculation. Then we wonder why we are anxious with minds running every direction, with uncontrolled thoughts and zero peace or joy!

By realigning our thinking up with heaven's, we will live out the gospel, the truth, the things we have learned from Him. When we do those things consistently, the God of peace will be there to help us overcome any lie we encounter. Right actions lead to right emotions, joy in the Lord and the peace of God ruling our hearts. There is victory over anxiety, and Philippians 4:13 assures us we can live in this victory through the strength we have in Christ.

"I can do all this through him who gives me strength," Philippians 4:13.

DIVING DEEPER

Prayer and Practicals

If this is you, I encourage you to join with me in a prayer, breaking the chains of anxiety once and for all!

Prayer for freedom:

> "Lord, I confess I tend to believe that I am alone and without any protection. Lord, I know that this is a lie I've been believing, and it works me up into worry and fear. I repent of that worry and fear now... ultimately, I know it stems from not trusting in Your goodness toward me. Reveal the lie that I have been believing that has kept me in bondage to anxiety. (He will show you something, bringing to memory a situation or conversation that planted an idea, which made you feel a certain way, a form of pain.)
>
> Father, I release the pain into your hands and receive your healing from deep hurt, anxiety and the bondage of fear. Help me to not be so hard on myself. I want to walk in your grace so that the next time I get hurt, I turn the pain over to you quicker and quicker. You haven't given me a spirit of fear. Replace my fear with your power and your love so I may have a sound mind to live each day in victory. Thank you Lord Jesus! Amen."

Practical changes that create an environment of truth:

1. By making some adjustments to your routine, like reading the Bible daily, will open your eyes to how God sees your real identity, getting the truth down into your heart. This is a practical to start realigning your thoughts to heaven's.

2. A second suggestion is start playing the audio Bible in your home, at night or and listening to it during recreation times. As I can personally attest, the Living Word of God cuts through all confusion and tormenting noise. It is literally alive!

   Not to mention, playing the audio Bible through the airwaves has scientific proof to change the atmosphere. Scriptures spoken into the atmosphere release so much peace, life and His healing love.

3. Finally, I encourage you to write out your favorite verses on a post-it or notecard. Then go find a mirror. Speak out the Bible verses nice and strong addressing that dear one looking back at you in the mirror! The Word of God is alive and active!

Prayer of declaration:

I *believe* that God has everything I need. I choose to rest in the belief of the finished work of Calvary. His love has everything I could ever need. I am whole, I am found, I am His child, and I will shine for Him today.

CHAPTER 22

When He Means More Than Our Own Life

A story in the Bible that blows my mind is the one about three Hebrew guys who were punished because they stood up for what they believed. In fact, they were so rooted in their convictions, they purposefully broke the law, because of their beliefs. Shadrach, Meshach and Abednego were Jews that were on the royal court of the Babylonian king. Babylonian society was a monarchy but because this particular king had a big head, he wanted to be worshipped. The King had ordered a statue in his image to be worshipped like a god. The rule that became law enforced everyone to bow down and worship King Nebuchadnezzar and no other god. Shad, Mesh, and Abe were sold-out men of faith however. These dudes believed in the uncreated God. They didn't back down, knowing the punishment to break a rule would mean they would be put to death. Now think about that, they already stuck out—they were Jews in the Babylonian courts, and now this law. Their lives on the line if they didn't bow down: if they choose to stand up, their "witness" would be cut short. They received the death sentence because they didn't bow down and worship the king as an idol.

As the story unfolds in Daniel 3 the three men were tightly bound and thrown into a fiery furnace for breaking the law. But here's the amazing faithfulness of God showing up and showing off! The guards to the furnace, were noticing there were no sounds of tormented screams and wondered just what was going on in there. They look inside and there's an extra person standing alongside the three convicted, described as looking like "a son of the gods!" The guards are witnessing something miraculous taking place. The three men and the extra one aren't being touched by flames at all! In fact, they were standing upright, unbound by ropes, and unharmed. The guards were scurrying around by now. The King who had grown to admire these brave men for their confidence in their beliefs, couldn't take it anymore—he had to save them, now evidently being protected by the God they had stood up for!

In the third chapter of the book of Daniel, scriptures say Nebuchadnezzar then approached the opening of the blazing furnace and shouted, "Shadrach, Meshach, and Abednego, servants of the Most High God, come out! Come here!" So Shadrach, Meshach, and Abednego came out of the fire, and the satraps, prefects, governors and royal advisers crowded around them. They saw that the fire had not harmed their bodies, nor was a hair of their heads singed; their robes were not scorched, and there was no smell of fire on them. Shad, Mesh, and Abe were brought out completely untouched by the experience. Boom! How's that for God showing up and showing off on behalf of His obedient dudes?!

We are the children of the uncreated God. His authority is our's and untampered, no matter what societal or cultural law may be enforced for whatever reason. He does not change. Just like the structural truth of oxygen to human lungs—it's real, active, and life-giving. He is so real. That is Whose we are.

We are the body of Christ, the embodiment of Christ...so Christ lives in us— literally! So we're chosen to be on the team: on the roster of Heaven. You are not a sub, not a benchwarmer, not a 2nd string. We were given the ball! So let your light shine! You are indispensable and irreplaceable.

I am a big believer in standing up for our convictions. If it's in the Bible, I believe it, and when being threatened to denounce the truths in the scriptures no matter if its social harassment or governmental laws, the Burning Ones shine even brighter!

No where is this more evident than on social media. Bold opinions and harsh comments can bully and pressure us to water down truth, stay in the shadows, and possibly lose the "saltiness" of our conviction to Biblical truth.

It's easier to be a follower of the masses, a people-pleaser than living out what we preach and sing about in the reality of Western Christianity. But for those who know and are truly dependent on the Heart of Father, there will be a strengthening in our convictions, a genuine belief and depth of dependence on Him, and I dare say in times to come of growing persecution and rejection, we will shine even brighter and find even more joy in the trails.

Tests make testimonies. Those tests strengthen our resolve even more, making our relationship with Him unshakeable and more of a reality. As an American I realize rattling off that statement means something completely different to me, as compared to someone who would be persecuted for standing up for their Christianity.

I read where a believer from a house church in Iran (whose name will be kept anonymous) explained that people who want to join the Church have to sign a written statement agreeing to lose their property, be imprisoned, and possibly even martyred for their faith in Jesus. Many believers are arrested in Iran and either killed or put in jail for years. (*** "Evangelical Growth," Operation World, accessed April 4, 2019, www.operationworld. org/hidden/ evangelical-growth.)) That puts everything into perspective doesn't it? What is so fascinating, is that some research shows that Iran has the fastest-growing evangelical population in the world! The Christians in the Middle East teach the way Jesus taught. They are required to count the cost, surrendering everything up front; otherwise they cannot join the Church. That's when your faith gets real!

The underground Church in China is another great example of how man-made laws cannot quench the fire of God among His people, who have had an encounter with God's love. It is real and those precious ones were left never the same. Hundreds of unofficial "home" churches are sanctuary to groups who meet to pray, sing hymns, and study the Bible. They run the risk of harassment, and even possible detention by the authorities. Nonetheless, these Burning Ones have tasted and seen that the Lord is good and real. Some estimate that there are more Christians in China than communist party members.

Are you connecting the dots here? There is a blue-hot burning flame in the hearts of those who *chose* to stand up while their lifestyles, and very lives are being threatened. That blue-hot flame can be called holy conviction. Those willing to lay down their lives in these dangerous, anti-Christian societies, I can imagine over time have come to know the reality of who Holy Spirit is: He's real, He's alive, and with them.

The Bible talks about a coming persecution. In no way do I understand the severity of trials my brothers add sisters on the other side of the world face. Would the American church be unshakeable? That blue-hot conviction is captivating to me as a Westerner. I struggle to find words that express how deeply I admire those giants of the faith, who know they are breaking laws by worshipping the one true God.

How are they able to do this? In Francis Chan's book, *Letters to the Church,* he shares about a conversation he had with a pastor in China, exposing the stark difference maker. "In America, pastors think they have to become famous to have a big impact. In China, the most influential Christian leaders had to be the most hidden." ((** Chan, Francis. *Letters To The Church.* Colorado Springs, CO, David

C. Cook. 2018. Print.)) Tests determine why and who you are really in it for. Do you really love Him enough when your life may be at standing up for Him?

Pride has no place in the costliness of the Gospel. In fact Jesus modeled and laid out the price tag front and center. It was a death to self. Becoming a Christian is a complete and total surrender to your own desires and flesh to the higher purpose of serving God's glory. Dying to your self and putting on Christ. "Then he called the crowd to him along with his disciples and said: "Whoever wants to be my disciple must deny themselves and take up their cross and follow me. For whoever wants to save their life will lose it, but whoever loses their life for me and for the gospel will save it. What good is it for someone to gain the whole world, yet forfeit their soul? Or what can anyone give in exchange for their soul?" Mark 8:34-37.

"I have been crucified with Christ and I no longer live, but Christ lives in me. The life I now live in the body, I live by faith in the Son of God, who loved me and gave himself for me." Galatians 2:20.

Sobering? This is what Jesus said it would mean to be His true follower. There is no room for self. **Do we really believe in what the Bible says?

How come we marvel at these stories of the zealous faith of Christians in the underground church, when here in the West that level of being on fire is so foreign to us? Church leaders, I believe we need to re-examine the vision of our local churches. Are our churches preaching a deep, deep commitment to prayer?

Secondly, are pastors preaching the commitment to the Word of God? It's not about the speaker, but a reprioritizing of the membership's focus to be on a personal pursuit of Christ through scripture reading and application daily. This is how the church will mature!

Thirdly leaders should be committed to share the Gospel and very intentionally teach their congregation how to do this regularly. Fourth, expect More of the supernatural, healings, miracles, and redemption stories. By our faith levels Father will use us to demonstrate his power! I believe we can all take a lesson from the hidden fellowships of the underground church. Their pastors are embracing the promise of suffering for Christ's sake. This level of real-faith living is producing a group of people who are on-fire for Jesus, willing to go wherever and do whatever, no matter the cost.

So how do the inspiring stories from the underground church and the book of Daniel pertain to our Western Christianity? I feel it can serve as a motivation- check. In America, there are more churches and ministries than ever. Some are bored in their callings, and may be honestly struggling, lacking true communion with

God. The absence of the presence of God is glaring in many places, and sheep are starving for the true Word of Life. Holiness has been replaced by hype. The lure of appearance has been exalted over anointing.

Generally speaking, it's also been very encouraging to witness believers laboring in obscurity, pressing into God in the Spirit, and taking an uncompromising stand for the Lord. Still others are growing increasingly discouraged. Some are feeling a need to be fixated on member growth. Feeling the pressure and eventual exhaustion, some will give up and quit because somehow their focus shifted to hitting numbers. Burnout.

Francis Chan calls that proof of misplaced focus saying it has created consumers more so than servants, followers of Jesus.[28]

My worry is we can become dependent upon the package, distracting us from recognizing or feeling the awareness to engage with the Holy Spirit, Who it's all about! We need a central and passionate focus from all the pulpits of America right now: to pursue the presence of Holy Spirit, and respond to what's on His heart...developing a full-reliance on Him alone. We have some of the largest churches we've ever had in the history of our nation and yet the greatest departure from the true faith. What a paradox! Many professing Christians don't read their Bibles anymore, but only trust in what their favorite preacher says.

I may sound like an alarmist, but I can't deny the urgency and conviction I have felt about this matter affecting The Church. We need a genuine pursuit for His presence alone. In Him we find healing, peace, joy, strength, hope, the answers to our heart's deepest needs. It's in Him alone! When we encounter His presence, it's undeniable; we never leave the same.

Overseas missionaries, underground church members, and persecuted Christians throughout history all have something remarkable in common: their reliance on God is real, they have staked their very lives on Him. How would that kind of complete reliance on God change how you see and live for Him? When we acknowledge that He holds everything together, and that in Him and through Him we move and have our being, that humbling thought should put our true allegiances in check. As Christian hip hop artist *Lecrae* said in my favorite song, *Background*:

> *"It's evident you run the show, so let me back down You*
> *take the leading role, and I'll play the background...*
> *Praying the whole world will start embracing stage fright*
> *So let me fall back, stop giving my suggestions*
> *I'm who I are, a trail of stardust*
> *leading to the superstar."*[29]

DIVING DEEPER

Prayer and Promises

If this is you, I encourage you to join me in a prayer of repentance and to awaken to our First Love once again.

> "Father, I want that blue-hot flame of conviction and boldness to be legitimately burning for You and you alone. My heart sometimes draws me away from You to other things—sometimes subtly, and sometimes deliberately. This fallen world, my flesh, and the enemy have at times lured my heart into distractions, pursuing hype in what the world defines as greatness, or even "an image" instead of loving and honoring You as Creator. Why would I turn to anything else that cannot heal me or love me as perfectly and completely as my Creator does? Give me a pure and undivided heart that comes before You in awe at Your power, majesty, glory, and mercy. I want to grow in a hunger for your word and to be captivated with the personality and character traits of Jesus Christ. I want to fall head over heels in love with Him, and develop a real, deeper, active relationship with him. Amen!"

1. Read Mark 10:29-30
   Colossians 3:5
   2 Timothy 3:1-4
   2 Timothy 3:12
   Matthew 28:19-20

2. Thank you Holy Spirit who doesn't leave us the same!
   Write down your insights

____

____

____

____

____

____

After praying, did the Lord put a slight "unction" in your heart, conviction or reveal something new to you about what it looks like to be living as the activated Church today? Write down your insights here.

Prayer of declaration:

I *believe* that God has everything I need. I choose to rest in the belief of the finished work of Calvary. His love has everything I could ever need. I am whole, I am found, I am His child, and I will shine for Him today.

CHAPTER 23

Marionette: The Strings We Allow To Pull Us

A marionette is a puppet controlled from above using wires or strings. A marionette's puppeteer controls the strings, and is normally hidden. Pinocchio may be one of the most famous marionettes thanks to Disney's adaptation of the storybook character. He was a magic puppet who came to life, his creator, Geppetto, called him his son. But Pinocchio had a lying problem, and the film shows Pinocchio getting led from one mishap to another.

Even though the magic puppet had no strings controlling him, he allowed people's opinions to persuade him to do wrong things. In the end, Pinocchio learned some hard lessons about telling the truth, and he realized the voice of his father, Geppetto, was the only one who really had his best interest in mind.

According to the dictionary, the Greek word for "puppet" literally means "drawn by strings or string-pulling."[30] How often do we allow opinions from others persuade us to believe something that's not even true? We second guess ourselves, fear can set in, and before you know it we are off chasing "something" that seemingly makes us feel valuable.

Many people have an identity crisis because they don't really know who they are and they base their worth and value on all the wrong things – what they do, what they look like, who they know, what they know or what they own.

What do we think of ourselves? How do we feel about ourselves? Do we ever compare ourselves with other people and feel "not as good" if we can't do what

they can do or be like them? Have you ever said "I wish I looked like her," or "I wish I had what they have," or "I wish I could do what they do"? Everyone experiences insecurity at times. Anybody remember high school?

The good news is, we don't have to live insecure lives because it's God's will for us to be solidly secure and not to live in fear. We were created to feel safe, secure, confident and bold; it's part of our spiritual DNA as Believers in Christ. But the key to living a secure life in Christ is knowing who you are in Christ, really receiving God's love for you, and basing your worth and value on who God says you are, not what you do.

> *"But no weapon that is formed against you shall prosper, and every tongue that shall rise against you in judgment you shall show to be in the wrong. This [peace, righteousness, security, triumph over opposition] is the heritage of the servants of the Lord," Isaiah 54:17.*

As children of God, it's part of our adoption to sonship, blood-bought right through our relationship with Jesus Christ to be secure. We are joint heirs with Jesus and whatever He has, we get! But we have to take it by faith, which means we believe it before we see it. And since we believe what we say about ourselves more than what others say, we each need to speak what the Bible says about us as children of God to overcome the negative, defeating opposition in the world that wants us to see ourselves compared to others, never recognize who we really are in Christ.

The perfect, whole, complete love that God has for us... if we could just "get it," that revelation would be a game changer for all of us! What would happen? We wouldn't get caught up in competition, comparing ourselves to others, be afraid to make mistakes or afraid of admitting weaknesses if we were secure in God's love!

"There is no fear in love...but full-grown love turns fear out of doors and expels every trace of terror!" 1 John 4:18

Getting a personal revelation of God's unconditional and perfect love has helped me understand that my worth and value are based on the fact that I'm a child of God, not on what I do, or what someone says or doesn't say to me. This is so important because if we believe God loves us based on what we do or how well we perform, we will never be truly secure and stable in our relationship with Him.

Society has recreated a standard for perfection, based on having it all. Messages about body image and what perfection should look like are created through computer generated images on screens, written in song lyrics, images in commercials, messaging that says you're not worthy unless you've become this, gotten that, and look like this. These lies based in consumerism that can affect how we see our self-worth over time, it can enslave us.

Satan wants us tormented, on a short leash of comparing ourselves, and rendered ineffective for demonstrating what real security, peace and love look like to the world around us. The thing is no one else can do you and do it as well as you! Your Creator designed you with strategic purpose, filling you with dreams and wired to bring unique and creative impact to the world around you. No matter what you do for a living, whether you're single or married, have children or not, you're well educated or not, rich or poor, you are just as important to God as everyone else. We are all equally valuable to God. He wants us thriving in a real and stable relationship with Him, so we can be used to show the world what His love really looks like.

DIVING DEEPER

Prayer and Promises

If this is you, I encourage you to join with me in a prayer, breaking the chains of fear of others' opinions that have effected what we believe about ourselves and even how we behave. It's time to declare our freedom and shine bright as He intended!

> "Father, forgive me for allowing other's affirmations and opinions of me to matter more than what Your Word says about me. Lord, please search me and take away any doubt, uncertainty, blindness, and denial that would prevent me from seeing clearly. I repent for any of my actions or the actions connected to my family that have opened the door to allowing insecurity, fear, manipulation, oppression, bondage, comparison and inferiority. I am your Beloved, a child of God, accepted, and my heart and life were worth You sending your son to the Cross, you wanted to have my heart that much. I am your inheritance! Lord, I am asking for you to show me specifically how you see me. Open my eyes today to the unique ways you will be answering my prayer. I declare the promise that you saw me in my Mother's womb, and I was fearfully and wonderfully thought of and designed. I have a purpose and I bring you joy. Thank you for healing my image of myself. In Jesus Name, amen!"

1. Read and highlight in your Bible these passages.
   2 Cor. 3:18
   Ephesians 5:8
   Romans 12:2
   Ephesians 1:5-6
   Romans 8:17
   Cor. 3:16
   Col 3:12

2. I encourage you to write these out on a notecard and stick it where you can see it frequently.

Prayer of declaration:

I *believe* that God has everything I need. I choose to rest in the belief of the finished work of Calvary. His love has everything I could ever need. I am whole, I am found, I am His child, and I will shine for Him today.

3. Creative Gush: Doodle, write lyrics, poetry and share how the scriptures say God sees you.

CHAPTER 24

Looking Like Revenge: Body Image Bondage

In 2004 a teen comedy was released called *Mean Girls.*[31] The movie exposed the cold reality of High School cliques, and the unwritten teen-girl law recognizing the sense of power Queen Bee herself, Regina George, reigned in, making sure she stayed the most popular. It always seemed to be about image. High school right? I believe in enhancing our unique God-given beauty. However, to play into argument, what happens once your skin starts aging, things start migrating 'south', and your teeth start to turn yellow, do you believe less in yourself once you notice you aren't getting as much attention as you used to? And that's exactly what started happening to Regina George in Mean Girls. As soon as someone else knocked her off her pedestal of being 'the prettiest' she was left feeling like she had no influence and it affected her confidence, and later decisions. It's real and real sad to ever let superficial beauty become that critical to walking in your God-given identity.

Body image is a person's perception of the attractiveness of their own body. The phrase *body image* was first mentioned by Austrian doctor and researcher Paul Schilder in his book *The Image and Appearance of the Human Body*. "Our society has at all times placed great value on beauty of the human body, but a person's perception of their own body may not correspond to society's standards."[32]

Our society has made a perfection standard for body image almost intrinsic. Perfect bodies are computer generated and strategically used in sales gimmicks to portray ideals of power, beauty and sex to sell units. This standard of physical perfection applied everywhere has had its effects. Also other standards of "perfection" as misapplied in our own mind during impressionable years would also play into our feelings. Aside from having low self-esteem, Schilder explains from his book how body image can lead some people to fixate on altering their physical appearances. He says long-term behavior could lead to higher risks of eating disorders, isolation, and obsessive behaviors.

I come from a beauty pageant family. I saw firsthand the lengths gone to achieving physical perfection: boob tape, 6" tall heels, thousands of dollars spent on makeup and hair products, and coaching lessons. And on the night the pageant winner is announced, just one name is called. All the hard work, rumbling hungry bellies of the contestants who voluntarily skipped some meals, and financial sacrifices spent, only left the other 99%with a sour taste in their mouth. What's worse is the cruel mind-game that takes root in their heads the next morning. My heart breaks for the girls who don't know their true identity and go through a broken system that is based on a few judges levels of perfection, and whatever personal value system they draw from. If not careful, they can get trapped in setting those standards as goals and they strive to attain: an identity rooted in outward perfection, that is not from God.

What happens when we are rejected based on our presentation? If we aren't grounded in our identity as sons and daughters of God, we can easily slip into a rabbit hole of comparison and insecurity. Sometimes we let that "prize" or standard we were going for, which was based on performance or image shape our goals and decisions, and it becomes almost like an idol we live to attain. I need to stop right here a minute.

Our society's focus on being skinny is way out of control. Culture's standards of what is desired only makes it worse, glamorizing unrealistic physical body types, and unfortunately, those common standards are everywhere: in music videos, in movies, commercials, photoshopped, and filter-altered. These images of perfection are brainwashing everyone, even children! They are telling you over and over what they want you to think, and especially what they want you to want. Psychology 101. What can start to happen is a new mental program is engaged: redefinition of happiness. We start believing we won't be happy until we hit that goal of perfection in our own mind. We start making decisions off a timetable of "when" we hit that perfect standard in our own mind. Though gentleman and women are both affected by these standards, and comparing ourselves, I believe women feel the pressure the most. It's all absolutely a lie sold by commercialism, and it's ridiculous.

No matter if it's a relationship based primarily on the physical, beholding to another human's need, or a beauty contest, inevitably we will fail to meet some standards. Rejection, guilt and shame are cruel step-sisters that work together taunting us to chase "perfection". Shame spawns and wraps itself around our identity, driving unhealthy performance, and perfectionism. When we believe the message that we are flawed and unworthy, we endlessly strive to change ourselves, and especially, to manage the way others perceive us so that our flaws remain undetectable.

Our looks will fade, it's a fact of life for everyone. Gray hair, wrinkles appearing, muscle tone isn't what it used to be; aging is inevitable for all of us. When we allow our looks to become an idol, we will be devastated when we discover that new wrinkle because it will disrupt the joy of our journey. Looks can't make life more meaningful, make us wiser, or even happier.

A friend of mine once told me she struggled with insecurity most of her life because her weight would fluctuate. Coming to the Lord with this insecurity, He revealed to her some key scriptures just for her that she clung to as personal promises. She began declaring them over herself daily. She told me a lot of them were found in Proverbs 31 which praised attributes like integrity, honor, dignity, and wisdom. I have never forgotten that perspective of "attractiveness," virtues that truly are captivating.

While poise and queen-like dignity can be taught, nothing can convince ourselves that you are enough except *believing* what your Creator adores you. God knows what He was thinking when He designed beautiful and unique you! He broke the mold!

We must learn the truth of who we really are. We were all created in His greatness and likeness. Like prisms with thousands of radiant angles and beams shining bright, we are uniquely designed with purpose to attract the nations for His kingdom purposes. So let's start seeing ourselves as Christ sees us, maintain the temple we have been entrusted with, and never again let anyone make us feel less important than anyone else. We are each irreplaceable and so treasured.

A Broken Record

Perfectionism and performance are fear-driven, leaving us feeling ashamed, powerless, and mistrusting. These are orphan identities. We must break these cycles. The enemy of fear is love. Perfect love drives out fear, because fear has to do with punishment. The one who fears is not made perfect in love. When we are ruled by fear, we form relationships where there is little authentic love, but mutual agreements to control and use each other to meet our needs. At the core it's selfishness and conditional according to what the other person does. Anxiety, disconnection, conflict and dysfunction reign in these relationships. There is not safety, trust, vulnerability, or genuine connection.

In the same way fear can mar how we see ourselves from a fallen world's standards, our new identity as sons and daughters comes not only from knowing we are adopted into His family but receiving His Spirit of adoption. 2 Timothy 1:7 says "For God did not give us a spirit of fear but of power, love and a self- control." As we learn to follow His Spirit inside of us we come to know our Father, what He says about us, and we are empowered to live in our true identities, walking in His power, love and self-control. Over time our experience of walking in relationship with Him, receiving His love and seeing ourselves from His perspective drives out our old fear-based thoughts. We will learn to think like sons and daughters, we will feel more and more secure in knowing who we are.

We will start to *believe* it! As a result, we will have the ability to recognize when we start to step outside of our identity and we will be able to receive correction to change course, staying rooted in the freedom of His truth. We will also start to see mistakes and flaws as opportunities to grow rather than signs of unworthiness and shame.

God's perfect love sets us free from any human validation. No human should ever have that power over us that drives how we behave and see our identity as His child. We have a God-shaped hole in our heart that only He can fill, no human will ever make us feel whole. We were made by Love and for love.

DIVING DEEPER

Prayer, Practicals, and Promises

If this is you, I encourage you to join with me in a prayer, breaking the chains of comparison and fear once and for all! He is so ready to open your eyes, begin the healing, experience true freedom in this area, and start you on the awakening of how He really sees you. This will be a game changer!

Prayer:

> "Father, Help me to release the burden of physical perfection. Retrain my focus from "sculpting my arms", to finding beauty in the duty they fulfill, working at the tasks you have called me to, opened up to love and ministering to others. Help me be at peace with my body. Please release me from envy and comparison to others. You created me, You chose my shape, and my DNA. Thank you that you made me with a plan and purpose. Your Word said I was fearfully and wonderfully made. Help me to appreciate the magnificent machine that is my body, and to celebrate how unique and beautiful I am.
>
> Show me how much I am worth to you, and Lord, change my heart to accept it. Thank you, it's done in Jesus Name, Amen."

Practical Application:

1. Pay attention to your self-talk. While there may be a ton of negativity happening in your mind, what is the *most pervasive* thought (lie) that you are believing. Write it down.

____

____

____

____

____

2. Start meditating on Bible verses that speak truth to that lie. For example, when I was younger I struggled with believing that my worth was attached to my weight. To renew my mind, I searched for verses on how God sees my worth and His love for me. The verses below are a great starting point.

   Scripture Promises on Worth:

   Jeremiah 29:11
   2 Corinthians 5:17
   2 Corinthians 5:20
   Ephesians 2:4-7, 10
   1 Peter 2:9
   1 Corinthians 6:20
   Isaiah 49:16
   Proverbs 31:10
   Proverbs 31:25-31
   1 Peter 3:3-4
   Psalm 139:14
   Philippians 4:8
   1 John 4:18

Prayer of declaration:

I *believe* that God has everything I need. I choose to rest in the belief of the finished work of Calvary. His love has everything I could ever need. I am whole, I am found, I am His child, and I will shine for Him today.

CHAPTER 25

Captivity: Freedom From Approval Addiction

Do you ever live under a heavy blanket of guilt or condemnation, feeling unworthy and insecure? Maybe like me you've struggled with being a people pleaser, looking for the approval of others. God doesn't want us to stay stuck here, because it will affect our relationships, maturity, and ability to be promoted. I can tell you first hand, this "rut" steals joy and peace, and that's not God's will for us at all!

I have always struggled with the "need" for approval. It started when I was in elementary school, and because I found the other conversations in the class more fascinating, I tuned in more to the chit-chattery of my friends, not listening to the teacher. I loved to join in, of course, but one particular day, I was made the example, and separated from the group. My new seat assignment was next to the teacher's desk. At the front. As a child, I was humiliated. I felt picked on because I was the only one singled out. I never forgot the feelings of shame, and tried not to

cry as I processed hearing the chuckles from the other students, my face growing more and more flushed. From then on I decided to be the most attentive student I could be in the third grade.

Over the corresponding years in school, similar situations would happen because I was naturally a talker, but I tried hard to rein it in. My conduct grades came up! But one day in High School, I was asked to step outside of the class and boy did I get an earful!

The teacher yelled in my face. Not for talking in class, but for a paper I had turned in for his creative writing class. The assignment was "how do you define success in creative writing." He really didn't like my analysis. Since creative writing is totally subjective, I thoughtfully wrote that I believed "success" was defined by what mattered most to the teacher, thus in order to gain "success", the student needed to build and craft their writing around what he valued. Made sense to me; but apparently I had crossed some line with him. I thought he was going to have a stroke! He yelled so loud at me in the hallway, his face was turning red! My body went numb, my mind froze. I can see where my paper may have nicked his pride, but how he expressed his disdain, exploding, screaming inches away from my face, scarred me. Later, I realized I blocked out the words he actually said to me that day. I couldn't remember the words, but I did remember his blaring voice, flashing eyes, and spit flying out of his mouth as he screamed.

That incident scarred me. To this day, when someone starts criticizing me, I can easily click into a resignation mode, feeling the need to comply. Over the years that default has cost me a lot, most valuable of them all: having confidence in my own voice.

We all love to be affirmed and encouraged but to have it drive our decisions is another thing entirely, it can become an addiction. It has nothing to do with chemical dependency or substance abuse, but it does wreak social, spiritual, and relational havoc. The need to prove ourselves comes out of a source of dependence upon another human's opinion or behavior towards us. To give someone that much influence that it affects how we think, is a form of idolizing which builds ceilings in our own heads of what we think we deserve. When other people's opinion becomes the organizing principle of our life, how we perceive our own identity can be put on the line. What happens is that we end up giving people access to our heart, attitudes and behavior that should not have that access.

Though "captivity" is a broad stroke to title this chapter, I believe the constant seeking of people's approval can become a form of mental and emotional enslavement. Captivity in a psychological definition is a period of time of being confined. If God's plan for humankind was to set us free, then by nature our hearts, and lives are meant to experience that on this earth, living in relationship with God who is all love, meeting all of our heart "needs."

Living in the gracious acceptance and approval of God will liberate us from the approval addiction. The converse is true too. Living as an approval addict will keep me from living in the love of God.

In my season to pursue total freedom, I desired all my entanglements to be exposed and die off. For several months I cried out to God to get truly free from other's responses and opinions of me. I can't control how people view me, only how I think and respond in love. Even further, I wanted a soul healing from "survival" behaviors I had developed over the years from how others had treated me. I had given people way too much power over how I perceived myself. God started peeling dependency crutches I didn't know I had since I was a kid.

Feelings with strings attached to other people's opinions of me validating how I saw my worth. The Lord started opening my eyes that my confidence, belief in who I was, and that my unique purposes on the earth were solid. They were promises predestined for me and meant for only me to carry out. That was revelatory! And as far as other's input received in my life, albeit critical and opinionated, or lovingly correcting as edification in maturity, the Lord showed me how to discern and keep their voices in check.A huge lesson learned later in life for this girl right here! Their praises would not make me, and their shame would not break me.

My experience from High School was borderline abusive, an extreme case of "criticism" that I intended to get rectified as a student. The way things are expressed can emotionally damage people. I wrote a letter, my parents got involved, and we had a meeting with the principal of the school about the teacher's behavior. The principal assured us a meeting with the teacher would be made to discuss what had happened. What I took from that painful experience sadly set off a pattern of approval addictive behaviors in me that followed me from relationship to relationship and job to job. I wish I had known then what I know now.

We can take the criticism of others and instead of reacting to it or allowing it to define us, we should ask ourselves, a few questions. If its professional in nature, be open to their perspective in how to make your presentation better. If its a personal character issue, consider your source. Is it a trusted friend, someone that really knows and loves you? If yes, then consider what they are sharing with you. If it still bothers you, take it the Lord and ask Him if it "fits". Does it line up with scripture, will it help you grow in integrity, maturity, or excellence? We must be pliable, teachable in order for our character to further mature in the ways God is wanting to grow us. For instance, I prayed to be a better wife and mother. The Lord started convicting me of things I had never noticed before until I yielded to be more teachable. I asked some close friends who I saw modeling out a healthy marriage and relationships.I valued their instruction because I saw the fruit in in their life! They had solid, committed marriages. They were content, at peace, secure in themselves, and navigating through life with focus, leaving others feeling uplifted every time they left their presence. He showed me some choices I had been making in how I was spending my extra time. I was convicted and I needed to make some adjustments. I started carving out more time out for quality one-on-one time with my husband, listening more, and being more present with my kiddos. I had to make some adjustments in my schedule and how I managed my extra time. It was so worth it to me to hear out my friend's suggestions and be teachable in order to attain a healthier marriage and ensure further trust bonds with our two treasures, our boys.

Corrective criticism can only make us better. And God wants you to win! He also wants to answer your heart's prayers to heal you, growing you further in maturity and Christ's character.

So in a nutshell, if the criticism "fits" we have the option to take corrective steps to deal with our character or behaviors and become better. If the criticism it does not "fit" then we can set it aside. In this whole process the key is to stay connected to the unconditional love, acceptance, and approval of a Heavenly Papa who beams with pride over you! You're the twinkle in His eye.

DIVING DEEPER

Prayer and Promises

If this is you, I encourage you to join me in a prayer to break the fear cycle of approval addiction once and for all!

> "Father, I want to seek Your approval above anyone's. We can't love people well if our need for affirmation, or fear of rejection, is greater than our love for You. Forgive me for holding onto other's opinions of me and being so fearful. I confess the guilt and shame I have held onto for so long. I want to love others as Jesus loves me; so help me to take back the power I've given certain people over my heart. I don't want to shrink in the presence of anybody; and I don't want to look to any human being to "complete me." That's your role, Father. So by the power of the Holy Spirit, keep blasting my heart with Your truth, Your love, Your promises for my life, and freedom. Thank you Lord! Amen!"

Scriptures:
Read 2 Corinthians 12:9
Psalm 27:1
Romans 8:31
1Thessalonians 2:4-6
Proverbs 29:25

1. What is God showing you through these truths?

Prayer of declaration:

I *believe* that God has everything I need. I choose to rest in the belief of the finished work of Calvary. His love has everything I could ever need. I am whole, I am found, I am His child, and I will shine for Him today.

CHAPTER 26

Monsters In My Head: Freedom From Anger's Grip

As you may have already guessed I enjoy Superhero movies. I have equal respect for the two founding houses: DC and Marvel. One of my favorite superheroes is *Marvel's The Hulk*. His origin story as a comic book hero is pretty interesting. His character was written as a nondescript, kind of "mousy" scientist named Bruce Banner who had a little radiation accident in the lab. The incident turned him into the Hulk, the strongest being in the Marvel universe. What triggered Bruce's transformation into the "force of nature" called the Hulk was his anger. He then morphed into a huge, volatile creature unleashing his blind rage on anything or anyone in his path. Fans have coined his behavior, "The Hulk Syndrome."[33]

Because the Hulk was so volatile, the public was always petrified of him. He was a danger to everyone around him. Bruce no doubt struggled with anger management. Anger and rage can consume us, rob us of our joy, drain us, and hurt those around us, sometimes creating such deep damage, people may not be able to recover fully from it.

Now, sometimes anger is a healthy sign that something is not right. It's our natural justice-radar going off. However, most times anger is a fruit that springs from a root of bitterness. Anger that's unchecked can sprout into other damaging fruits that can eventually keep us in bondage to the emotion making us toxic to those around us. Ephesians 4:31 gives the warning, "Get rid of all bitterness, rage and anger, brawling and slander, along with every form of malice."

The root of anger is *anghos which means "tight, painfully restricted, painful,"[34] The word "anger," has action built into it, stemming from a root of bitterness and can lead to rage. *"Thermo" is a root word connected to the origin word *"rage", which means, "a violent anger, fury, nuclear, ready to detonate." Rage can easily manifest physically as brawling or attacking someone. This is abusive and if you have ever witnessed this climax in a home dynamic, you know it turns a once safe home into a nightmare.

The other manifestation of rage is slander, as seen in Ephesians 4:31. Slander is a false tale meant to dishonor reputations and dishonor people.[35] Proverbs 18:21 also says, "There is power of life or death in the tongue." Our words can give life and encourage those around us or speak death, killing the joy, hope, and security of others.

We are easily aware when other people slander us, but it's not so easy to realize when we are escalating out of control, fueled by bitterness and anger in a moment, and lash out attacking others with our words. This behavior is especially damaging to the innocent and precious children we are responsible for, for those of us who are parents. If we let anger simmer and take root, we become just like the Hulk: bitter, angry and toxic to everyone around us.

My husband used to be involved in a prison ministry years ago. He has witnessed miracles take place in the hearts of some of the inmates during worship services. Almost every time, he would notice the hardest of criminals break down, singing *Amazing Grace* during a jail ministry service. "Amazing Grace, how sweet the sound that saved a wretch like me. I once was lost, but now am found. I was blind but now I see." Come to think of it, I don't really know anyone who doesn't get a lump in their throat singing one of the most sung hymns in history. What many attribute to the power that lies within *Amazing Grace*, was that it was written by John Newton in the late 1700's, who also struggled with anger management.

Described as a reckless young man, in England, constantly drinking, he needed work and took a job in the royal navy, then became a captain of a slave ship involved in the slave trade in England. The cruel reality and injustices he witnessed on the slave ships compounded his rage. His behavior grew more volatile, Newton was captured, enslaved, abused. Later he planned revenge, to murder the ship captain he blamed for his situation.

John Newton was a liability. However, the anger in his eyes soon would be overcome with helplessness, fighting for his life. Heading back to England, the ship encountered a severe storm off the coast of Ireland and almost sank.

Newton woke up in the middle of the night and, as the ship filled with water, called out to God. The cargo shifted and stopped up the hole, and the ship drifted to safety. Newton marked this experience as the beginning of his conversion to Christianity.[36]

To sing *Amazing Grace*, is more a declaration than anything. It carries inside its melody a posture of surrender, an end of oneself and need for God's help. When we get to the end of ourselves, ready to stop being controlled by a root of bitterness, when we stop running, and legitimately want freedom, the Holy Spirit always shows up. Why? The truth is He has been waiting on us the whole time. The truth is He has never left us. The truth is, He didn't bring the condemnation into that situation in the first place, that was another human's voice. He sees you. He knows you. His love is strong, and won't let go.

That's the message from The Great Messenger, Jesus Christ. A prayer that I pray daily that has changed my life and how I behave, is: "Help me to have your heart for your people Lord." To feel his heartbeat for another human being, changes how you see them. That prayer is remarkable. How it changed me was that I started to see every person I encountered through his eyes. He sees us as whole. He sees us as free. He sees us as restored and at peace.

Forgiveness. (Breathing a long sigh here...) It ain't easy sometimes is it, but then again it's the most effortless thing, to just let go of the offense, placing it in a capable Father's hands. The act of forgiveness takes trust. Trusting that a good, perfect Father has you. Forgiveness releases us from the weight of carrying offense, building walls, and isolating our heart. Forgiveness frees us to live in healing. He makes all things new!

Forgiving hearts understand the power of one of Christ's most powerful personality traits: grace. "Grace" has a mind of its own. It's unmerited favor, a movement that carries inside it a haunting posture of surrender, the end of our self. As our will takes a knee, grace lifts off a cover of blindness revealing Who has been intently staring at us the whole time, the King. He is waiting for us to wave the white flag in the middle of our war. To take a knee of surrender, let the hurt, the betrayal, the loneliness, the judgements carried that have kept us feeling like caged animals, misunderstood, and simply let them go... and trust Him. He will free you from you. He wants you to realize restoration. This will open your eyes to life, in Him, where He is our peace, scripture promises are the Truth you stand on and declare in prayer to move your circumstances.

He has always had a purpose for you, and for you to enjoy this life! After all, how will we be a beacon in the dark unless we shine bright?

If you are reading this, and have been mistreated by someone in the church, judged for years that may have allowed bitterness to take root, I want to extend a sincere apology. No human has the right to judge another, no one. To families, sometimes we become blind to how we treat others and especially our own. We don't think about the words coming out of our mouth that can either build up or destroy our loved one's happiness. If this resonates, I challenge you to ask them what it's like living with you. The truth is the first step to finding freedom.

2Corinthians 10:4 gives us the strategy on how to get free from a bitter root of anger. "The weapons we fight with are not the weapons of the world. On the contrary, they have divine power to demolish strongholds." Ephesians 4:2-3 tells us what specific tools will rebuild, bringing healing to those broken relationships, "Be completely humble and gentle; be patient, bearing with one another in love. Make every effort to keep the unity of the Spirit through the bond of peace." Humility puts others first and I daresay is a holy root that brings forth fruit like kindness, gentleness, compassion, and forgiveness.

Jesus embodied humility and kindness, after all his very reason for coming to earth was for others. Each human was created in God's image, so each human being has a divine imprint on them, as such each human is loved with an unconditional love, was created in love, and is to replicate this love to others. We can carry His servant-love, preferring others. This is how we are to shine and advance his empire of love on Earth.

DIVING DEEPER

Prayer and Promises

Let's get good and free from bitterness, anger, and tormenting thoughts. Are you ready to get this process started? Please join me in prayer.

> "Father, I confess my struggle with anger to you. I am tired of being tormented, going off and feeling out of control, hurting those around me, and draining myself. This is not how you intended me to live. Forgive me, I forgive those who have betrayed me and hurt me. Please heal my mind, somehow restore those relationships you gave me as a gift that I may have fractured with my words and actions. For those who intentionally wronged me, help me to forgive them. I want to live in freedom, help me to see others as you see them, preferring others. I want to be known as humble and kind, I want to be known for that! Thank you, in Jesus Name. Amen!"

Scriptures

1. Read 2 Corinthians 10:4 Ephesians 4:2-3
   Jeremiah 29:11
   Colossians 1:17
   1 Corinthians 13:1-2

2. Commit to memory 2 of these passages today.

Prayer of declaration:

I *believe* that God has everything I need. I choose to rest in the belief of the finished work of Calvary. His love has everything I could ever need. I am whole, I am found, I am His child, and I will shine for Him today.

CHAPTER 27

Braveheart: Breaking Free From Insecurity, Self-Shame and Addictive Behaviors

Years ago, our family had just enjoyed another sweet Christmas holiday, and we were about to enter into a new calendar year. Jorge and I normally go into a time of prayer and fasting for the Father's agenda as we position our faith, and pray into what's on the Lord's radar for the coming new year. In praying I also asked for freedom in some very personal areas. I had always struggled with my weight, where I had been every size during my adult years. I was tired of the mental and physical roller-coaster that I had put myself through time after time. True to the Lord's faithfulness, He began answering my prayer: opening my eyes to a pattern I had fallen into with why I ate in extremes. I never thought I could actually get healing from the root, the trigger that set me off eating like a bottomless pit, it was a self-sabotaging behavior.

I would hide my binge eating, sneaking into the pantry at night when Jorge and my kids were asleep. This behavior continued for years. But God didn't want to leave me there. He was about to answer my prayer, like coming out of a dark fog.

I started waking up, and seeing just how ridiculous it was to allow my emotions so much control over how I felt about myself that I would eat my feelings!

Feelings of unworthiness spiraled into hopelessness which usually had a box of Oreo's attached to it. This behavior was almost a coping mechanism for me somehow, and the Lord was opening up my eyes to the real hurts buried deep down that were my emotional triggers. For example, if a circumstance made me feel rejected, defeated, or discouraged for whatever reason, I would allow my mind to subconsciously "chew" on that. It would feel definitive, and I began to take on thoughts of why it was my fault somehow. I fell into victim mindsets often because of it. Then if I spoke that insecurity or lie out loud, like "I'm so fat," or "if people knew the real Kathryn, they wouldn't really like her," or "I can't do anything right," inadvertently I would be giving that lie power to take root inside my mind. I would start to believe those dramatic one-liners that would fly out of my own mouth! For our tongue is so powerful, even to our own ears! Proverbs 18:21 says, "The tongue has the power of life and death, and those who love it will eat its fruit." I began to realize that the words I used, especially during times of insecurity, were critical to my thought life.

During the process of realizing that I was binging out of feeling emotional, I decided to take control back. My first reset attempt was noble. I had a plan! I started strictly focusing on how to regain my mental wellness and physical health. I went to my Doctor and got some blood work done to see what hormone levels were a little low. Then I ordered a bunch of high-quality vitamins and like 3 different kinds of B vitamins for energy. Then I turned my focus on regaining control over my body, I started exercising regularly during the week to manage my stress, and eating for health. But I still struggled from time to time with those same trigger thoughts that made me want to start binging, grabbing whatever snack I could find in the pantry late at night, hiding (typical behavior of those who struggle with eating disorders.) And the obvious ridiculousness was I had no

"good" guilty treats, I was stealing and eating my kids snacks for school— a sleeve of graham crackers, Cheezits, or Poptarts in multiple packs. Sheesh!

The next day I felt like garbage from the sugar and gluten overload. I knew I had to run off those extra calories, so I started falling into a pattern of excessive exercise from Poptart binging. Inflammation in my joints from the sugar didn't stop me from hitting my running mileage however. After months of this, my body started to break down. Pulled hamstrings, shin splints, a rotated hip...it was ridiculous! I hobbled around my house most days during that season. I knew the problem was the sugar overload in the middle of the night, almost every night. So again, I had to revisit the motive behind why I always fall back into this pattern?

What exactly was triggering this out-of-control behavior? Over weeks of asking the Lord to show me, in his gentlest way, he allowed a series of painful events to happen, and I was able to recognize what was going on this time. It was coming from a wrong belief system. A sense of disappointment was stemming from a root of self-condemnation, that was still working deep down inside my heart. That shame root had wrapped around my identity. Shame, tsk, tsk, tsk. I had allowed it to have a field day with my emotions most of my life. And this shame feeling came from what situation today? Somehow I knew I needed to trace back the source of when I first felt shame in the circumstance. Did it actually happen?

Was it something I presumed from a conversation? Why did I presume that? Okay, okay, this was good. There was a lot of tracing back and dots connecting for me. I was learning through feeling the shame and actively taking back the control! I wouldn't eat that Poptart after all. But I knew I needed to process, and plan a way out of the power shame had on my emotions and behaviors. So I journaled. I did a lot of journaling.. I also become more aware of seeing my emotional and behavior patterns. In those patterns, I would ask the Lord to bring further healing into those "false narratives" and correct my thinking. This was a start, it was challenging, but it was so good. I was starting to receive freedom and healing in areas I had never even recognized before! Thank you Jesus for answering prayers and the start of emotional healing, this was some serious progress!

I started praying again for the Lord to complete the deep healing process once and for all. I wanted to be free from this emotional, knee-jerk reaction. The inflammation in my joints was real pain, not to mention the standards I was trying to keep up physically. I prayed and asked the Father to help me see myself as He sees me. I desperately wanted to *believe* it too, though I had a feeling I was about to walk into a huge process if I really wanted a new mindset, to start *believing* in how He saw me.

I am about to get vulnerable with you. What I had inadvertently been doing was emotionally eating out of a need for people approval and shame. I grew up a chunky kid so I wasn't used to getting attention for my looks... like ever. Once I started losing weight, because I was committed to my strict exercise program, I had a different shaped body, but that wasn't the remedy for feeling worthy or valued. The same feelings of discouragement, anxiety, and disappointment came in waves, triggered by life circumstances. The root of self-condemnation can create a vicious cycle inside our minds, and women are especially prone to it because of society's unrealistic fixation on being skinny.

My perception was so warped and rooted in insecurity so deeply it had affected my being able to accept any compliments at all. I didn't feel worthy of it, I didn't feel value at all! The dramatic and confusing lies were bearing toxic fruit in my head, but now I was aware that the Lord was exposing the traps purposefully for me to renounce them. I also recognized where I needed to set up some boundaries with people who were operating from a broken spirit.

As more revelation to this "root" came up, I continued to pray for complete healing. Then, I found a key strategy. Remember when I told you that I prayed to really start *believing* how Father saw me? I started praying scriptures that talked about my true identity. I would even substitute my real name into the verses as I spoke them out loud into a mirror. "I am the elect of God holy and beloved..." Col. 3:12. "In Christ all the fullness of the Deity lives in bodily form, and in Christ I have been brought to that fullness..." Colossians 2:9-10, and that I was made in the very image of God!

It felt a little weird speaking verses out loud, but I knew it would make a huge difference as my own ears received those truths daily. I stopped getting so irked out at the sound of my own voice, and over time, I began to be aware that I had been missing out on security, confidence, peace, and feeling comfortable in my own skin.

I started to *believe* that God made me in his image with His divine imprint, and His opinion was the only one that mattered anyway. Once I got that settled, I didn't care what anybody said to me from a cat-call from someone on the street, someone trying to intimidate me, or even cursing me straight to my face. I was being set free from past insecurities and human affirmation completely! I was starting to really *believe* that I was loved, the object of a pure, binding, jealous and relentless love as old as time itself! I started Believing what the Bible said about that: I had been on His mind before the creation of the world, and that Jesus would have planned to come to the Earth, be tortured and hung on a cross...if I was the only person here! The transformation on how I started seeing myself was evident in the peace I started carrying. The anxiety, fear of people's opinions was disappearing, and I began to feel a freedom that I never had experienced before. This revelation of my real identity was effecting what I believed about my purposes too. The more I reminded myself of those truths in scripture, the more fearless, and bold I grew in walking out assignments the Holy Spirit would put on my radar.

I am thankful I had the experiences that I did stretching over all those years. They were lessons I needed to learn in order to grow, and really *believe* who God made me to be. Painful experiences, broken people hurting other people will continue. However, we will be able to abstain from letting the pain break us. We will be able recognize more quickly the bait and trap of the enemy, how to grow through, and make choices based on Whose we are and His truths. Keeping the seed of insecurity from taking root continues to be an on-going process, however the quicker I recognize the bait of offense, the quicker I am convicted to let it go, because the truth was inside me like a steel backbone. I can see a bigger picture and purpose at work: we are to shine, free from anyone's opinions and walk in complete "fondness." Honesty with a loving Father is the key that unlocks our prison door that has kept us on a short leash of emotional survival behaviors.

Just as I would ask Him to cut through the lies and navigate me through the emotional stages of healing, He would walk me through gently, a step at a time. More and more peace would come and I would even feel a new lightness, joy return and notice that I would be laughing more! He was restoring my emotions, because He really does want us whole and free. He is so good!

Pain is inevitable in this life. Our job as Christians is not to live in denial, act like nothing ever happens, and put a fake smile on our face, that's not showing others how to shine in a fallen world! As Christians living in truth, and knowing and *believing* in Whose we are, means we are never alone even in times of abandonment, He never turns His back on us. He meets all of our heart's needs, especially through the painful times of life.

The freedom I am now living in makes me kinda regret not thinking to take my thoughts to Him earlier in my life. I had to keep going around the same tree, because the root of shame had grown so deeply grounded into the foundation of my identity!

What happens when we start to read, meditate, and declare out loud scripture promises is that the scales over our own eyes will fall off. We will start to *believe* the power in our own God-given voice, our own purpose, and that we are unconditionally adored. Once we believe that we are so loved, we notice that our cup is brimming over with God's love! Then we can truly shine, being The Church, forgiving, living out compassion, humility, patience, and kindness to everyone!

A Braveheart is one who is called to action, who steps out in courage, and who follows through an assignment to completion. We are able to be brave because He was brave first for our account. His action on Calvary and the completion to conquer death frees us from shame and all insecurities forever once we receive Him as Lord of our life. He has everything our heart's deepest needs could want.

We were all created with an innate need to be loved, however our needs can only be met by a perfect loving Father. He made you. He knows you, and that God- sized hole in our heart will always ache until you surrender, and are pulled back to Him. He is love, the source of everything good. It frees us from being dependent or disappointed by any human who simply can't fill our love reservoir.

It's in our spiritual DNA to be so filled with truth that our true identity is solid. No matter what comes our way, He will always be there with us, guiding us, holding our hand, as our source of love and security, and that is how we get to know Him better. It's a transformational relationship that changes everything. Then we will start *believing* and *thinking* like God's children. All of creation is waiting for us to wake up to that transformational truth! And during volatile times living in a fallen world, we will be able bring His Kingdom to renew it because we are His: a generation of Bravehearts.

DIVING DEEPER

Prayer and Promises

If this is you, I encourage you to join me in a prayer to break the cycles of shame and insecurity and get free once and for all!

> "Lord, please help me to break free from the bondage of insecurity, anxiety and shame. I am done with this bondage and the destructive way I am trying to cope. Forgive me for letting my emotions control even my health for so long. I have let the pain of disappointment or feeling like a disappointment to others influence my thoughts and feelings. Your word tells me I am fearfully and wonderfully made, (Psalm 139). Your word tells me I am not rejected, but I am accepted in The Beloved, (Ephesians 1:6). Your word says I am blessed and not cursed. I am the apple of Your eye. I have worth. I have value. For a long time, I have had a hard time believing that. Today I want to surrender rejection, self-hate, feelings of abandonment, fear, insecurity, inferiority, shame, bitterness, self-pity, and unforgiveness. I receive your perfect, healing love. Open my eyes and show me how you see me, Father. I want to *believe* what your word says about me. Thank you! In Jesus Name I pray, Amen."

Scriptures to quote over identity:

1. Read Colossians 3:12 Colossians 2:9-10 Romans 8:31
   Philippians 4:13
   1Corinthians 15:57
   Romans 8:37
   Romans 8:39
   Psalm 139:14
   Ephesians 1:5-6
   Numbers 22:12

2. Write out a few of these scriptures on a notecard and stick it somewhere where you can see it frequently. These are your declaration of Truth!

Prayer of declaration:

I *believe* that God has everything I need. I choose to rest in the belief of the finished work of Calvary. His love has everything I could ever need. I am whole, I am found, I am His child, and I will shine for Him today.

CHAPTER 28

Identity Based on Habitation

My husband and I produce a couple of film series, our latest program is called *Your Story Is Not Done*. The dramatic biography highlights the redemption turn when God showed up in the most hopeless situations. In every testimony we hear, we have noticed how much human beings are naturally story-driven. Bob Hasson wrote the book *The Business of Honor* and describes it like this, "We constantly look for meaning in our experiences, tying those meanings together that makes sense to us."[2]

In a nutshell, we are searching for our identity. Since we live in a fallen world, painful experiences, the people who should be pointing us toward setting it all straight don't or can't, and we are like that lost person in a novel searching for their identity. We search for it in what we have, what we don't have, what we do, and the people we associate with. The person who can only tell us who we really are is our Creator.

In Genesis the word tells us humans were made in the image of God. Each one of us has God's divine imprint! When we ask Jesus to be the Lord of our life, that's when everything changes; it means so much more than just getting a ticket to heaven. It means we can start living like Christ!

One of my favorite evangelists, Dan Mohler, posed this mind-blowing dialogue that's pretty telling of how we can think as Christians, "Yea, I asked Jesus into my heart, but do you have Him in your life? Yea, I'm going to Heaven, but is Heaven inside you? Yea I'm forgiven, but have you forgiven *them*?"[37]

Now walking as a Christian looks like transformation of the heart and a renewed mind. How does that start? To *know* Jesus as in, being in relationship with Him, will change how we think, and live as believers on this earth, carrying Him inside of us. This type of transformation looks like how Jesus lived: being a servant to all and seeking first the Kingdom of Heaven. There was no selfish will influencing Him at all, because He knew He was not His own. He changed the world one person at a time.

One of my favorite examples of His selfless character can be seen in John 13, the accounts of Jesus final hours on earth during the events of Passover. If we read between the lines we can pick up on just how deep his love, trusting His Father and how solid His belief was in God's perfect will and plan. His actions and the timing were extremely symbolic. In parallel to the 13th chapter of John, Luke 22 explains that in the days leading up to Passover, He asked his friends, the disciples, to meet for what would later become known as one of the most famous moments in history, the Last Supper.

The first thing the Son of God did was bend down, began untying the laces of their sandals, and then hand-washed the disciples' dirty feet. What an act of humility and unconditional love! He honored them putting them first just hours before Jesus knew He would walk through the most painful and history-making event on earth, His crucifixion. If anyone needed attention and prayer at that time, it was Jesus himself! But He put His flesh in its place, positioning his heart on the precious ones He was with at that exact moment. He stopped, and looked into the eyes of his friends displaying such an act of love by washing the filth and dust from their feet.

His voice, I can imagine, was gentle, and reflective as He said to them, "the greatest among you should be like the youngest, and the one who rules like the one who serves. For who is greater, the one who is at the table or the one who serves? Is it not the one who is at the table? But I am among you as one who serves," (Luke 22:26).

That is how Christ saw people, it's a testament of how firmly He trusted in His Father's will, knew who He was, and why He was there. His love for humanity outweighed preserving His own human life.

Being a Christian means He is in us, just like His nature is in us waiting to be awakened. It's a revelation that is meant to lead us into the natural transformation. Christ came and died for us to have: to become, think, and behave like the sons and daughters of God. We put on his nature, putting others first. Our own wants, "needs," and selfish nature are put in check, in fact we are to crucify our fleshly nature. Any thought that is contrary in truth to the truth and unconditional love of God is anti-Christ.

When we intentionally invite the Lord into our decisions, recognizing that He literally lives inside our hearts taking up habitation, He not only has everything our heart could need, we are free to turn our attention to others. Through that understanding we can see them as Christ did, worthy of a second chance for eternity, through the eyes of Love. It was the very reason He was marred unrecognizable on Calvary. He came to win our transformation into His nature, as the sons and daughters of God.

In order to transform, we must *believe* that He literally takes up residence inside us and that we have access to everything our heart needs. It's all in Him! When we start thinking and acting like his children, that's the game changer! That belief carries all the setup to change the world a person at a time. We don't have to strive, coming up with the perfect prayer formula, then it would become about our words, wouldn't it? We don't have to rely on our "righteousness" or "works," because then it would be about how perfect we act. No, we simply believe He is Who He says He is. It's a surrender to His goodness and unconditional love for people.

In our unshakeable belief in His identity is when walking in miracles starts to become a regular display of His love and desire to free his creation. How do we keep ourselves useable for Him? A huge key is to walk in humility and be active in forgiveness. This keeps our hearts pure for the Holy Spirit to show off through us. It's all about revealing His kingdom, not our own selfish promotion of any kind.

This is key to walking in the manifest habitation of the Holy Spirit where our lives as believers would look faith-filled, powerful, joyful, and seeing every person as Christ sees them: restored and unconditionally loved by God.

The transformation is about becoming The Church, His glorious Bride. The battlefield is in our mind. Renewing our thoughts with scriptures, memorizing them, and being aware of how active and real your relationship with the Holy Spirit is. This starts the process of aligning our minds with scripture truths. As we set our mind on things above, our heart will synchronize to His, we will start believing, thinking, and behaving like Christ intends for us to, the lifestyle He died for us to live out.

The habitation of the Holy Spirit starts to get real as we let his unconditional love overflow into how we see others. We will be a pure vessel, trusted with more souls to share the Gospel with, love unconditionally, believe when you pray for healings and miracles when the Lord stirs that unction in your heart. It's most definitely all about how much He loves people, and your purity to see and believe that will make all the difference, because you are bearing witness to his real nature. Living the life of a Believer is radical and exciting! This is how we advance his empire of love on the earth.

There is a difference between facts and the truth. A *fact* is like a piece of a puzzle. It's an object, an article, a fragment of information, or a bit of trivia. *Truth*, on the other hand, is all about *meaning*. We must choose to believe the truths in scripture that clearly tell us who we are as The Bride of Christ. It defines our meaning and therefore our purpose on this Earth. Before the foundation of the world was woven together, our identity was already set! We were called a chosen people, priests and kings, sons and daughters of God, the Bride He is returning for!

Our life is the only barometer anybody will ever have to God's Kingdom. We were made in His image and likeness, we weren't made *for* our *selves*. Dying to our selfish desires, and living in unconditional love as Christ, the Hope of the World, is how we promote, reveal, and expand his Kingdom on the earth. We were called to this. We were created for this. He paid the price for this. It's our birthright, it's our destiny, and we just can't settle for anything less! So let's run well!

DIVING DEEPER

Prayer, Promises and Reflection

Prayer exercise:

"Father, first I want to pray for the awareness of my motives, forgive me when I have been overly focused on myself. I'm asking for the courage to surrender those real motives to you. I am realizing that self-promotion and servanthood don't mix. In fact, I am aware how it leans into performance and how that keeps me focusing on my words, works and actions instead of relying on what you came and died for already: YOU inside of me.

Can you help *that* revelation get settled in my heart? Forgive me for "excluding" others because I was protecting my feelings of entitlement. Lord, our next breath isn't guaranteed and yet you allow our lungs to expand, you hold everything together! Lord, thank you for starting this realigning in my thoughts: that I am not my own, that I was not made for my *self* but I was made in Your likeness, Father. I want to be truly transformed into Your nature, preferring others. In Jesus Name, Amen."

Scriptures:

1. Read 1 Peter 2:9, 1 Cor. 6:19-20, Romans 8:9, Romans 8:22, 2 Cor. 2:14-15, Luke 9:23

2. "Take up your cross and follow me." Luke 9:23. Denial of self is the ultimate challenge we face as humans.

How does understanding the character of Jesus and how He treated people shed light on how we are to take up our cross and follow Him. Share your insights here.

____

____

____

____

____

____

Prayer of declaration:

I *believe* that God has everything I need. I choose to rest in the belief of the finished work of Calvary. His love has everything I could ever need. I am whole, I am found, I am His child, and I will shine for Him today.

CHAPTER 29

It's all Greek to Me: The Exousia The Ecclesia Carry

My Dad likes to tell a story on me of the first time he saw me completely lose it. I was 5 years old and completely sucked into this super old TV show that didn't even have any words! I was watching a "talkie" featuring Charlie Chaplin. I thought he was so hilarious, and I would get tickled laughing so hard I would sometimes get hiccups! From then on I fell in love with the typecast classic characters in the old movies. It kind of became my family's thing to watch together.

Sometimes when my Dad was around, we would end up watching an old cowboy movie starring legends like John Wayne or Clint Eastwood. There was always that one scene, normally the climax of the movie where the sheriff faces off against the outlaw. You know the one, the segment filmed in front of the saloon, usually meeting at "high noon," called the showdown scene between sheriff and outlaw. Sheriff facing due east, outlaw facing due west, pace off 10 steps in opposite directions, and then spin around on their jingling boot spurs. Lightning-fast they reach for their holster, whipping out the Colt. 45 and unleash hell on each other.

They both show courage but normally the sheriff would prevail. The cameras would catch the nervous bystanders draw in a dramatic sigh of relief. The town was saved yet again!

The classic showdown scenario got me thinking. Both sheriff and outlaw carried power, the Colt. 45, but only one held legal right to enforce the law. Anyone breaking the law has to comply to the law officer or face the legal consequences. The same principle can be applied to how we see our true identity in Christ. When we recognize our bloodline is royal, we are entitled to Kingdom authority, it's a legitimate right. The authority just comes with the territory so to speak.

The Greek origin of authority is a word called exousia. I dove into this same concept in an earlier chapter, but I wanted to revisit it, focusing more on our authority. Exousia is used in terms of jurisdiction or dominion over a certain realm, right, privilege, or ability.

We can look at countless scriptures in the New Testament where Jesus's divine rights were demonstrated in his earthly ministry. His authority was active to heal, forgive sins, to judge, to rule over men and angels, for both the elect and non- elect. His authority was for the Church and evident when He raised Himself from the dead. There are a ton of scriptures that demonstrate Christ's authority (Matthew 7:29; 9:8, 10:1, Mark 1:22, 27, Luke 4:32, 36; John 1:12, 5:27, 17:2, Jude 25, Revelation 12:10).

I know we are getting text book here but hang in there with me as I unpack a game changing concept. The word exousia is also found in the scriptures mentioning the delegated authority that the apostles and disciples of Jesus Christ received from Him (Luke 10:19, Acts 8:19, 2 Corinthians 10:8, 13:10). The noun is mentioned speaking of the authority in the millennium that Christ will delegate to the overcomers. "To the one who is victorious and does my will to the end, I will give authority over the nations," Revelation 2:26.

Exousia is supposed to be evident in all of our lives as Christians! Yep, all of *that* we're also supposed to be walking in! The Bible says in John 16:13 that, "the truth will be revealed by the Holy Spirit, who has been given to guide us into all truth." So are you ready for your mind to be blown as we dive into this deep yet simple revelation?

Ok, so let's first start with the simple breakdown. Where does this power come from and how do we get it? It comes out of a relationship with Jesus Christ. When we accept Jesus as our Lord, because of God's exousia and position, He delivers us from the power of darkness and translates us into the Kingdom of His Son. "For he has rescued us from the dominion of darkness and brought us into the kingdom of the Son he loves, in whom we have redemption, the forgiveness of sins," Colossians 1:13-14. Later in 3:3, it says, "For you were dead, and your life is hidden with Christ in God." At the point of salvation, positionally we are in Christ, seated with Him in heavenly places and all demonic powers are under His feet (Ephesians 1:3-5, Col. 1:15-20). Also when we accept Him as Lord into our hearts, the Holy Spirit comes in us, and we are adopted in sonship to the Body of Christ. "Just as a body, though one, has many parts, but all it's many parts form one body, so it is with Christ," 1 Cor. 12:12; where Christ is the Head of the Church and we are His Body.

So that means we are the bearer of The Firstborn's power and authority, as we are in Him and He is in us. We are His priests, co-heirs with Christ, and ambassadors of Christ.

"But you are a chosen people, a royal priesthood, a holy nation, God's special possession, that you may declare the praises of him who called you out of darkness into his wonderful light." 1 Peter 2:9.

"Now if we are children, then we are heirs—heirs of God and co-heirs with Christ, if indeed we share in his sufferings in order that we may also share in his glory." Romans 8:17.

"We are therefore Christ's ambassadors, as though God were making his appeal through us. We implore you on Christ's behalf: Be reconciled to God." 2 Cor. 5:20.

This is a mind blowing revelation when it comes to our faith life. This revelation is especially effective when you feel you're under a spiritual attack. It's no contest. When you know Who already fought, securing your victory, there is no fear. For we are hidden in Christ, and every need has already been provided for. Christ was marred unrecognizable to offer us manifestation into the sons and daughters of God, giving us the same Kingdom authority Jesus has. It's nothing we can work up, it was already bought for us.

There is a difference in being a carrier of authority: we are beholding to His higher law. Our rule is God's love. As we were made in His likeness and image, when we become followers of Christ, our new royal position activates a purpose. We will be used to free people from darkness, and reflect His nature. Our hearts will synchronize to His, and we will be drawn into a process to be transformed in how we see others, because He literally is living inside us now. His love sees people restored and set free, with heaven living in them on earth.

Our new positions came at the most expensive price: Calvary's Cross. When we accept His amazing gift of grace and forgiveness of our sins, we become His adopted heirs, and it all becomes relational. We are His, with a divine imprint on our hearts, meant to bring His kingdom come to earth. Our exousia reflects the truth that we are not our own. We were called to this. We were created for this, and He paid the price for this.

If you are reading this and honestly feel convicted, and can't say you've asked Jesus to be the Lord of your life, let's take care of that right now. Would you pray with me?

Prayer of Salvation:

> "Father, I come to you as I am. I recognize how my sin has separated me from you. Please forgive me...
>
> I believe that your son, Jesus Christ died for my sins, was resurrected from the dead, is alive, and hears my prayer. I invite Jesus to become the Lord of my life, to rule and reign in my heart from this day forward. I don't want to do this without You anymore. Thank you that You had everything planned out for my needs to be met through the guidance of Your Holy Spirit. I commit the rest of my life to You. In Jesus' name I pray, Amen."

Now what? Even though a king was crowned, he has to start thinking and believing like he is one. As co-heirs and carriers of Jesus, we can begin a process to renew our mind and start thinking like the sons and daughters of God. As we read in The Word daily, asking Him for wisdom, clarity and pertinence to what we are reading, we will start to mature as his children. The Bible really does hold the answers to everything in this life we would face, and we all need wisdom.

Renewing our mind also means protecting it. What we see, listen to, experience, and get familiar with easily becomes accepted into our life as thought patterns and habits. Our thought life is key if we are to start believing and acting like sons and daughters of God. Edit what you allow into your ears and eyes. Protect the gates. Personally I have to change the music station if a depressing song comes on, and change the channel when a perverted show starts. I fought hard for my peace of mind, and don't want to waste time in a struggle with something that I know can be a personal weakness for me. Further, I really do believe that I am not my own, but I am a daughter of God, meant for predestined purposes that were planned out before the creation of the world. I really do believe that I was called to this. I really do believe that I was created for this, and that He paid the ultimate price for us to carry His Kingdom of Heaven on earth. I want to run this race well!

One of the coolest results of renewing our mind is that we will start to better hear His voice. When we go to Him in prayer for wisdom, waiting on what He tells us to do, He will always answer. His dialogue with you may feel like an unction, audible words, visions, dreams or an idea. Make sure you wait on Him to answer you, this will save you a lot of confusion so you won't jump ahead of Him. That is listening to the King in the middle of the reality of living in a fallen world. It's seeking Him first, there is no one like our God. For in Him we move, think, and have our being.

As we mature in hearing Him clearer, we will start to act on His leading, He will use us to share His love, and the hope of Jesus in the Gospel message with people. We will start to think and behave out of His love for people and desire for them to be restored and set free. This is proof our hearts are being synchronized to His.

As a final note on renewing our minds, and becoming the empowered sons and daughters of God, we are capable of breaking free from mental torment and bondages. Reoccurring events or occurrences noticed reciprocating in our life can sometimes be defined as generational patterns. Those that are negative are called generational curses however as a believer in Jesus Christ, that's not who we are, and we don't have to receive or submit to those old patterns.

2Corinthians 10:4 tells us, "The weapons we fight with are not the weapons of the world. On the contrary, they have divine power to demolish strongholds."

Breaking Negative Generational Cycles

Generational curses are reoccurring problems that steal, kill, and destroy. They are demonic influences that can manifest, and cycle through generations as emotional instability, fear, suicidal thoughts and depression, chronic sickness, impotence, barrenness, family breakdowns, divorce, abuse, poverty or lack, bondage, slavery, alcoholism, or addictions.

Take courage! You are who He says you are. Those influences don't define or shape your identity, and they stop with you because the finished work of Calvary freed you from any dark influence. Jesus was the spotless lamb who was slain to take on our broken patterns, and He overcame them all!

We can be the first to break the cycle in our family! You and your children can be free from that negative thought pattern or behavior. Jesus came so you could be free! Ephesians 1:19-21 says, "and his incomparably great power for us who believe. That power is the same as the mighty strength he exerted when he raised Christ from the dead and seated him at his right hand in the heavenly realms, far above all rule and authority, power and dominion, and every name that is invoked not only in the present age but in the one to come."

So even though the subject of deliverance is controversial, I believe once demonic influences are exposed, we are meant to stop agreeing with their influence. They are trespassing in areas rightfully belonging to Christ: your mind! The power of Jesus' blood is against them.

DIVING DEEPER

Prayer, Reflection and Homework

If this is you, let's break agreement with fear and negative generational strongholds once and for all! Please pray this prayer along with me.

> "Father, in the matchless Name of Jesus I submit my thoughts to you. By the Blood of Jesus I am healed, saved and delivered, and my thoughts are your thoughts, how You see me! I go back to my parent's decisions and situations, and
>
> I break and renounce every bloodline generational curse! I forgive my ancestors for all past sins, transgressions and iniquities that have fallen down on me and my kids, and I ask You Father to forgive them also. Because I am of Your bloodline, adopted into sonship, I have a blood-bought right to stand here today, and break any negative influence that has recycled through my family, and stolen my peace and joy. I do it now in the name of Jesus!
>
> I break any addiction to worry, fears, I confess anything that I was involved in that opened the door of death or doom (occultic practices, or tools of witchcraft).
>
> I break depression, molestation, victim mindsets, abusive relationships. The Bible says I have the mind of Christ, and that He literally lives inside me! Instead of fear, I acknowledge that I am a carrier of trust, peace, favor, protection, provision and security, in the Name of Jesus! Amen!"

Disclaimer

"Caution lights" are flashing here, it's important we get completely honest in this next chapter, dear family. He wants our hearts whole and healed above anything else. We can renew our mind through scripture that will start the transformation, a seed of belief that grows into the becoming. The becoming turns into the fulfillment of a great plan set into place before the creation of the Earth: the revealing of the sons and daughters of God. How do we start this process? If you really want change in your life, your thoughts will need to be healed, pray and ask the Father to personally reveal His perfect love to you.

Secondly, and this is the tough love challenge: ask Him to highlight willful sins. When He exposes them to you, you may need to write them down somewhere safe.Tomorrow we will dive into His truth versus the enemy's plan to sabotage your life that will be exposed. You will be amazed at what you discover tomorrow!

REIGN: Restoring Identity is about awakening to the purposes we were created for. We can't start to heal and truly live in freedom if we don't face our darkest parts, dragging them out into His light. The Lord will start gently exposing the lies that have affected our beliefs, peace of mind, and kept us in a locked cage. This will start a realignment in our thought patterns. We are not our own but bought with a great price. We are being positioned for greatness, so hang in there with this exercise in preparation for tomorrow's reading.

Homework

1. In your private prayer time ask the Lord to highlight the willful sins you are holding onto. Write them down somewhere safe if need be.

Prayer of declaration:

I *believe* that God has everything I need. I choose to rest in the belief of the finished work of Calvary. His love has everything I could ever need. I am whole, I am found, I am His child, and I will shine for Him today.

CHAPTER 30

Willful Sins and Their Root

We can sound holy, saying just the right words and praying poetic prayers that would make a nun cry. We can even nail the "righteous" look in outward behavior, but are we deliberately denying the Lord's divine power in and through us, because we have intentionally given ourselves over to a lie? Willful sins are dangerous and actually symptoms of deeper issues.

We all have been there in some form or fashion. Examples of willful sins can show up as toxic fruit in our lives that could look like a body image addiction, obsessive insecurity, porn addiction, drug use, overspending, overeating, and (my personal way of "hiding" my hurt without getting shamed) overeating in secret. Serious addictions such as porn and drug use if not brought into the light will destroy our life and those around us. We all have things, forbidden fruit, we have continued to circle back to, like a default behavior. But the real issue is not the fruit itself, it's the root or trauma that triggered it all.

If those root issues are not addressed, we can set out on a track that can sear our conscious over time, become hard-headed, and even lose our holy fear towards God. Willed sins create internal torture, a wrestling inside ourselves, that leads to torment, oppression, and shame. Those decisions steal our joy, potentially our unique voice and influence, and platforms He intends for us to use for His Kingdom ways. What can happen, when we acknowledge the obvious lie but then callously say, "whatever...the Lord will forgive me," has spiritual and emotional ramifications. Once we decide to fully agree with the "temptation" and submit to it, it creates a spiritual apathy. We are plugging our ears to the voice of the Holy Spirit and pushing Jesus to the side.

When we intentionally give ourselves over to vain imaginations: lust of the eyes, lust of the flesh, or the pride of life, we deliberately agree, and participate with deception. If we don't settle it once we feel that initial pain of conviction, it can create a sort of mental stronghold, even obsession. Anyone relate? He wants all people complete, whole, and free because that's what Calvary afforded us! He wants us set free from the captivations, snares, and enslavement to these baits and hooks. The bait is always custom tailored to our weakness.

For example, when a husband is caught up in pornography he may ask for forgiveness once the truth is exposed. When a wife's excessive spending "shows up" because hidden bank statements are found, she is repentant for the consequences of her decisions. Both the husband and wife may then try to stop their individual expressions of sin, and for a season be successful, but this behavior is normally a front, a bi-product of some deeper heart issues. Until the deeper root problems are recognized, the willful behavior will likely come back or look slightly different.

The Lord desires us completely free. His heart breaks seeing us in torment, living behind walls of lies. He will expose the truth once we ask Him, showing us the depth, and origin of the real problem. At the root of these issues, there normally is a more foundational issue in our hearts that is found in misplaced identity, and our need to feel loved. Some common roots to willful sins are unforgiveness, idolatry, selfishness, unbelief, pride, anger, and bitterness. Until we recognize the real issues, and bring them out into the Lord's light of healing, these core vulnerabilities will continue to give birth to behavioral sin.

How do we get out of this bondage? In times where I've felt conviction and humbled myself, choosing to face the truth I was hiding. In that vulnerable state, I came to the Lord right where

I was, stuck in a mess, confused, and hurting. My ways weren't working. I asked for His forgiveness. And because His grace is so sufficient, He would remind me that He had already taken care of the dust I had swept under the carpet, and the skeleton I had shoved in my closet. Thank you, Jesus, for Your blood shed at Calvary!

A beautiful song by artist Riley Clemmons further sorts through this mystery, "You're not afraid of all the things I feel; So why am I afraid of being real? You want my tears, every messy word; Every scar and every fear. You want all I have with no holding back. When I'm hurt, at my worst, You meet me there. Cause you see the beauty in my broken prayers."[38]

He not only forgave our sins, but He wants to open our eyes to the Russian Roulette game we play when submitting to willful sins. When we drag our darkest parts into His light, He stands there beside us, wanting to free us and start the healing. It will take bravery to release of our white-knuckled grip on that "thing," that has become an obsession. But He is such a good good Father, He is more than trust-worthy! He wants you to experience healing, peace and restoration more than anything.

In a moment we will be going into prayer asking Him to expose the truth of our willful sins and more importantly their roots. If we listen, He will explain how and why it was all a plan of deception. Ask Him to show us how His standards of love are for us, above our routine understanding normally, but through what He reveals, we will see how we are choosing to live far below our real pay grade as His children.

The Lord is revealing our true hearts, because He wants our hearts healed. This is a first step, that exposes who or what is really on the throne of our heart. He will reveal the motivations from our will, why we intentionally held onto that sin.

Normally at the very root of willful sins, there is a core issue. The motivation may have sprung from a situation.

Do you want set free from bondage, maybe a stronghold that has held you captive for years, decades even? Let's pray for Him to realign our thoughts. Get ready, He will reveal some situations and initial motivations. So let's let him unpack it all and get this surgery complete, get all that junk out. And remember, His plans are *for* you!

Disclaimer

As you walk out this revelation, as memories come up, maybe even old conversations, your flesh and emotions may continue to struggle with the addictive craving that is the stronghold in your heart. I do believe in deliverance ministries, and encourage anyone who feels they are wrapped up in such torment to seek out a deliverance prayer team who has been trained in this area. But practically we can submit to the truth in the scriptures, and have effectiveness.

We are whole and healed in Christ Jesus! He paid for that at Calvary. That's who we are! That's the *believing* part. Some days we struggle in the battlefield of the mind. In those moments, even in the heat of the craving, keep talking to the Father. You can be in the very act of struggling in your flesh and old mindsets, and suddenly you recognize you're convicted—that's huge! You are recognizing the struggle, and you want to be free: this is growing, family! God can work with that!

DIVING DEEPER

Prayer and Promises

If this is you, take advantage of this moment, allow Him to remove the residue from years of running, the hurt, the resentment, the vendetta, and let Him in. Please pray this prayer with me.

> "Father, I thank you for running hard after me even in my deliberate sin. I ask forgiveness for willful sins and agreeing with the lies that have kept me in mental bondage. Help me, I want to be completely set free from my deep hurt, the abuse, the offense, shame, misunderstanding Your character and not believing that You can be trusted to fully heal my heart.
>
> Expose the root of where my willful behavior came from. I want to be healed from that soul wound. Show me where the seed was planted, and help me to see your perspective... (go still for a moment and listen as He will answer you).
>
> Thank you, Lord, for what you are showing me, exposing the root lies I have believed, forgive me. Please give me just as much deliberate resolve *desiring* what you have for me: peace, wholeness, and true freedom as you intended for me. I believe that You have plans for me, a hope, and a future. I want everything you have for me. I submit my situations, and the people involved to you now.
>
> Bring me answers and resources to get me out of this mess, in Jesus Name, Amen!"

We have been delivered because of the blood and stripes of Jesus! The battlefield of our thought life can be realigned to the truth of what He paid for on Calvary, for us to walk in freedom! And this is the exciting part, in time, saved, regenerated people will start to demonstrate behavioral change as a byproduct of their transformation. I don't want to just "do good" and survive to the end. I want to shine to the end! This is what we are called to, created for, and what He paid for on Calvary! He wants us to be lights on the Earth, His sons and daughters who carry the hope of Jesus!

Scripture promises:

1. Read 2 Corinthians 5:17 Ephesians 2:8-9
   Romans 8:18-21

2. Commit to memory:
   John 8:36

Prayer of declaration:

I *believe* that God has everything I need. I choose to rest in the belief of the finished work of Calvary. His love has everything I could ever need. I am whole, I am found, I am His child, and I will shine for Him today.

CHAPTER 31

Realm of Fantasy

"She stood at the window, her heartbeat beating loudly in her chest. She scanned the horizon looking for the western palace wall, where the woods lie just beyond. If only she could break free, to run so no one could find her, or demand anything from her, or tell her how to think, and what to say. Her life didn't belong to her any longer, she was a sovereign, expected to be everything the ideal represented. She couldn't breathe.

The racing thoughts and loud pounding of her heartbeat hit a fevered pitch. The woods, she had to get to the woods. She had to get out of the palace. Without anyone's notice somehow, she had to get out, and make it to the wood's tree line, there she could disappear. Only there would she be free to sort things out, to meet her own thoughts on her own terms.

She spun around, her back to the window and now facing the bedroom door. She clamped her eyes shut, fists clenched, and whispered a prayer under her breath,

"Please let there be no one outside my door." She opened her eyes and drew in a deep breath. With decided strides, she crossed the expanse of her bedchamber to the door.

Perhaps it was just as well that the insurmountable pressures of being queen brought her to a breaking point, for had she not run to the forest she might never have met the one who set off a new dream inside Rey."

Years ago I started writing a fantasy novel based on the power of choice, and a queen's temptation to break free from the pressures she felt in her royal position. Rey's character chooses to break away from royalty. Because of her choice to leave the protection of the palace boundaries, she experiences perils and alluring temptations that would lead her into great dangers, deception, and heartbreak.

Her appearance even starts to change. She learns the hardest lessons at the expense of nearly losing her beloved family who had been searching for her, heartbroken after learning she had left.

In a moment of self-reckoning Rey recognizes how her terrible selfishness left much destruction in her anxiety-driven exit; she was about to lose the truly invaluable treasure that her family was! She begs and prays for a second chance to be reunified with them again. Through a series of misadventures and enchanted meetings, Rey meets The Clockmaker, who is the character representing God in the story. She shares her lament with him, and he gives her an incredible gift. Out of his pocket he pulls out an elaborate looking glass.

He explains that she's living in a dual reality where retracing her steps would rewind history back to the moment she was standing at the window, on the cusp of deciding to turn her back on her royal identity. Because of the impulsive choice Rey made, and the terrible heartbreak that happened on her journey chasing a deceptive dream, she lost a great deal, at the brink of losing the most valuable gifts forever. Gaunt from despair, bruised from her dangerous encounters, lonely and exhausted, she realized the painful truth of all she had, and had been so reckless with. She had thrown away all the blessings and the powerful responsibilities that influenced an entire kingdom. Areas given to her in dominion and effected only by her voice and presence alone. But the most painful truth was how her selfishness separated her from the most treasured gift of all, what she desperately wanted back more than anything: her family.

Fantasies, Daydreams, and Imagination

Edgar Allen Poe wrote, "Those who dream by day are cognizant of many things which escape those who dream only by night." That's so true! Daydreams can help us harness our creativity, and reach our full potential. God gave us this wonderful gift: a two-fold ability to see. We can visually observe what goes on around us and also "see" pictures in our minds. It can help us achieve wonderful things. Or, that same imagination can hold us back when use it in a negative way.

The Gift of Imagination

There are some differences between fantasies, daydreams and imagination. Imagination is a creation of the mind, the ability to form a mental image.

Daydreaming is normally a wishful creation of the mind. Fantasy is using the imagination to create mental images that are often unrealistic. Daydreams have been responsible for some of our greatest discoveries and human creations.

French composer Claude Debussy created some of his music by viewing reflections of the sun on the river. Every great cathedral once existed only as an idea in someone's mind. That imagery was translated into magnificent reality.

Fantasy can also be used as a powerful magnet to draw out our abilities to unlock problems and tear down barriers blocking progress and growth. Athletes often claim mental imagery is about 50% of their game, imagining where they want the ball to finish. The key is to ensure we're using our imagination in a positive way.

Vincent Collins, author of *Me, Myself and You*, explains the process in this way: "Imagination is to the emotions what illustrations are to a text, what music is to a ballad. It is the ability to form. As soon as we perceive a feeling and begin to thing about it, the imagination goes to work. The imagination reinforces the thoughts, the thoughts intensify the feelings, and the whole business builds up." (Vincent, Collins, *Me, Myself and You.* (St. Meinard, IN: Abbey Press, 1974), 30.)

When our real life feels unfulfilled, we may fall into the recesses of our thought life for satisfaction. Satan has been gunning for our imaginations from the dawn of time. The world of fantasy that we create in our mind's eye, presents the possibility of human desire restrained by nothing more than the imagination. Any alluring idea planted to sidetrack us, if not put into the light of the Lord's wisdom, could lead us down a dangerous off-ramp to pursuing a desire. And we pursue it one decision at a time, one day at a time until it becomes our reality. This type of unrestrained imagination can hinder us from ever realizing the truth of our real identity, in God's will for our lives and purposes. A human's subconscious can be influenced by our selfishness, where we start to view others through the filter of our own imagination. How often do we recreate others into our desired image within the parameters of our own minds? Such re-creations can take the form of fantasies, or unspoken expectations played out and pursued over the real, God- created person. Cutting through to the heart of the matter, we ultimately would trade the image of God for that made in our own likeness.

The enemy is panicking, he is so threatened by the sons and daughters of God being told the truth, starting to believe, think and behave as Christ's heirs. He knows what's going down right now, the preparation of the children waking up to their identity, living free from offense and selfishness, and being used to usher in God's love on the Earth. This signals a great fulfillment of the ages, the Lord's imminent return to co-rule and reign with His people on a new Earth and new heaven.

The enemy's feverish ambition is to do anything to sabotage us from recognizing the Father's love for us, and consequently keeping our relationship with God estranged and apathetic. The original sin planted in the Garden of Eden is the perfect example. The twisted manipulation was an idea whispered that made Eve think God was withholding wisdom so he could retain dominion and control.

This was the furthest thing from the truth. God created humans with a brain to make choices and decide. Nonetheless, the enemy's contrary idea planted in the fertile seed of Eve's imagination took root. She made a decision, told Adam, and it caused the change in history that impacted all mankind thereafter. That's the only card the enemy knows he can play: to plant lies. He bets that if we chew on those lies for long, they just may take root if we don't know the truth, address the lie, and take back our thought life in the truth of knowing who God is, and who we are in Him.

This is where daily time in the Word and prayer is key. We will begin to know and realign our thoughts back to what He lovingly desires for us: love, protection, freedom, and provision on every level, entering into a real, active and dynamic relationship with the Lord. The war for humanity starts in the battlefield of the mind.

Imagination is the faculty where new ideas and concepts are formed. It's the place where creative power explodes, and vision is birthed in the mind's eye. The act of imagination is beautiful. Further, its power is limitless. When an idea is planted, entertained, chewed on over and over, scientific studies have proven it connects certain neurons in the brain where obsessive thoughts can begin to form. However when these thought patterns are contrary to what God has for us, and we don't recognize it, the seeds of our imagination can bear fruit manifesting into ideas of desire, offense, judgement, wanderlust creating a yearning "need" to seek and satisfy that insatiable desire, sometimes in complete abandon. A thought not examined against the Word of God can sidetrack our life.

Deception conceals and misrepresents truth. If a Christian is deceived by satan it is one thing, it is something totally different when a Christian deceives oneself.

James 1:23-25 tells us, "Anyone who listens to the word but does not do what it says is like someone who looks at his face in a mirror and, after looking at himself, goes away and immediately forgets what he looks like. But whoever looks intently into the perfect law that gives freedom, and continues in it—not forgetting what they have heard, but doing it—they will be blessed in what they do."

Examination is the main purpose of a mirror. As we look into God's Word, we see ourselves for who we really are. James mentions a couple mistakes we must avoid when looking into God's mirror. *They simply glance at themselves:* this is not studying or examining oneself and then dropping it. A casual reading of God's Word will not reveal the deepest needs in our hearts. Don't simply glance into a mirror and forget what you see. Look intently at The Word, not just a quick glance, because blessing comes from doing (James 1:25 says, "blessed in his doing"). What happens when we choose to obey, walking away from a trap of mental deception? God sets us free! We break the bondage of sin, and we choose to conquer those thoughts.

Once we are in the process of being completely honest, turning over those deceiving thoughts to the Lord, He begins restoring our minds and healing our identity. That's the beginning of transformation. We are made to recognize and conquer lies planted on the battlefield of the mind, no matter if those ideas were sown by others, the enemy or our own misguided thoughts.

I want to address two other types of dangerous thought patterns: taking the bait from someone intentionally wanting to hurt you like rejection, where our thoughts continue to spring up in a cycle of responses or defense. Secondly, misinterpreting a word spoken, action or silence from someone in a misunderstanding, which digested through our insecurity or other root issues, can cause us to lose focus on the Father's affirming love for us.

Living in response to someone's words or actions taken shouldn't have any impact on how we see our value. However, we very often are effected, subconsciously reacting or treating the offenders differently after, either in contention or by building defensive walls for distance, or even retaliation. No other human should have that much power over us that it ruins our day. If another human is "acting out" in anger, judgement, or offense, we need to be so rooted in God's love and knowing who we are, it doesn't phase us at all. Sound impossible?

Renewing our mind with the truth of scripture, and asking to have Father's heart for that individual will keep us grounded.

We aren't responsible for other's words or decisions, just our own. "Finally, brothers and sisters, whatever is true, whatever is noble, whatever is right, whatever is pure, whatever is lovely, whatever is admirable—if anything is excellent or praiseworthy—think about such things," Philippians 4:8.

The truth is God wants us free from others, and our own thought patterns that can bounce around like a wild, unruly kite in the turbulence of life's hard winds. Disciplining our minds with scripture is key! It's absurd to think our thought life shouldn't be in check, left completely open, unprotected by circumstances, or anything another human could throw our way.

Thoughts like judgement, offense, seduction, and lust are a byproduct of someone else's presence and "power to plant" in our life. They are what we have allowed. Learning how to renew our mind as a royal daughter or son of the King is critical to being trusted with more people for His Kingdom impact. We must learn the art of controlling what thoughts we agree with, not being affected by unfiltered and disrespectful comments directed our way. In fact, we are to impact others in the world, not the other way around, letting our light shine! Glowing in the dark, now that's attracting attention! Standing out from the crowd may not be popular, but that's why we are called the Ambassadors of God on this Earth! We carry Heaven's Kingdom, the Firstborn Son's heart to a fallen world desperate for restoration.

We have this one life; our life is the only barometer other humans have of God's character! So please be aware how we handle other's words, and actions when we seemingly are an innocent caught up in crossfire of anger or misunderstanding. It is critical that we stay aligned in His truth. "We demolish arguments and every pretension that sets itself up against the knowledge of God, and we take captive every thought to make it obedient to Christ," 2 Cor. 10:5.

We are free from others and ourselves when we submit every thought that contends with His love and character. Pray, candidly share with the Lord how a thought is "digging" at you. Release that to the Lord, and ask Him to show you the truth in how He sees you. This is a powerful strategy, and a key to reigning in our thought life as His ambassadors.

Misunderstandings

Sometimes we misunderstand something someone says or does to us, or maybe it's their silence or lack of presence in our life when we come to a conclusion— whether it's reality or not. Compounding people-approval addiction problems, and then processing it as rejection, we can start to believe and behave like we're living in a fantasy land of made-up scenarios. The realm of our imagination is powerful. We can chew and chew on just one conversation, and all of a sudden we have convinced ourselves of something that isn't even reality.

Over the years I have learned a simple rule when it comes to having relationships with people: take it at face value. As the character playing Elizabeth The Queen of England says in the TV drama, *The Crown*, "Don't think too long or too hard. It just gets one in a muddle."[39] Living above and not succumbing to people approval addictions and anxiety cuts us free from drama.

Satan works hard to sabotage how we see God, his true nature and who we rightly are. He is so ridiculously desperate. He feverishly schemes to build contention between people and even create misunderstandings in the hurting, fractured soil of our mind, normally when we have trouble trusting in general. He knows this and works overtime to sow seeds of hurt, rejection, misunderstanding, anything to plant lies in our imaginations, seducing their thought life to believe lies. The enemy is desperate to keep us from resting in, thinking, and standing firm in the truth.

We are called to rule and reign with Him. It's all about *who* He is, and who we are to Him as His inheritance, His beloved. Don't reduce your life to managing emotional pain. Pain is the symptom. The real issue is recognizing we are whole and worthy of every bit of what Jesus did on Calvary. How do we break these cycles, and start renewing our mind? Build a culture of wholeness around yourself with boundaries and truth.

Talk about self-care! This is how we do that: be aware of what you watch and listen to, and try playing more worship music. When you feel doubt, hear a negative thought, or rejection whispering, declare out loud scripture. Repeat that truth over and over. Write the verses out, and post them where you look most often. This is how we get the truth down inside us, how we war with it, believe it and how we start conforming to His image.

Imagination is a powerful tool, when put to the stories of our faith, breathes life into them again, and helps us to fall into their rich, deep, and complex narratives. It transforms our beliefs from a rule book or an ethic of life, to a story of ourselves and of God. God's living storyline is intertwined with ours. It's where divine inspiration births wonder, awe, doubt, faith, and hope into our imaginations.

That's why it is so vital to be reading the Bible daily to learn the truth. Our eyes will be opened once we read in between the lines, and see how God's love story for humanity fills the scriptures. He made a way for us to be free from ourselves. The very act of salvation means we are saved and free from our neediness, and are being renewed by choosing to get out of the snare from our thought patterns.

How do we get out of the snare? Through a simple heart-examination exercise we will go through in just a moment. It's a simple process where we ask the Lord to show us where deceptive thoughts have crept in. Secondly, we ask His forgiveness that we chose to line up our thought life and faith with the lies. Finally, we must choose to walk out the restoration, by obedience to protect our minds, and possibly setting up new boundaries with people who have sown the discord while we retrain our thinking. We are stronger than the power of deception. We are conquerors! Stop making excuses and rationalizing, and make some choices to protect your mind, your eyes, what you hear, and who you let into your heart.

When we as children of God look into the mirror of The Word, we should see the Son of God, a transformation that's taking place by the Spirit of God. This change is a metamorphosis, a change that comes from the inside out.

Do you want to get well? Stop accepting resignation in the pain. Let's make this your liberation day from deceptive thoughts that have kept you in bondage for too long! This will require you to act in faith, it's a mental commitment. Don't just sit down and believe you're stuck, get up and show up!

Deceptive thoughts of rejection, guilt, shame, believing you're hopeless, not worthy, too far gone... He wants to heal you, not numb you! Stop going around the same tree for the millionth time, you've made a rut in your mind by doing that!

Same. Tree. End this today, and take up your crown!

Creation groans for us to recognize who we are! God knows who you are, the devil knows, and even creation knows who you are. We are indispensable! We are the ambassadors of God. As Romans 8 tells us, we carry His restoration and liberation on the Earth. To recognize that greatness God placed inside of each of us, and resting in Who we belong to, we will begin to recognize and conquer any distracting thoughts, remaining captivated by our unique purposes. This will be our new normal, and how we reign in our thought life. Thinking like His children will keep us moving straight as an arrow, flying towards our purposes. Get ready, sons and daughters of God, and brace for impact!

DIVING DEEPER

Prayer and Promises Prayer:

"Father, show me how I have let deception rule my thoughts (Pause to listen to what He exposes to you...)

Lord, forgive me for believing those lies I know down deep aren't even true, they have been a trap, and I am done with living in this mental bondage over this lie. Heal where the real need is coming from. Help me to forgive that person that spoke that hurt and rejection to me. I release that person to you... (This frees us from carrying the burden anymore of hurt, shame, blind-folds of lust or coveting). Father, heal my mind and help me to see the truth. Help me to see how you see me, and the impact I am called to make. Can you give me a "cookie trail" of hope today? Give me the discipline to resist deceptive thoughts. Help me to stay focused on who you have made me to be, to know your plans are for me. Show me where I need to make change for real transformation in my thoughts. Thank you Lord that I am restored and resting in your truth! In Jesus Name, Amen."

Reflection

1. He will highlight to you what areas of your life need attention and change in order to have transformation in your thought life. What is He showing you? Jot down your insights here.

2. What you do to make your thinking less futile as described in God's Word?

3. What steps will you take to train your imagination?

Scriptures promises:

1. God designed and gave us our minds to think creatively, a unique pinnacle of His creation. He also gave us instructions on how to protect and use that precious gift.
2. Read Romans 12:2, Mark 12:30, Luke 24:45, Philippians 4:8

Prayer of declaration:

I *believe* that God has everything I need. I choose to rest in the belief of the finished work of Calvary. His love has everything I could ever need. I am whole, I am found, I am His child, and I will shine for Him today.

CHAPTER 32

Heartbreak and Pain

Loss. Sometimes the unthinkable happens. When life interrupts our plans and leaves us dropping to our knees in shock, we start asking where is God in the heartache, and feeling as if we were abandoned. There's nothing more traumatic than to experience a life ripped away from you. Tragedy that impacts you at the core. It certainly wasn't your plan. The void and painful journey to get through minute by minute... to function without the presence of that person you were so looking forward to seeing, depending on, dreaming of, who brought a smile to your face. Life isn't the same after. Tragedy has a way of changing us.

Loss has touched all of our lives in some way. When Jorge and I were five years into our marriage, we talked about starting a family. If I could be brutally honest, having a baby was kind of a hard subject for me because up to that point, I had been content without children. I had always been laser-focused on my career.

However, when Jorge and I got married, we shared a future including each other's dreams that would make impact long after we were gone. I started to wake up out of dreaming just for my own goals, and could see that "us" meant legacy; legacy as in, something that would live and make impact far beyond our individual selves. Kids are our legacies and God has plans for them that will far exceed our own singular impact.

So I got honest with God and with my husband. We started to pray into it. I took the limits off God this time, trusting Him to heal the hindrances I had erected in my mind from starting a family. He showed me some things I needed to address within myself, and then Jorge and I decided to intentionally go for a family.

We got pregnant shortly after and since I had received so much healing from my anti-family hang-ups, a mama's heart was starting to warm up inside of me. As time went on, my heart started beating wildly to meet our little one! I let my imagination go free in expectation to meet our future little world changer.

As the pregnancy progressed, I would go to my regular doctor checkups. I had all the normal symptoms every pregnant mama experiences: morning sickness and exhaustion. One day, I went in for the routine tests, and received the news no mom ever wants to hear. They couldn't find the baby's heartbeat. I was miscarrying. A procedure was scheduled after confirmation that our baby had died inside me.

I couldn't speak. I was silent for about an hour after, my body weak and drained from crying, and processing the cruel reality. How could this happen? Just when I thought God had finally gotten me "straightened out," I finally wanted to be a mom—and to just take our little one away from us?!

At this point, we were sitting in the car, it had been several hours after the procedure, and Jorge told me he felt like he needed to go to a bookstore. He felt like God wanted me to read a certain book. "What?!!" I was cussing though. "Are you serious? No. I don't want to read a book, in fact I never want to see the Bible ever again. I am *so* done with you, God!"

Jorge who is always the cool balance to my machine-gun mouth, turned to me and said, "Just wait here in the car for a minute. I promise I'll be right back." Left alone in the car I balled my eyes out again. I still remember how flushed my face felt, my eyes were swollen almost shut. There is no pain like the loss of your baby, someone made of you and by you, who dies inside you. Jorge came back a few minutes later, and as he sat down at the wheel, he hands me the book. "*The Shack*" by William Young. It didn't look like a self-help book, in a bizarre way I felt like reading it all of a sudden.

I'm so glad my husband hears the voice of God and is obedient. The message in that book was about the tragic loss of a child but in the most horrific way possible. God shows up to journey through with the main character, the father of the child. It was a hard book to read, but exactly what I needed at that time. The universal question of "Why does such horrible stuff happen on God's watch?" Is a difficult one, but through the sum of hard experiences I've journeyed through personally, I know His heart breaks too. The only thing I can say here is that He never leaves us, He walks with us even closer, through the valleys of the shadow of death. I felt Him through the grueling days to come when reality started to sink in.

That tragedy was over ten years ago, and I still remember the emotions like it happened last week. I remember how helpless I felt. I remember feeling like a ghost, feeling hollow. I remember the weeks it took me before I wanted to open up and talk to anyone, let alone talking about our miscarriage. I remember crying at the drop of a hat months later inside the grocery store when I saw a mother put her baby in the cart. I just ached.

I also remember that I didn't want to pick up a Bible for a while, because I was desperately trying to rationalize why God allowed this. Tragedies such as the loss of a loved one can become a sort of threshold experience, when everything before that is "before," and everything after is "after." Little did I know it at the time but I was actually in a process of healing, it was more reckoning that He would be with me and hold me closer still even when the cruel and unthinkable happens. He becomes more personal and alive, intentionally comforting during those times somehow...if we pay attention.

I think we all cope with loss and grief differently. When we realize we are capable of losing someone so central and important to us, it can trigger fearful thoughts and anxiety. We usually go to great lengths to avoid thinking any further about it.

The way people cope with tragedy is just as unique as their relationships with the people for whom they are grieving. In *A Grief Observed*, C.S. Lewis explains the extremely painful, sometimes conflicting nature of his own grief after he lost his wife, *"I see people, as they approach me, trying to make up their minds whether they'll say something about it' or not. I hate if they do, and if they don't." The process of grief is unpredictable."*[40]

Dr. Dean Nelson, has researched the impact and process of grieving. In his book, *God Hides in Plain Sight*, he shares how grief can be an agent in opening the door to healing and grace if we allow it.

"Grief shows us how attached we were to a specific person," he wrote. "It slowly points to grace and gratitude, which shows us how much of the person is still around us in our memories, our routines, and in the unexpected if we are paying attention."[41] With the understanding that this slow and difficult process we call grief can point us to grace and thankfulness, we can see a huge need for the body of Christ to come alongside those suffering loss, and be family to them, bringing comfort and even provision.

I can personally attest to how important it is to have another aware of how honestly you are struggling. My husband's part was critical to my grieving and healing process. If it weren't for him praying, and being there for me, I don't know what I would have done. I was in a frightening hole for weeks.

We are not designed to be an island. It's pretty important to have a strong "family," or core group of friends who have your best on their heart. Isolation is dangerous and though reaching out initially for prayer is the last thing we feel like doing, it's key for recovery. There are amazing recovery groups at most churches these days.

I believe a key to coping on the other side of tragedy, is to intentionally have a raw and honest conversation with the Lord about everything we are struggling with. This is what an authentic relationship with God is all about. If we pretend everything is fine, even though it isn't, then we aren't leaning into His grace and comfort. This can lead to bitterness and resentment toward God, where underlying fear and anxiety still remains at the core of our heart. Just from not taking a deep breath and bravely facing the reality of how we are feeling. As a result, we lose out on the relationship with Him because we're not totally honest about our struggles, anger, and fears.

As I mentioned above, no man is an island. Especially during the process of coping with tragedy, there is something undeniably intrinsic about human connection that takes place only in physical presence. Loving someone in their grief is never as simple as quoting scripture, praying with them, giving them space, or even crying with them. Healing happens when someone comes alongside them without answers or expectations, in total grace. I have been on both the receiving and giving side of grace while walking through sorrow.

Tragedies change us, but I hope I have been changed in some good way from experiencing loss. I hope a deeper capacity for compassion and tenderness has been developed inside of me through the painful journeys. There is a humility that has been deep-seeded in me, accepting that God is in control of our lives and in the lives of those we love. It is by God's grace that we hold loosely both joy and sorrow, living a life under the influence of trusting in a God who has overcome the world.

DIVING DEEPER

Scripture Promises

Psalm 34:18
Matthew 5:4
Psalm 73:26

Prayer of declaration:

I *believe* that God has everything I need. I choose to rest in the belief of the finished work of Calvary. His love has everything I could ever need. I am whole, I am found, I am His child, and I will shine for Him today.

CHAPTER 33

Tests and The Power of Choice

"Heartbreak. Temptation. Pain. I am no stranger to the cold feeling of outstretched arms...empty. Where the heat should be, but is not. "Did I dream this? Where did I go so wrong?"

Like an old clock, the mind games click into gear. The arm strikes the hour, triggering the chimes "for whom the bell tolls." How could I let this get so far in my own head?

Then the sickening swell, the undertow of betrayal washes over me... Chime. The shame... Chime. The guilt...Chime." (from Eclipsing Rey)

Two years ago I began writing a fantasy novel that I couldn't bring myself to publish. It was based on real emotions I was experiencing at that time. Ironically, I am grateful for the heartbreak, even the test, and especially for the answer of God's resounding "no."

At that time, my life wasn't happening the way I wanted. I had swallowed back a deceptive load of lies that was pushing me to abandon so much the Lord had already built up for and through me. I slipped dangerously deep into the recesses of my thought life and imagination for satisfaction. It was a convenient escape. I began to desire it over my real life, instead of making real changes to begin a healing journey. My will and imagination were contending daily for my future.

As described in Chapter 30, imagination is far stronger than any other power we possess. Scottish preacher Alexander Whythe explains the power of imagination Hannah Hurnard's *Winged Life*: "It makes us full of eyes, without and within...

Psychologists tell us that on occasions, when the will and imagination are in conflict, the imagination always wins. How important therefore that we should vow by the Savior's help never to throw the wrong kind of pictures on this screen in our minds, for the emotion literally has the power of making the picture real and effective."

But God.

Looking back now I am beyond thankful that God isn't surprised by our humanity. After all, temptation either makes us stronger or breaks us. Also I am aware that He answers prayers, including those prayed by family members, and that He stays faithful to His promises even when my thoughts don't line up. All those prayers for God's will to veto mine were clearly active in my life. Sometimes His perfect will usurps permissive will. Behind the scenes, He was working even though I felt very much alone.

With time, I learned to appreciate the pain of correction. To appreciate "the silence" that came after I imagined risking everything. To experience the strong undertow and surge of the temptation to bolt, even to redefine, and restart my life. But what got me to this "mid-life" breaking point were cracks in my foundation. I was feeling undervalued, believing lies that I wasn't worthy, and a deep seed of resentment was beginning to bear toxic fruit. I started fantasizing about living out a completely different future. However, the saving grace in my mess was that I had not shut out God. In fact, through that hard season I believe I grew into an even more authentic relationship with Him as I challenged myself to give voice to the pain and talk it out with my Savior through prayer. I couldn't contain it. The pain and desperate desire to run was brimming out. I recall feeling like I was fighting minute by minute within myself during that season. Nevertheless, I kept the line to my heart open to God. He answered with a sort of silent comfort. It felt like a parent who knew their kid was making some wrong decisions but loved them unconditionally anyway. He was allowing me to go through a monumental test.

Character and integrity. These were being chiseled into me. I quickly grew to having a healthy fear and respect for the power of choice. A choice is simply that, it's not a divine mandate even if you call yourself a Christian. However, because we have free will, and every one of us are faced at some point with acting on temptation, it comes down to how we respond in that critical moment.

I am a different person today. I am stronger because I kept the communication lines open with the Lord during a test of my flesh, and I made the choice to yield to His "no." I was at a place in my relationship with the Lord where I *knew* He was good. I believed that His plans *were for me*, and somehow I also knew this test was originally sent to destroy more than just my voice and purposes. It was meant for destruction beyond what I could imagine, impacting other lives that would have damaging effects.

I had asked a bold question of the Lord in the middle of my lament one day. I asked to see the big picture. I asked Him why I was allowed to walk through a test of such strong allure. He didn't have to answer me, but He did. The Lord opened my eyes, and I became instantly aware of the favor He had put on my life and my family for His Kingdom purposes. Even though I never realized how many people our lives impacted, I was starting to wake up to it for the first time. Our unique mission was Family. How to model it and reach out to others creating it.

Then He showed me something that sealed the argument for me once and for all: the enemy was definitely behind the custom test. My imagination was playing reruns of the fantasy scenes, spawned from deceptive lies of feeling unworthy and unfulfilled. My thought life had been hacked. But the more I prayed for help, the more the Lord exposed the enemy's plan. Satan wanted desperately to sabotage the legacy God had in store for my children. Thousands of hearts could be impacted, destinies included, because of how my decisions would impact my kids. Realizing the cataclysmic chain reaction my decision to "escape" would set off, I saw how selfish my thought stream had become, how intrinsic, and how it could negatively impact people even beyond my life on Earth. Talk about big picture!

I am human, but I also know I am spirit. When the Lord graciously answered my prayer to see the big picture of why I was allowed to go through such a tormenting test, He showed me the breaks in my foundation of how I saw myself. They were pressure points I had allowed, impacts from depending on others to feel secure.

He also showed me where I had swallowed a lie that my need to feel valued would be satisfied "when" I reinvented my life, escaping from my troubles. This coping mechanism was only a Band-Aid for the real underlying issue in my heart. He wanted, more than anything, to completely heal and realign how I felt valued. No other person, no other dream fulfilled could satisfy that need. The feeling of worthiness is only quenched by our Creator, the master maker of our gifts, vision, and author of our pre-destined purposes. He is the only one who has that answer, and in meeting His hungry gaze that's longing, desperate only for you, that's where we are found!

I am more aware of my acute need for Him, no matter how I feel, and what I am walking through. Now instead of feeling rejected, aware of the chill of empty, outstretched arms left stuck in the middle of a deceptive plot, my flesh was eclipsed. I am beyond grateful for a rare, divine intervention when God answered my prayers with "no." Now I am aware of the warmth as I press my head into His chest. It brings me to tears recalling how He turned my mourning into dancing, and I even believe that one day when I'm in Heaven I may fully understand the grand scope of my personal choice to stand for something bigger than myself.

"I know the plans I have for you, declares the Lord. Plans to give you a hope and a future," Jeremiah 29:11.

We overcome by the blood of the Lamb and word of our testimonies! So for every story out there of struggling temptation, hopeless dead ends, feeling desperately backed in a corner, if we keep the communication lines open with the Lord, yielding to Him in the midst of the fire, rest assured, He will deliver you! You will arise with a new authority, as an overcomer, carrying a depth and strength of grace that looks like a weapon used to combat future attacks from deception. As we are spiritual beings first, made in the likeness of God, we can temper our flesh with spiritual truths. It is then that we experience a new level of dunamis power: a strength wielded out of a choice to stand for virtue.

"For God did not give us a spirit of timidity, but a spirit of power, love and self-discipline," 2 Tim 1:7.

If we allow the Master Physician to really heal the root issues in our hearts, where issues like worthiness and value stem from, we will begin to see ourselves as He sees us. We will be wise, discerning deceptive setups that will come down the road, and stronger to make choices based in the truth as his sons and daughters! Dunamis power will be evident in our lives, peace, favor, and power to overcome traps from the enemy.

When we live by our born-again spirit and not by the flesh, we will naturally produce the fruits of God's character, holiness. We may mess up because we are spirits inside flesh but that's why John the Baptist emphasized "keep with repentance," meaning humbly confessing when we miss it (Luke 3:8). Those who mature spiritually will become more and more freed-up from the flesh and become more godly. This is the awesome power of Christianity: being like God!

So come hell or high water, Jesus paid the price for you to live victoriously, as an overcomer and to participate in godliness! The author 1 Chronicles 28:9 writes, "And you, my son Solomon, acknowledge the God of your father, and serve him with wholehearted devotion and with a willing mind, for the Lord searches every heart and understands every motive behind the thoughts. If you seek him, he will be found by you; but if you forsake him, he will reject you forever."

God understands our thoughts and our motives. His instruction about our thoughts is clear: we are to serve God with total dedication and an open and willing mind. Remember, God knows what's behind every thought we have.

Our choices are effected by our thought life and birthed out of motive and will. Depending on how its used, imagination can be a blessing or a royal pain, leading to a choice. It's like a giant movie screen, and all day long we throw various episodes on it. As in most movies, someone has the leading role. We cast as ourselves as the central figure. It's normal. But how do you see yourself? A hero or a villain? Positive or negative?

The mind is a unique and wonderful creation. With it we can solve problems and craft masterpieces. With it we can also create problems that don't even exist.

In the images of our mind's eye, we may depict ourselves as a capable hero, or as an ineffective and disqualified. We make judgments about ourselves and others. And sometimes, we see these imagined events as reality. So we must first guard our imagination, our thought life, and keep the communication lines open to Him to begin a healing process that will lead to your freedom!

You were an individual chosen in Christ Jesus before the creation of the world, a child of none less than God Himself, and greatly loved. You are a person through who the Holy Spirit works for the blessing other others, someone triumphant in all circumstances—the list could go on and on! Create imagination films that portray you in the positive, Biblical light, and that is what you increasingly become!

That's when we take charge, choosing instead to play the mental images that feed our mind and imagination and mold our character with the truths of God's Word.

DIVING DEEPER

Prayer, Reflection and Promises

"Father, I want to thank you for Your amazing grace. You know my secret thoughts, you see how much I have been struggling in (name the specific area). I know You hate to see me in pain, but what I really feel is... (be honest and share exactly how you feel to Him). Father, would You please show me the truth in this mess, can I see Your bigger picture for my life? Forgive me where I have agreed with a lie and lingered making excuses to hold onto it for so long. Show me the real underlying issue behind this temptation and struggle. Show me how You see me, I want a complete healing. Thank you for the victory at Calvary You gave me to overcome the lies! I want Your peace, and Your power so I can reign as an overcomer. Please give me a key scripture that's my personal weapon for this situation. Thank you Lord Jesus, it's in your name I pray, Amen!"

Reflection

After praying, the Lord will highlight what the real underlying issue is. He wants to heal you completely. Let it go. Trust Him.

1. Jot down the truth of how He sees you. He may even show you in a dream, poetry, song lyrics, or through a picture. Feel free to use this space to write what He shows you.

____

____

____

____

____

____

____

____

____

2. Further describe the significance of the choice the Lord highlighted to you. How could it effect your life and other's around you?

____

____

____

____

____

____

____

____

____

3. What will getting control over your thoughts during challenging times look like for you? What steps will you take?
   Scriptures promises Read Galatians 2:20
   2 Peter 1:4
   2 Cor. 5:17
   1 Peter 1:23
   Hebrews 4:15-16
   Romans 5:17

___

___

___

___

___

___

___

___

___

Prayer of declaration:

I *believe* that God has everything I need. I choose to rest in the belief of the finished work of Calvary. His love has everything I could ever need. I am whole, I am found, I am His child, and I will shine for Him today.

CHAPTER 34

Integrity's Rebirth

Pornography and the human sex trafficking industry are epidemics that are impacting generations. Children, as well as adults, have been violated by perverted masochists, treated like currency. This epidemic breaks the Father's heart. These industries have inadvertently shaped standards of objectivity, easily accessible on any Wi-Fi device. The epidemic has not only broken apart marriages, but has proven to affect human brain function, creating "addiction tracts" in areas of the mind. Viewing pornographic images traps the viewer in a pattern of animal instinct. However, justice is starting to fall on this perverted behavior. Victims are breaking their silence.

Recently a miraculous boldness has come upon people in the film and TV business exposing years of exploitation of actresses and actors by some high- ranking industry "professionals". The definition of exploitation "is the action or fact of treating someone unfairly in order to benefit from their work. To take advantage of, abuse, misuse, ill-treatment, unfair treatment, or oppression."[4]

I applaud the bravery of victims to break their silence and name names, setting those accused on a path of justice, but also rewriting the rules to protect others against such disgusting perversion. This will most assuredly impact future generations. Integrity becomes a stronger value, usurping the years of sexualized objectivity, and hopefully challenging the role "sex" and "objectivity" has played in media and film.

As God's children, I believe we carry His kingdom come. In our new identity as sons and daughters of God, we represent the nature of God. We are His ambassadors on the Earth. As we live in a fallen world it is our right to free the oppressed.

Thousands of years ago, the Lord spoke through the prophet Isaiah reminding the Jewish people to stand up for social justice during a time in history marked by racial, gender, and societal hierarchy. The scripture remains today one of the most referenced verses on social fairness.

Isaiah 1:17 tells us to "Learn to do good; seek justice, correct oppression; bring justice to the fatherless, plead the widow's cause."

Reading between the lines, the laws of love from one of Jesus' most famous sermons comes to mind in Matthew 7. We have come to summarize the famous message on ethics as the Golden Rule, "Do unto others as you would have them do unto you." When the orphans and widows are neglected, Christians are not living out what God describes as *pure religion.* "Religion that God our Father accepts as pure and faultless is this: to look after orphans and widows in their distress and to keep oneself from being polluted by the world," James 1:27.

At its simplest form, Jesus tells us what religion is in this verse. It's a responsibility to speak up for the voiceless being exploited.

"Open your mouth for the mute, for the rights of all who are destitute. Open your mouth, judge righteously, defend the rights of the poor and needy," Proverbs 31:8-9. In this verse, Solomon passionately writes, *"Open your mouth,"* clearly this wise King discerns the need for action faced with societal injustice. The fact that he repeats the phrase *"Open your mouth,"* prefaces the importance of speaking up for those who are being treated unfairly, and most often it's the poor and needy, including those who are disabled, and have no other means to seek justice on their own. "Thus says the Lord: Do justice and righteousness, and deliver from the hand of the oppressor him who has been robbed. And do no wrong or violence to the resident alien, the fatherless, and the widow, nor shed innocent blood in this place," Jeremiah 22:3.

We can learn significant lessons from the contextual stories in the Bible. A study on the history of the ancient Jewish society shows concealed or civic injustice swept under the rug. The Jews had not been administering social justice. They had been favoring those in power and those with money, while turning a blind eye to the laws they knew. Leviticus 19:15, "Do not pervert justice; do not show partiality to the poor or favoritism to the great, but judge your neighbor fairly." If you read many of the Old Testament prophets, the neglect of strangers, aliens, widows, and orphans are mentioned so many times that these things were an ongoing problem with the nation...and today, we see much of the same thing.

However, as the people of God, we are called to rescue the victims and correct injustice. As the Church we have no excuse for neglecting the poor, the widows, the orphans, the disabled, the homeless, and others who are pushed to the fringe of society. Notice that all the above verses mentioned here are not written to unbelievers in the world, but to the nation of Israel, Judah, and specifically to the people of God. That doesn't mean that society is off the hook, but it does mean the church has a legitimate responsibility. When we ask the Lord to show us how to do this personally, He absolutely will highlight a need.

As His ambassadors, we should be burning with passion to correct injustice in our society, just like King Solomon did. We should have a radically different perspective on reality, to take action! Our biggest obstacle is looking beyond ourselves to see the great needs that lie not just around the world, but also in our own backyards. Human trafficking is an epidemic. Money, power, and greed are the core strongholds of this perverse infrastructure. The corruption of certain companies and organizations behind these trafficking rings is disgusting.

However, there are real life, on-the ground saviors. There are some amazing ministries resourced and connected to local governments to help save victims caught up in the sex trafficking industry. As Christians, we should at the very least seek out these amazing groups, and financially support them, giving them a platform to share the good they are doing.

In *The Christian Wallet*, author Michael Slaughter shares a convicting message, "*Conscientious and compassionate use of our money in a world where people spend $310 million on costumes for their pets and $5 billion on entertaining ringtones for their phones is not an easy task. The temptation to spend now and think later (or never!) is ever-present, but with good intentions and prayerful hearts, we can slow down and reflect on how we spend it, who is affected by it, and who we can share it with.*"[44]

As Christians we are called to live with a conscience. Too often how and where we spend our money is a reflection of our own heart. Church, let's shine the brightest in our giving! Let's take action with our money, supporting organizations who are saving innocents being exploited. Let's be intentional! After all, money brings in more help, more supplies, giving organizations what they need to save more people. Those groups are being the hands and feet of Jesus in the trenches, some doing very dangerous rescue operations, because they are passionate to save the vulnerable victims, it is their call! As the Church, we are to be the examples of how to intentionally use our money to accomplish God's good.

We carry His kingdom come to the Earth, a fallen world filled with hurting people. When we truly grasp that we are catalysts for Christ's kingdom of love, our whole way of thinking is affected! We are called and created to bring restoration to all things, and at the very least we can financially support groups who are doing the hard work, rescuing innocents who have been exploited in our society.

DIVING DEEPER

Prayer to X End It X

> "Father, thank you for exposing the lies, the corruption and we pray for supernatural protection and lives saved out of the human trafficking market. We speak resources and finances to dry up in Jesus name that have funded these rings across the world. We pray for more Godly rescuers to be placed at the right time and place to rescue victims and give them wisdom and resources to invest in restarting the lives of those who need second chances so desperately. Thank you to those ministries around the world, whose hearts are all in for saving these precious ones. We pray blessing, favor, finances and mighty open doors to supernaturally unlock. We believe in angelic visitations and miraculous rescue plans to happen more and more. Move on the hearts of people to give more to these rescue ministries, to feel your heartbeat and conviction to step up for the victims. I thank you for passion for integrity and purity to be rebirthed in Your Church. And show me how I can play a role in being your hands and feet, Jesus. Show me what group I should assign my money to, and pray for real change in the lives of the victims and in the world in Jesus Name. Amen!"

There are countless wonderful organizations that are equipped to rescue victims from the vicious clutches of the sex and human trafficking industry. Personally we know the founders of the Hookers For Jesus Ministry, Destiny House, Scarlet Hope, Harbour Hope, and Run Against Traffic foundation but there are many more acting in various positions to help rescue victims and spread the awareness to stop trafficking. It's easy to think to its too big of an epidemic for us to make much of a difference ...but everyone can do something! At the very least you could make a donation or signup to volunteer for the program! It is a worthy mission since human trafficking is rampant, and one the Church should be passionately seeking to end. Ask your local church if there is a group they are connected with and start supporting them.

Prayer of declaration:

I *believe* that God has everything I need. I choose to rest in the belief of the finished work of Calvary. His love has everything I could ever need. I am whole, I am found, I am His child, and I will shine for Him today.

CHAPTER 35

The First Women's Lib Movement

Misunderstood and labeled wrongly. Have you ever been there? I think we all have been at some point. I have been throughout my life as a woman, as a woman in the workplace, and definitely as a woman in ministry. Back stabbed, passed over, shamed in public (by someone speaking in a microphone), and no one came to my defense. Being misunderstood is a very painful and lonely place. But nothing I have ever experienced comes even close to the prejudice treatment of a Samaritan woman living in ancient Palestine.

John chapter 4 is the story of Jesus' encounter with the Samaritan woman at the well. I love this story! If we read between the red letters, we can see just how our Creator saw this sassy, amazing woman, as unique and loaded with so much greatness! But first we need to highlight how Jesus's unique personality was God-designed, and used to disarm, drawing "all men unto Himself."

Let's have a quick history lesson and compare how Jesus Christ, as God wrapped-in-flesh, lived in an ancient Middle Eastern society. His sermons, His conversations were considered scandalous for His society. He read the holy scriptures in the Jewish synagogue, and then cleared out "the fog" of religion in His sermons. He lived by a higher standard of love, honoring people that society and the Jewish religion treated unfairly.

Society back in Jesus' day was extremely prejudice. Women were treated as outcasts. Jewish men couldn't even talk to their wives in public! There were rules and religious expectations if you were a man. What makes Jesus even more of an interesting figure was that he was a Jewish Rabbi, a teacher. As a Rabbi, He was considered a sort of religious celebrity, generally untouchable. But Jesus was the fulfillment of the law, the Way Maker. And God had certainly not forgotten about an entire gender group of women living in a prejudice culture.

Ok so that was the scene, let's go back to John 4, and the story of the Samaritan woman. This story was so scandalous in the fact that it kind of "raised a middle finger" to cultural norms of that time. Jesus started up a conversation with the society outcast, she was being singled out, and there was nowhere to hide, no way to avoid this man standing at the well. It was almost as if he had been waiting just for her. Now just who was this mystery girl, the Samaritan woman? Her story: she was not a typical, submissive Palestinian woman. She was feisty.

"The Samaritan woman said to him, "You are a Jew and I am a Samaritan woman. How can you ask me for a drink?" (For Jews do not associate with Samaritans.)" John 4:9.

In verse 9, we see her wheels were turning. She may have been thinking, "This man is talking to me, how do I interpret this? Is he coming on to me? She drops a hint in verse 17 saying, "I'm not married," but then He reads her mail! In fact, Jesus already knew she had gone down the aisle five times. She is starting to see there is more to this "prophet." In fact, the whole prophetic encounter sends her straight into a theological argument, she knows this man has the answers. "Sir," the woman said, "I can see that you are a prophet. Our ancestors worshiped on this mountain, but you Jews claim that the place where we must worship is in Jerusalem."

Then the dots connect on a grand scale. The whole encounter at the well, the theological discussion was leading up to "the close," which was so epic! "The woman said, "I know that Messiah" (called Christ) "is coming. When he comes, he will explain everything to us." Then Jesus declared, "I, the one speaking to you—I am he," John 4:25-26.

By breaking through society's norms of prejudice, racism and sexism, Jesus zeroes in on this woman's life. Yet he is so gentle, clever, and sees her totally free as the Father sees her. This is just another example of how awesome I imagine Jesus's personality really was. He was disarming, truthful, and he gave hope so specific to this woman's heart and situation. He was rebuffing all the social rules by talking to her at all!

What happens next? Well, what do you expect if you had just met the One who the ancient scripture prophesied about? And, He read your mail, freeing you from years of guilt and shame, giving you renewed life, just being in his presence!

Yeah, she told everybody! The story impacted a region. God wrapped-in-flesh bucked the system, and was healing hearts in the racist society of Palestine.

The Samaritan woman's story had a snowball effect. Jesus ended up spending two days there—in Samaria! A Jewish Rabbi hanging out, loving on, and healing a bunch of Samaritans. He was a rebel with a Cause.

I think we can all take a lesson from how Jesus reached across "party lines," societal norms, and saw straight to the Samaritan woman's soul. This meeting at Jacob's well couldn't have been "coincidence." Clearly this scene had been ordained by God. In fact, The Word describes the process like this: "Long ago I ordained it. In days of old I planned it; now I have brought it to pass," Isaiah 37:26. And Psalm 139:16 says, "All the days ordained for me were written in your book before one of them came to be."

Jesus didn't give up on the Samaritan woman, just like he won't stop pursuing our deepest need. "Everyone who drinks this water will be thirsty again," John 4:13.

Nothing on this Earth truly satisfies. Not even good things, not even the love of a Godly person can quench our spiritual longing. If we settle for the kind of water this world offers, we will soon be dying of thirst, guaranteed. "But whoever drinks the water I give him will never thirst. Indeed, the water I give him will become in him a spring of water welling up to eternal life," John 4:14.

Jesus wanted to give her more. He wanted for her to experience eternal joy like only He can give. If you are reading this and its resonating, maybe you genuinely never asked the Lord into your heart, will you pray with me?

Prayer of salvation:

> "Father, I know that my sins have separated me from You. I'm stuck...please forgive me. I believe that Your son, Jesus Christ died for my sins, was resurrected from the dead, is alive, and hears my prayer. I invite Jesus to become the Lord of my life, to rule, and reign in my heart from this day forward. Thank you for guiding me, Holy Spirit. I want to be in your will, do Your will for the rest of my life. In Jesus' name I pray, Amen."

Ancient Samaria isn't that much different to our self-promoting, modern society today. I believe the Lord is highlighting His children who had their fair share of battle scars. He sees us equally brilliant, and carrying loads of greatness. The Lord wants to bring miraculous redemption to lost or stolen opportunities of influence, and speak truth where twisted lies have kept you in the shadows of shame. He desires to see you restored to how He created you: charged with hope, trusting in His truth, secure in the reflection you see in His eyes. Of you. He wants to settle some things in our hearts.

DIVING DEEPER

Prayer and Promises Prayer of healing:

> "Father, I am coming to you, acknowledging the hurt, feelings of betrayal, intentionally being passed over, resentment, offense and feeling misunderstood. Anger, hatred and bitterness are not of You. You are the God of grace, God of peace, God of mercy, and the God of love. Restore Your peace in me. Teach me to forgive and resolve any conflicts which may arise, immediately, and peacefully.
>
> And deeper, show me how you see you me. Just like the Samaritan woman, I'm desperate for Your Living Water. Help me to begin to put my security and trust in what Your Word says about me. And thank you for redemption of lost opportunities that You meant for me to carry out, in Jesus Name, Amen."

Scripture promises:

John 4:4-26
Galatians 3:28
1John 5:4
Philippians 2:3
Romans 8:6
1. Commit to memory: Isaiah 43:1

Prayer of declaration:

I *believe* that God has everything I need. I choose to rest in the belief of the finished work of Calvary. His love has everything I could ever need. I am whole, I am found, I am His child, and I will shine for Him today.

CHAPTER 36

We Are Ambassadors

2 Corinthians is one of my favorite books in the Bible! In it Paul is addressing the church in Corinth however the revelation he unloads in his letter stands to challenge all of who call ourselves Christians. Paul challenges us all not only to represent Christ well, but to participate in it.

"We are therefore Christ's ambassadors, as though God were making his appeal through us. We implore you on Christ's behalf: Be reconciled to God," 2 Cor. 5:20.

The job of an ambassador is to represent someone or something. Everything he or she does and says must intentionally be proxy for a leader who isn't physically present. An ambassador doesn't clock in or out on the job, that person is always the stand-in, on call, and representing the king. In other words, their actions, character, and words embody the king who isn't present. It's a lifestyle.

When we become ambassadors for Christ, our purposes completely change. In fact, our lives cease to be our own. When we ask the Lord to be our Savior, we are really submitting our rights to Him; our lives belong to Jesus from that point forward. This is where it gets real. If we are honest, we don't really want to surrender our lives as ambassadors, representing all the time. That means, taking on the true nature of Christ which is the opposite of *self*-promotion and service, and everything this world teaches us to run after.

As ambassadors, we start to see a difference between how we live on this Earth; our identity and purposes are meant for a

Kingdom much bigger than "my kingdom." What we used to cling to that shaped and defined our identity formerly, like certain people we hung around, certain desires and goals, may not fit like they once did. When we really say "yes" to living like Christ's ambassadors, our perspective shifts from the kingdom of self to His Kingdom.

This is why Christ said to his disciples, "Whoever wants to be my disciple must deny themselves and take up their cross daily and follow me," in Luke 9:23, and why no one can serve two masters in Matthew 6:24. We, as ambassadors, must sacrifice our own kingship before we can properly represent the one true King.

In the scripture, Paul challenges us further, "We implore you on behalf of Christ, be reconciled to God," 2 Corinthians 5:20. Look back a few verses, "For the love of Christ controls us, because we have concluded this: that one has died for all, therefore all have died; and he died for all, that those who live might no longer live for themselves but for him who for their sake died and was raised," 2 Corinthians 5:14-15.

Paul is saying that the purpose of the Cross is not just to secure an eternity for sinners, but to recapture the hearts of God's people. Our sin not only separates us from God, but even after we've be reconciled to God through justification, our remaining sin causes us to be incredibly self-absorbed, with potential to reduce us to worshippers of self.

The focus of Christ's work is to deliver us from our bondage to ourselves, even after we've been saved! As long as sin indwells us, which it will until Jesus returns or we're taken home, we tend to wander away from the worship of God, serving ourselves. God is intent on owning our hearts unchallenged. His goal is that our lives would be shaped by a worship of him and nothing else. He desires us to come running to Him alone for any heart-need we may have, after all, our Creator knows us best. And the most amazing truth of all: He has chosen to send us as His ambassadors to make His appeal for people's hearts.

When we realize that we were made by God and for God, and we pledge our soul to Him eternally, something remarkable happens! The Divine literally comes inside to live in our heart! And I believe that's not figuratively, but the Holy Spirit really moves in and takes up residency. Think about that! He is inside us, when we ask Him to become Lord of our life. So everything we would ever need: wisdom, comfort, discernment, patience, kindness...it's all in Him and we have access! The God-shaped hole in our heart can be filled and whole when we ask Him to meet our need.

Practically, journeying through our daily routines we will be challenged by hurting people and disappointing situations. According to 2 Corinthians, Christ's ambassadors are meant to engage in the ministry of reconciliation. It is a mental decision to see with Christ's eyes, forgiving others, and believing in the truth that we are meant to participate in His glorious grace. This is how we impact the world with His Kingdom: by the love of Christ controlling us. Any thoughts and lies that try to distract us into negative emotion or rejection, is a sign of the self- kingdom trying to reign again. Those thoughts are just distractions from our real identity as ambassadors. We not only represent Him on this Earth to others, but our actions reflect how we think as sons and daughters of God.

We can only represent the King well when we relinquish our former title and crown from "my kingdom," and enter into His Kingdom for our new purpose of living. This is what it means to be an Ambassador of Christ. Because of the indwelling, the helper, the Holy Spirit literally living inside us, we carry His promises, answers, and truth into the world.

Our impact? Get this! In John 14:12 it says, "greater works will you do." So not only do you have what you need personally to reign through life, we also should be looking outside ourselves to others, and doing what Christ did out there: healing the sick, casting out demons, and sometimes the hardest thing of all: forgiving people. He wants you to see yourself as He sees you: adopted into royalty and given authority to set things right for His kingdom of love.

One of my favorite passages of scripture is found in Ephesians 1:4-7, it is so loaded! "For he chose us in him before the creation of the world to be holy and blameless in his sight. In love he predestined us for adoption to sonship through Jesus Christ, in accordance with his pleasure and will— to the praise of his glorious grace, which he has freely given us in the One he loves. In him we have redemption through his blood, the forgiveness of sins, in accordance with the riches of God's grace."

Before the foundations of the world he chose us, and it's in accordance to His pleasure and will, to the praise of his glorious grace, that we have redemption through the forgiveness of sins according to his rich grace—dude! No matter what you have done, does not change how God sees you! We are his sons and daughters! We just have to start thinking like His ambassadors!

Let's shake off the lies of the identity crisis. Ready to activate your faith? Let's speak this truth out loud together!

Identity Declaration:

"I am God's greatest creation.

I was born to do greater works than Jesus. I was born for Glory.

Nations are attracted to me.

I have the mind of Christ; therefore I think like God. He's my inheritance. I'm His Inheritance.

Creation knows who I am. God knows who I am.

And today, I know who I am!"

Feel different? Now check this one out:

"As for the saints who are in the earth, they are the majestic ones in whom is all my delight," Psalm 16:3.

Our identity is clear. We are not nameless or faceless. We are called the "majestic saints in the Earth," meant to carry out Kingdom purpose!

Reflection:

1. Where is God specifically calling you to "die to yourself" so you can live for a kingdom much bigger than your own? Jot down what He shows you here.

____
____
____
____
____
____

2. Who is God calling you to engage with in "the ministry of reconciliation"?

____
____
____
____
____
____

Prayer of declaration:

I *believe* that God has everything I need. I choose to rest in the belief of the finished work of Calvary. His love has everything I could ever need. I am whole, I am found, I am His child, and I will shine for Him today.

CHAPTER 37

Our Bodies: An Instrument of Worship

This book in large portion has been to challenge our way of thinking about who we really are as the sons and daughters of God. To change the way we see ourselves impacts how we approach our purposes will affect us as a whole being. What I'm about to dive into is not profound in context, but not talked about very often by Christian speakers. Our bodies are significant; they are in fact instruments of worship.

God designed us as a three-part being: spirit, soul, and body. Our spiritual health has significant impact on our emotional health. Our emotional health has influence on our physical health. Just as discussed in the previous chapter, The Bible calls us God's ambassadors. We were made in His likeness and when we understand the great significance of Calvary's Cross, treating our bodies with honor is put into a whole new perspective.

"Do you not know that your bodies are temples of the Holy Spirit, who is in you, whom you have received from God? You are not your own; you were bought at a price. Therefore, honor God with your bodies. Another level to realizing this identity is the physical and emotional health of our temples," 1 Corinthians 6:19-20.

Kat's Story:

I want to briefly share my journey, more like a rocky-road of trial and error, that eventually lead me into better understanding of how to respect this living machine I call my body. I was a busy Mom, always putting myself last. The kids had their checkups and doctor appointments, and honestly I never scheduled mine regularly. I had always been a high-achiever, add on that my word was my bond, so when I told someone I would show up or do something, come hell or high water, I would, and it would be done well. But because I also was a people pleaser, I had a million spinning plates, anxiety was my constant companion. But with two kids, running a production company, and being active in ministry projects was taking a toll physically and emotionally on me.

I had no idea that our blood chemistry could affect our energy level and consequently our moods. After I had my two kids, I personally discovered this physical dynamic of chemical and hormonal levels. I suffered from mild to moderate postpartum depression with both children. I can remember feeling sluggish, foggy, and drained. I was getting desperate, barely able to care for my infant, and exhausted from lack of sleep on top of it all. Weeks after my first son was born I called my Doctor for help. I had an amazing OB who recommended a trained nutritionist and medical professional who suggested I get my blood levels checked. I was way off in some basic chemistry levels like iron. I was amazed at how good I was starting to feel, like a new person for the first time in my life! I was put on good-quality vitamin supplements, started eating healthy foods for my specific metabolic structure, and committed to making exercise a lifestyle habit for the first time ever. I am so grateful for medical and scientific information out there that can help enhance our vitality!

From my experience with postpartum, I began to respect the correlation of fueling my body for optimum results. I was eager to learn more! I remember talking with a friend about health one day and she shared with me that she had suffered most of her childhood and early adulthood with chronic fatigue. She began to research and ask her doctors the source of her constant exhaustion. Discovering the culprit of her symptoms, brought her so much relief but sadly noted that it's a widespread problem: food allergies.

Hearing her personal struggle with a food allergy fueled my passion to pursue total health. I began to do some research myself on certain ingredients like gluten, fructose and aspartame found in common foods we ate as a family. Our pantry was filled with Pop Tarts, Pringles, and sugary cereals. Even my favorite salad dressings, beloved Diet Dr. Pepper, and coffee creamer were offenders! I was amazed to learn of all the "side effects" our bodies manifest when I was feeding it foods filled with sugars and preservatives. Those ingredients trigger inflammation in various areas of our organs. Symptoms of a mild food allergy vary from feeling exhausted, and the inability to focus clearly, to skin rashes like eczema or nasal congestion. Severe reactions can be life threatening.[45] Learning just how common food allergies are in foods my family ate normally was eye- opening. Sure enough, I had some mild allergies to gluten, as a lot of people do. If you think you may have a food allergy, I urge you to talk with your primary care doctor, get evaluated, diagnosed and treated by a medical professional, like a board-certified allergist.

The revelation that I had been feeding my family and my temple with inflammatory foods was eye-opening and about to be life-changing! It was all part of our journey to vitality. Personally, I experienced so much more energy and even sharper focus while working, after a just a few weeks of simple health changes. I reduced sugars (including sugar-alternatives like aspartame), added in at least 30 minutes of exercise almost daily, drank eight or more glasses of water a day, and consistently took a good-quality vitamin supplement.

Restorative sleep was just as crucial for me as a busy mom and a working "creative" during the day. I committed to getting in bed no later than 10pm, aiming for 6-8 hours of sleep. This may have had the quickest impact for me. Shutting off electronics at least one hour before bedtime, not watching shows right before bedtime that induced anxiety (that meant the Nightly News), and no mid-night snack. This last factor was imperative as it allowed my body to naturally recover, wind down, and get fully recharged without having to work digesting sugary foods.

I have to explain here that eating sweets at night was a form of "comfort" for me. I was drawn to the cupboard and would sniff out that hidden box of Oreos like a bloodhound.

Snacking on sugary treats before bedtime or during a midnight pantry raid had become almost a reward or emotional crutch, depending on the day. However, armed now with the knowledge that too much of a bad thing often reflects some deeper seeded issues, I decided to go hard-core. I chose to be an overcomer. I wasn't perfect by any means, especially during those four days a month. But the next morning brought with it a fresh slate and with it, a field of choices. Sticking to these changes was hard but being the best version of myself for my family was worth it. My journey continues as I enjoy life in my 40's. I want to stay an example for my kids reminding them through my lifestyle choices that our bodies are called God's temple for a reason.

Breaking Addictions That Enslave Us

I believe that vitality isn't limited to disciplining the body alone. I also believe it means freedom from mental and emotional dependencies or addictions. Anything from addictions to sugar and chocolate, to drugs or alcohol, or anything that becomes a "have to have" in order for you to feel okay. Those defaults should be a warning sign to us. I'm just gonna throw this out there, but addictions aren't just limited to something you inhale or consume. We can be addicted to our phones, the TV, shopping, even certain people in our lives.

Think this is far-fetched? Ok, let's take a little test to determine if there's something in your life that feels like you can't live without it in your day. Ask yourself this: "Can I tell myself no to this certain thing or behavior?" That will show if that "thing" has a hold on you or you have a hold on it.

I heard a story from a minister of a gentleman who wanted to quit smoking. He was tired of the addiction controlling his life. He wanted freedom and was getting desperate. He went up for prayer, and God did something radical and rare! The minister recalled the conversation with the man. Instantly he realized he didn't even crave smoking anymore! Shocked but thankful for the undeniable healing that was taking place, in obedience he decided to stop buying cigarettes. The minister later shared, the miracle healing for that man opened his eyes and in faith to walk out his healing, made the choice not to buy cigarettes again. He lined up his thinking with the new reality of *not needing* a cigarette. The addiction stronghold was broken of that man!

The story of this brother being set free from a long-standing, addictive behavior was so encouraging to me! I wanted to apply this to my own mind battles, and addictive emotional patterns. I asked the Lord to clearly show me how to get free from my own emotional addictions. And what He showed me was exactly what the man who received the miracle had experienced: a perspective change. He believed he didn't *need* them, he took back a sense of self control in that initial decision, and applied that control each time there was a doubt.

I realize if we think about what initially triggers addiction behaviors, usually there's a deep heart issue behind it all. Whether it's running to the pantry stress- eating a row of Oreos (my addictive behavior), *having* to catch up on social media twenty times a day, to *needing* that entire bottle of wine...nothing should have that much control over us! Any activity or thing that we become dependent on to feel okay, is a warning sign.

Anxiety, stress, feelings of depression, hopelessness, loneliness, rejection, and shame; these are all cruel emotional masters. Our bodies and minds were fearfully and wonderfully made and we should honor them! Further, if we call ourselves Christians, we have The Hope of Glory living inside us literally, and there's no room for lies to abide in the same space!

"For in Christ all the fullness of the Deity lives in bodily form, and in Christ you have been brought to fullness. He is the head over every power and authority," Colossians 2:9-10. And He lives *inside* us?!—That is a game changer right there! When we believe, and bring our faith into that profound yet simple truth, any need our heart may ever have is met in Him! And that is exactly where the battle to break ourselves free lies: inside our beliefs, in our daily thought life.

There are board-certified professionals who are trained to help people wean off and break their addictions. I am all for these measures and would highly encourage that if your addiction is chemical especially! But I also believe at the core of problem, is a God-shaped hole. The simple truth I am suggesting has everything to do with the goodness of God meeting our heart's needs, and the finished work of Calvary. Our emotions can send us into a tail-spin, picking up habits that can keep us wrapped up in emotional cycles, dull our cognitive reasoning, or worse, potentially destroy our temples.

Addiction is enslavement! Jesus came to set us free and that includes from emotional dependencies, crutches, and ourselves. He desires for us to experience deep heart-healing only He can give! He can bring you freedom from years of addiction and emotional enslavement.

If you have asked Christ to be the Savior of your life, you were given everything He has access to: peace, trust, rest, and strength. What I'm telling you is not profound, but it's a critical first step. One that will bring you freedom from addictive habits. So start taking control of those negative thoughts! You know the ones that send us running to the pantry or Liquor Mart. Armed with the truth of scriptures that define *Who* really lives inside of your heart, we can learn how to reign through the moments of weakness. That will affect our thoughts, emotions, and also our physical vitality. Let's be declared the champions in the ring of our own thought life and temples. You are an overcomer! You are victorious! It was already bought for you at Calvary's Cross.

Reflection: Our Mental and Emotional Health

Let's take a mental survey: What in your normal routine is something or an activity that you feel you are dependent upon to feel "okay"?

How does the truth in Colossians 2:9-10 change how you view your own emotional dependency to that "thing"?

"I praise you because I am fearfully and wonderfully made," Psalm 139:14.

Our bodies, toes and noses, knuckles and heels, were knit together fearfully and wonderfully. The human body is the most complex and unique creation in the world, and that complexity and uniqueness speaks loudly about the mind of our Creator. Every aspect of the body, down to the tiniest cell, reveals that it is fearfully and wonderfully made. The Lord created the human brain with incredible design! A human brain that has the ability to learn, reason, and control so many naturally-automated functions like heart rate but also it can multitask, am I right moms out there? That being said, we should honor our bodies as God's masterpiece. "We are his masterpiece. He has created us anew in Christ Jesus, so we can do the good things he planned for us long ago," Ephesians 2:10.

In Romans, Paul brings up an interesting perspective that our bodies are living instruments. He even compares our temples to an act of worship.

"Give your bodies to God because of all he has done for you. Let them be a living and holy sacrifice—the kind he will find acceptable. This is truly the way to worship him," Romans 12:1.

There's a spiritual connection between genuine worship and bodily dedication. Track with me a moment, if we really consider Paul's advice and dedicate our bodies to God in worship, treating it with honor as the divine instrument it is, then we are, in some way, doing something all physical and all spiritual. Our total being is engaged, participating in the Lord's divine dance. Worship is not reduced to just the spiritual realm or just the physical realm. Worship takes all of our being: heart, soul, mind, and strength. Our bodies were created for so much divine purpose!

DIVING DEEPER

Prayer, Reflection and Promises

The Lord wants us to enjoy quality life. Thankfully with modern medicine and self- care approaches we can achieve vitality including balanced hormone levels. He also wants us to acknowledge when we have misused food or other substances to fill an emotional void that may be sabotaging our health. If this is you, let's invite the Lord back to heal the real issues.

> "Father, reveal to me how I can be a better steward of my heart, emotions, and body. I want to know exactly what you have for my unique body chemistry. Please provide the resources, renewed outlook, and strength to stick with a plan for increased vitality. Also I pray for freedom from anything I've become dependent upon as a form of comfort like food, alcohol, but also emotional things I've let become an addiction, like my phone, shopping, or even another person. Please open my eyes to really understand what it means to have the fullness of Christ living inside of me. Show me very specifically how my heart's needs are designed to all be met in You. By the stripes you received at Calvary, I thank you for setting me free and placing me on a new path to vitality, healing my emotions. Thank you, Lord Jesus. Amen!"

Reflection: Our Bodies a Divine Instrument

1. How does Paul's perspective from Romans 12:1 that our bodies are used as an act of worship change how you view your own temple?

2. What are some practical steps you should take to better your physical health?

*If you want freedom from a chemical addiction, please seek out a professional counselor. I suggest calling your local church for suggestions.

Scripture promises:

Read Colossians 2:9-10
Ephesians 2:10
Psalm 139:14
1 Cor. 6:19-20

Prayer of declaration:

I *believe* that God has everything I need. I choose to rest in the belief of the finished work of Calvary. His love has everything I could ever need. I am whole, I am found, I am His child, and I will shine for Him today.

CHAPTER 38

In Communion With Him

I have two precious little boys. One is five and the other is ten years old. When I want to have a heart-to-heart talk with my kids, we do this thing I like to call "getting in Mommy's circle." I sit down on the floor, cross-legged, but stretch open a space large enough that one can sit inside my circled legs. We have our important talks that way. My kids know it's a safe place, a tender place and trusted place where we are focused completely on where they are at that moment. They feel loved and secure. These special moments transcend from being just another conversation to a very intimate time where we intentionally get honest about our feelings.

Both my kids as well as Mommy leave those precious talks feeling like our hearts are full, and like we really understand each other. Our relationship is always stronger as a result, especially if we had to discuss some hard things. This is exactly how I see my conversations with the Lord, when I pump the brakes of my day, and stop to pursue a moment with Him on purpose.

To go from knowing about the Lord, to *knowing* Him, our communication with Him must be intentional. Intentional interaction with God is the starting point. For a lot of Christians, this may look like a morning quiet time of reading the Bible and praying. For others, listening to worship music, or even a change of scenery like taking a walk to clear our head, get quiet, and harness our thoughts on things heavenward really engaging with Him in His realm. This discipline enables us to grow deeper in our faith walk. Then, as we read from the Bible, God speaks into our life, revealing even more of Himself to us.

Knowing *about* the Lord, however, isn't the same as *knowing* the Lord. While reading about God's ways and attributes is important, communion is far more than collecting facts about Him; it starts with coming to Him in an alert expectation of experiencing His presence, and *interacting* with Him. In that way, we become vessels both containing God's life, actively engaging with Him, and expressing it to others. What makes the difference is approaching Him in an attitude of submission—a readiness to do life *with Him*, obeying whatever He tells us.

The key is being alert to His presence that's active and speaking all the time around us. In time, our initial connection with the Lord will naturally turn into an open-ended conversation continuing throughout the day. When we invite Him into our thoughts, being vulnerable, and talking with Him as in a regular conversation, we share our hopes, struggles, and concerns with Him and we will start to listen for His input. When He nudges us in a certain direction, we obey. And at night, we remember and thank Him for His love, care and guidance.

When we focus our attention on earthly concerns, it's possible to pass through life never realizing that Jesus is walking with us. We can become so busy that we never give Him a second thought during the day. Like "Mommy's circle" time, the Lord desires for a purposeful conversation with us, sometimes just meeting His eager gaze. He loves pursuing you!

When we decide to break away from the fast pace of our normal life and hear Him urging us to sit down at the divine table set for just two, something incredible happens when we choose to join Him in that intentional moment. Our eyes meet

His, and in His security, sharing His presence, His warmth, an unraveling starts to take place. You can hear Him ask, "Why are you weary, my love?" We feel the safety of His eyes and His hand reaching out to grab ours across the table. When we engage with Him, and "go there," acknowledging the reality of our real heart's longings: loneliness, needing to feel love, needing an answer and rest, in those intimate moments our eyes open. We recognize it is Jesus Christ only who can fill the deepest longings of our heart.

This intentional communion time with the Lord is critical to receiving healing, growing, and how we should do life all the time, carving out time to intentionally meet Him at the table set for two. At this time in my life, I have developed an "ear to hear," and I live for His creative voice to guide me through my day. I have become completely dependent on His guiding hand to highlight something He wants me to notice, because there's purpose in it for me. After all He is my Creator, He knows me better than I know myself, and is always eager to be invited into my thoughts and daily decisions.

Just as my kids have intimate conversations with me in "Mommy's circle," the Lord feels the same about His conversation time with me. He is always communicating with us. He is very much alive! He desperately wants a real and active relationship with you, and communication is key to building relationships. In your prayers start asking for an awareness of His presence. Soon you will notice He has been speaking through your dreams, creative ideas, highlighting things on purpose to you, and interacting with you throughout your normal routine. He has even highlighted random things to me like a license plate on the back of a car. And those ideas, if you keep the conversation up, asking Him the right questions, will be an adventurous, running conversation with the Lord, He has brilliant humor! I dare you to ask Him to show you His humor today!

He wants to be the One we turn to in every stage of life, not just the hard times, or times of need but also the fun times, and seasons of breakthrough. After all it is by His grace we are alive! "For In Him we live and move and have our being," Acts 17:28.

"He is before all things, and in him all things hold together," Colossians 1:17. Living aware of His constant presence and abiding in Him is where all our heart's longings are met. Always. He wants to have connection and closeness with us like only our Creator can, meeting His gaze at a table set for two.

DIVING DEEPER

Prayer, Promises and Activation

> "Holy Spirit, open my eyes, my eyes, all my senses today, help me to be alert to Your Presence interacting all around me and Your voice talking with me. I pray this hunger for more of Your presence consumes me so that I can't get enough of You! I want to know what it really means to abide in You. Blow my mind today, God, at how real and active You are, and how you are constantly pursuing my heart and attention, in Jesus Name, Amen!"

Scriptures promises Read Colossians 3:1-3

Psalm 4:4-8
Psalm 5:3
Psalm 25:4-5
John 15:1-11

Activation

The Holy Spirit is alive and active, and we're about to get proof! There are no parameters on Him! He will speak through nature, anything around you at all! It will strike your heart in a funny way. That's how you know He's speaking to you!

1. Ask Him to prove how real he is. Keep your mind and heart alert through the day and this evening, when you have a moment to reflect on the day, write down everything that strikes you as *coincidence*, that sticks out to you, however He highlights it.

Prayer of declaration:

I *believe* that God has everything I need. I choose to rest in the belief of the finished work of Calvary. His love has everything I could ever need. I am whole, I am found, I am His child, and I will shine for Him today.

CHAPTER 39

Community

"Art, freedom and creativity will change society faster than politics." Victor Pinchuk[21]

I have always loved art: painting, drawing, and I especially love soaking up inspiration when visiting art museums or galleries. The story and message the artist conveys through the use of shape, scale, color, and material can evoke our hearts. When you stand far away from a piece of art, you can take in one image and story, and when you walk closer, other details start to come into focus. Those details matter and make up the message of the whole piece, telling a complex and deep story. As a Christian, I have always been moved by the sacred storytelling of massive installations of stained glass inside church buildings.

I remember watching a show about an architectural salvage company who had been hired to remove a stain glass window from an old church. They were taking their time to plan their strategy of removing the leaded glass art piece. I was getting nervous watching them. They were going so slowly, maneuvering their crowbar carefully between the wall and casing. Then one of the crowbars got stuck inside the trim. The guy painstakingly worked to rock it back and forth out of the trim, in hopes to pull it out without damage. But there was just enough pressure put on the casing that a piece of glass broke. The snap and crack of the glass got the entire crew's attention.

My heart sank along with millions of other viewers as we watched the cracked glass fall to the ground and shatter. It left a gaping hole in the window. The film crew panned over to capture the horrified looks on the faces of the crew along with some choice words. The massive stained glass image, depicting a heavenly scene of the risen Christ, now had a noticeable hole in it. Now everybody's eye went straight to the gaping void! That image stayed with me.

Just like the massive image that a stained glass window shows, if we move closer, we can see the framework of millions of leaded glass shapes holding the entire image together. If one piece is missing, there's a noticeable void. Clearly the master artist, had designed, created, and purposed each piece as critical.

Every shape, color, bubble, swirl, and imperfection in the glass is highlighted when the light shines through it, and is absolutely necessary to the grand story of the stained glass window. It's a product of mastery. As the Body of Christ, we are a lot like the countless and unique pieces of glass. Each one of us bring different skill sets, experiences, personalities, and interests that are totally individual and God-created for purpose.

In *REIGN: Restoring Identity*, we have learned how to recognize these attributes in ourselves as sons and daughters of God, and also how we are to see others, especially those in our spiritual "family." When we change our perspective, seeing others as absolutely necessary, filled with unique purposes for impact in His Kingdom of love, we start to champion others, work in harmony, and see our

collective purpose as the Body of Christ. We are a bright beacon of light, carrying the hope of Jesus in the Earth. The image of a stained-glass window is at its most brilliant, taking your breath away, when the sun shines through!

Stained glass windows remind me of the family of God, the Church. We are just like the collection of unique and colorful pieces of glass. When we are in our purposed positions, letting His love shine through us, together we become a living depiction of Christ, the Hope of Glory.

The more we receive the Father's love, learning to live as sons and daughters, the more we will want to form loving, healthy relationships that endure like family, and grow stronger and richer over passing years. His love enables us to stop protecting ourselves from one another, and start to experience the healthy benefits of a real family of God, from those He brings to you to "do life with." Becoming a son or daughter means by definition belonging to a family, and this leads us to forming bonds of sisterhood and brotherhood marked by sacrificial love, loyalty, trust, edification, and friendship free of legalism and punishment.

Comparison, competition, jealousy, and insecurity are common symptoms in the Church that keep us distracted, burned out and divided! These are traps strategically set by the accuser, satan. Deny the accuser any ground in your mind. The last thing he wants is for the Church to do well as a family, embracing, and championing each other in our unique callings to spread the message of Jesus across the Earth.

We're not meant to look like a dysfunctional family, estranged from one another. We're meant to be a fellowship. And this is no polite and formal fellowship. It's a body, bound together by our individual decisions but also bound together by more than human decision—the person and work of Christ. It would be silly to say, "I'm not a part of the family," as it would be to cut off your own hand or nose. As Paul said to the Corinthians, "The eye cannot say to the hand, 'I don't need you!' And the head cannot say to the feet, 'I don't need you!'" 1 Cor. 12:21.

Once we recognize our individual purposes will only make impact when we show up in our unique zip codes, and path, it's a game changer. This holds true for our brothers and sisters in Christ, who were God-created for specific, creative impact that only they can make. It's time to cheer each other on; after all, we're all on the same team! Plus, do you think you can evangelize and be Jesus to everyone on the planet at any moment of need? We are all indispensable and vital to evangelizing His Kingdom!

As we see how necessary each part of the Body of Christ is, functioning as family, we will grow in becoming more courageous, vulnerable, trusting, and empowered people who are self-controlled. It would be ridiculous that we would need rules or "controls" to intimidate us into compliance. We will start to live by the internal law of love and honor by which we should hold ourselves as The Church.

"Love is patient, love is kind. It does not envy, it does not boast, it is not proud. It does not dishonor others, it is not self-seeking, it is not easily angered, it keeps no record of wrongs. Love does not delight in evil but rejoices with the truth. It always protects, always trusts, always hopes, always perseveres," 1 Corinthians 13:4-8.

The Church is a family and a fellowship, a body and a bride, a people and a temple. The Church is not really a place. It's a people—God's people in Christ. The Body of Christ gives a visual presentation of the Gospel when we forgive one another as Jesus forgave us, when we commit to one another as Christ committed to us, and when we lay down our lives for one another as Christ laid down his life for us. Together we start to look like a massive stained glass window, depicting a glorious image, and displaying the gospel of Jesus Christ in a way we just can't by ourselves.

Collectively, the purpose of the Church is to transform both society and individuals to be more Christ-like. And the Bible says Christ will be returning to rule and reign with His spotless Bride. It is imminent.

DIVING DEEPER

Prayer and Reflection

If you feel the Holy Spirit is tapping you on the shoulder right now, exposing some areas where it's been more about you than Him, please join me in a prayer.

> "Father, first off, please forgive me when I have fallen into the comparison trap, and start to get more inward focused than seeing your bigger plan at work between all my brothers and sisters. Forgive me for coveting how you used them. Help me to embrace the truth of the stained glass window, and see how critical my position is in it. Lord, also show me how I can cheer on, and champion others in their unique callings. I want to function well in the purposes You have for me to make impact in, and be a light to others. Please highlight those people you want me to reach out to and start leading as a big brother or big sister. Thank you for allowing me feel your heartbeat for people who desperately need to know how much you love them. I am so thankful you called me, created me, and that Jesus died for me to be a part of Your bigger plan. Thank you, in Jesus Name, Amen!"

Reflection:

1. How does the comparison of the stained glass window to the family of God change how you view other Christians?

____

____

____

____

____

____

2. What have you learned in *Reign: Restoring Identity* that addresses how we should be defining ourselves, instead of comparing ourselves to others?
   Scripture promises:
   Read Psalm 139:14
   Colossians 1:27
   Romans 8:19-21
   Romans 8:29

____

____

____

____

____

____

Prayer of declaration:

I *believe* that God has everything I need. I choose to rest in the belief of the finished work of Calvary. His love has everything I could ever need. I am whole, I am found, I am His child, and I will shine for Him today.

CHAPTER 40

The Church. A Bride. And Our Purposes in Establishing His Kingdom

REIGN: *Restoring Identity* was written based on what I've read and whole- heartedly believe to be true in the scriptures. It's up to us to share with everyone the love of Jesus Christ, and demonstrate that so that His empire of love spreads throughout the Earth. Jesus is the perfect example of a spiritual being who was wrapped in flesh and bone, sent to earth to testify as The Firstborn, fulfill an ancient plan, and as a man, to become the ultimate covenant offering. He was the redemption catalyst making a way for humankind to be adopted into divine sonship, embracing their real identity as sons and daughters of God. I am no theologian but I have read in the scriptures that He is returning for His Bride, and to rule and reign with the believers and saints collectively in a new Heaven and new Earth.

"Now if we are children, then we are heirs—heirs of God and co-heirs with Christ, if indeed we share in his sufferings in order that we may also share in his glory," Romans 8:17.

I felt the urgency to write this book because of a series of revelations, over the past few years that the Lord had dropped through dreams, visions and supernatural situations. Further, the scriptures are clear: Jesus is returning soon. The promises of God demand it, the teaching of Jesus demands it, the testimony of the Holy Spirit demands it, and the corruption of the world demands it, the vindication of Christ demands it, the destruction of satan demands it, and the hope of the saints demands Christ's imminent return.

The entire Bible is based upon this fulfillment, using humanity's critical and pre-destined position as the sons and daughters of God. The book of Revelation specifically outlines earthly signals of Christ's imminent return: wars, violence, lawlessness, increased selfishness, natural disasters, signs in the heavens, the rise of specific political powers, certain events taking place in Israel, specifically Jerusalem, the rise of global government, and the emergence of the anti-Christ figure.

As the Body of Christ, it's time we awaken to our real identity, making impact for His kingdom: we are His ambassadors, literally carrying the Hope of Glory that is Christ Jesus inside us! This truth is the game changer.

Satan, though an already-defeated foe as far as Christians are concerned, still exercises a level of dominion over the world. But Christ is the only rightful ruler of this world, and when He returns, He will overthrow and destroy satan completely. Scripture exposes the paradigm of a broken world, the lies woven and multiplied through the enemy of our soul. As time is drawing very short, he is desperate to ravage, ensnare, and destroy the lives of as many people as possible before his imminent destruction in the eternal lake of fire.

Christ is awaiting His return for a pure and spotless Bride. We are His Burning Ones who are ruled by the laws of love, filled brimming with security, a solid knowing of who we really are, and Whose kingdom we belong to. This revelation and its timing is critical for us to catch and implement in our daily thought life. I believe these concepts were already set in motion before the foundation of the Earth was created. I personally believe as the Bride of Christ, we can hasten the day of Christ's return to the Earth. The truth is right there in the scriptures: "Then I heard what seemed to be the voice of a great multitude, like the roar of many waters and like the sound of mighty peals of thunder, crying out, "Hallelujah! For the Lord our God the Almighty reigns. Let us rejoice and exult and give him the glory, for the marriage of the Lamb has come, and his Bride has made herself ready; it was granted her to clothe herself with fine linen, bright and pure"—for the fine linen is the righteous deeds of the saints," Revelation 19:6-8.

"Husbands, love your wives, just as Christ loved the church and gave himself up for her and to present her to himself as a radiant church, without stain or wrinkle or any other blemish, but holy and blameless," Ephesians 6:25-27.

We are destined to be one flesh with Christ. We are "the called-out ones," the Ecclesia, the New Jerusalem, the City on a Hill, the Saints, the Bride of Christ. So let's get stirred up about the critical part we play in His big picture, and show up!

This book, was meant to carry an offensive sound, a rhythm of advancement similar to how an army is aggressive and intentional. It will sound like a battle cry to those who hear it in their spirits. I believe He is not only calling us into a restored identity as His Bride, but into our predestined purposes for what is to come.

As Jesus prayed in the Lord's prayer, "Your Kingdom come, your will be done on Earth as it is in heaven." If he calls us His ambassadors then we are carrying His Kingdom come to the Earth. Let that soak in a minute—How is that even possible? Because we are who Jesus is returning for, His Bride. And His return is what the entire premise of the Bible is based on. The promises of God require it. The reality of this is chilling: He is returning to a new Heaven and new Earth, to His people. Our real identity is being called out. Do you have ears to hear?

"Let us rejoice and exult and give him the glory, for the marriage of the Lamb has come, and his Bride has made herself ready," Revelation 19:7.

CHAPTER 41

Prayers and Promises

Prayer of Salvation

"Father, I come to you as I am. I don't want to do this life without You anymore. I recognize how my sin has separated me from you. Please forgive me… I believe that your son, Jesus Christ died for my sins, was resurrected from the dead, is alive, and hears my prayer. I invite Jesus to become the Lord of my life, to rule and reign in my heart from this day forward. Thank you that You had everything planned out for my needs to be met through the guidance of Your Holy Spirit. I commit the rest of my life to You. In Jesus' name I pray, Amen."

Restored Identities Declarations

A Declaration about My Worth

"I am loved by the Father. I am adored by the Father. I am approved of by the Father. He finds pleasure in me. He calls me capable. He calls me worthy. I am His desire. I am beautiful. I am indispensable. Today I receive His great love for me."

Identity Declaration

"I am God's greatest creation.

I was born to do greater works than Jesus. I was born for Glory.

Nations are attracted to me.

I have the mind of Christ; therefore I think like God. He's my inheritance. I'm His Inheritance.

Creation knows who I am. God knows who I am.

And today, I know who I am!"

Scripture Promises on Identity

I am a new creation in Christ: old things have passed away behold, all things have become new. 2 Cor. 5:17

I am of God and protected for He who is in me is greater than he who is in the world. 1 John 4:1-4

I am called out of darkness into His marvelous light. 1 Peter 2:9

I am born again, not of corruptible seed but incorruptible, through the word of God which lives and abides forever. 1 Peter 1:23

I am a child of God and can therefore come boldly to the throne of grace, than I may obtain mercy and find grave to help in time of need. Hebrews 4:16

I am assured that all things work together for good for those who love God and are called according to His purposes. Romans 8:28

I am confident that He who has begun a good work in me will complete it until the day of Christ Jesus. Phil. 1:6

I am more than a conqueror through Him who loved me. Romans 8:37

I am the elect of God holy and beloved. Colossians 3:12

I am the righteousness of God in Christ, for He made Him who knew no sin to be sin for me. 2 Cor. 5:21

I am filled with strength as I can do all things through Christ who strengthens me. Phil. 4:13

I am victorious for thanks be to God who gives us the victory through our Lord Jesus Christ. 1 Cor. 15:57

I am no longer a slave but a son, and heir of God through Christ. Gal. 4:7

I am a joint heir with Jesus Christ. Romans 8:17

I am a child of God. 1 John 3:1

I am a son of God through Christ Jesus. Gal. 3:26

I am a fellow citizen with the saints and a member of the household of God. Eph. 2:19

I am accepted in the Beloved. Eph. 1:5-6

I am redeemed through His blood, and have the forgiveness of sins according to the riches of His grace with He made to abound toward us. Eph. 1:7

I am loved by Jesus Christ who washed me from my sins in His own blood. Rev. 1:5

I am the temple of God and the Spirit of God dwell s in me. 1 Cor. 3:16

I am a member of Christ's body. 1 Cor. 12:27

I am light in the Lord and walk as a child of the light. Eph. 5:8

I am delivered from the power of darkness and conveyed into the kingdom of the son of his love, in whom I have redemption through His blood and the forgiveness of sins. Col. 1:13

I am not conformed to this world, but transformed by the renewing of my mind that I may prove the good and acceptable and perfect will of God. Romans 12:2

For in Christ all the fullness of the Deity lives in bodily form, and in Christ you have been brought to fullness. He is the head over every power and authority. Col. 2:9-10

TheReignBook.com

# # #

REFERENCES

1. The Coronation, Anointed, Not Appointed". The Crown: Season 1, episode 5. Writ. Peter Morgan. Dir. Philippa Lowthorpe. Left Bank Pictures and Sony Pictures, 2016. Netflix.
2. Hasson, Bob and Silk, Danny, The Business of Honor: Restoring the Heart of Business, Loving on Purpose, 2017.
3. "Identity" from Oxford Advanced Learners Dictionary oxforddictionaries.com, 2018
4. The Victim Mentality – What It Is & Why You Use It. Counseling Blog. HarleyTherapy.co.uk, 2016).
5. The movie 'Justice League', 2017.
6. Coretta Scott King quote from brainyquote.com, 2018).
7. "Mother" from collinsdictorionary.com, 2017
8. "Greatness" from dictionary.com, 2018
9. William Shakespeare quote from brainyquotes.com, 2018)
10. Mahaney, C.J., Humility: True Greatness, Multnomah Books, 2005)
11. The symbolism of the eagle according to Indians from ancientpages.com, 2017.
12. Twain, Mark. The Prince and the Pauper, James R. Osgood & Co, 1881
13. Railway Mission, London, The Railway Signal, Vol. XI, 1893
14. Tim McGraw (transcripts.cnn.com, Larry King Live, 2004)
15. Daigle, Lauren and Ingram, Jason. "You Say," Centricity Music (Universal), 2018)

16. Definition of Power and Authority. Lexicon Greek, biblestudytools.com, 1999).
17. Vazquez, Jorge. No More Rejection, Stairwell Media, 2015.
18. Jacobs, Cindy. "The Seven Mountains," generals.org, 2014.
19. Marriage and Divorce rate. apa.org, 2018.
20. Fake news. dictionary.cambridge.org, 2018
21. Victor Pinchuk quote from brainyquote.com, 2018.
22. Halliwell-Phillips, James. "The Three Little Pigs," The Nursery Rhymes of England London and New York, c.1886), americanliterature.com, 2018.
23. "Perfectionist" from *en.oxforddictionaries.com*, 2018.
24. Brown, C. Brene. Daring Greatly: How the Courage to Be Vulnerable Transforms the Way We Live, Love, Parent, and Lead. New York, N.Y.: Gotham, 2012.
25. Brown, C. Brene. The Gifts of Imperfectionism. Hazelden Publishing, 2010).
26. Mildes, Erik. "Breaking the Cycle of Perfectionism: Tips from a Christian Counselor." seattlechristiancounseloing.com, 2016.
27. Trauma. "Hope For the Heart." hopefortheheart.org, 2001.
28. Chan, Francis. Letters to the Church. David C. Cook, 2018).
29. Lecrae. "Background." Rehab. Reach Records, 2010.
30. Puppet. A Greek-English Lexicon, perseus.edu.
31."Mean Girls." imbd.com, Paramount Pictures, 2004.
32. Schilder, P. The image and appearance of the human body. Oxford, England, 1935.
33. Hulk. marvel.com, 2018.
34. "Anger" from etymonline.com, 2018.
35. "Slander" from etymonline.com, 2018.
36. Aitken, Jonathon, John Newton: From Disgrace to Amazing Grace, Crossway Books, 2007.
37. Mohler, Dan. "Love and Forgiveness" sermon. Neck Ministries
38. Clemmons, Riley. "Broken Prayers." *Riley Clemmons,* Capitol, 2018.

39. Queen Elizabeth quote from the movie "The Crown". forums.previously.tv. 2017.
40. Lewis, C. S. A Grief Observed. New York: Seabury, 1963.
41. Nelson, Dean. God Hides in Plain Sight. Brazos Publishing. 2009.
42. "Seed" Greek meaning from Strong's Greek Lexicon. 2018.
43. "Exploitation" from oxforddictionaries.com, 2018.
44. Slaughter, Michael. The Christian Wallet. John Knox Press, 2016.
45. Gluten food allergy. Food allergies.com. 2018.

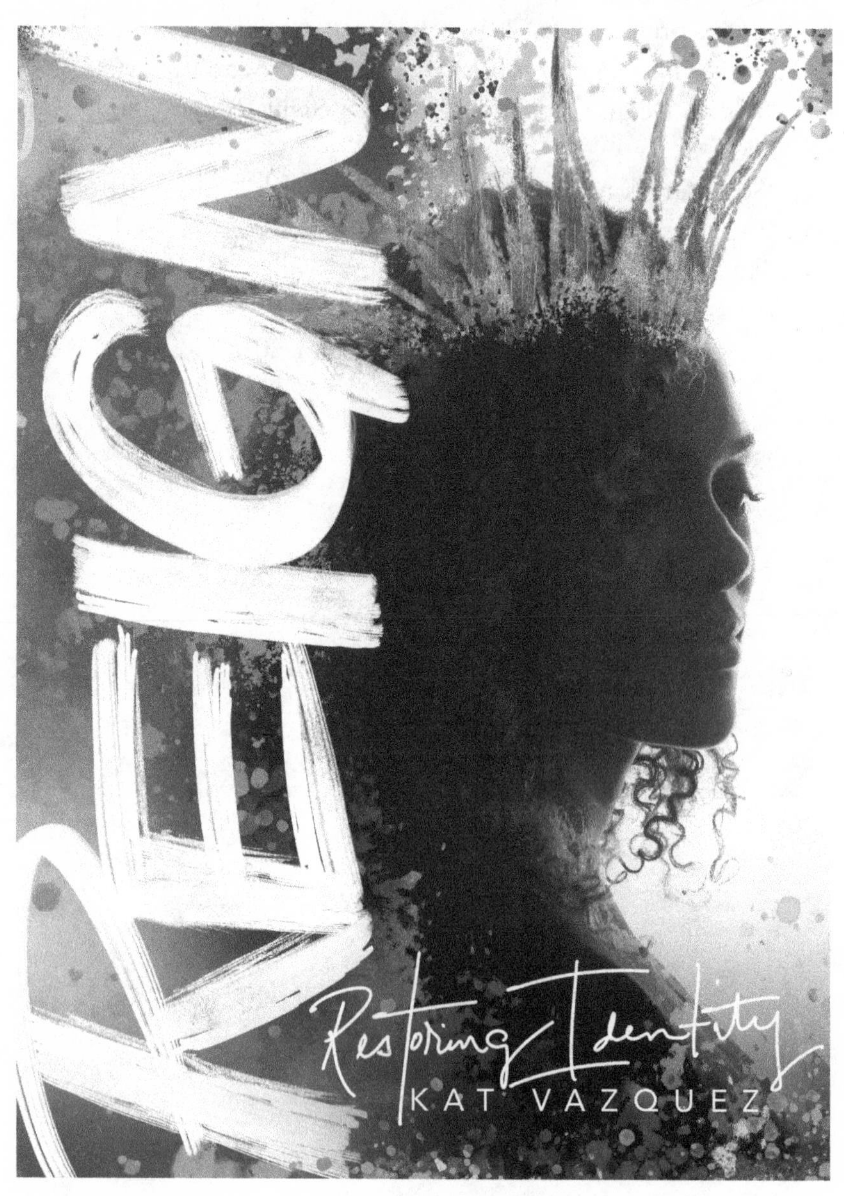

Photographer: Jordyn Myer
Artwork: Yeni Torres
Model: Analice Gonzalez

CPSIA information can be obtained
at www.ICGtesting.com
Printed in the USA
BVHW041443130922
646898BV00005B/156